Search
for
Harry Price

HARRY PRICE

Search
for
Harry Price

TREVOR H. HALL

DUCKWORTH

First published in 1978 by
Gerald Duckworth & Company Limited
The Old Piano Factory
43 Gloucester Crescent, London NW1

Distributed in USA by Southwest Book Services
4951 Top Line Drive, Dallas, Texas, 75147

© 1978 by Trevor H. Hall

ISBN 0 7156 1143 7

Printed in Great Britain by
Unwin Brothers Limited
The Gresham Press, Old Woking, Surrey

Preface

The late Harry Price's autobiography was published in 1942, six years before his death. What has been described as his 'official life', written by the late Paul Tabori, made its appearance in 1950. In my view both these books are misleading and inaccurate. I hope that the present work may be regarded as a necessary correction to what has previously been written by and about this extraordinary personality, a personality in which R. A. Lambert, the Editor of *The Listener* from 1929 to 1939,[1] discerned 'something of Beckford, the collector; something of Richard Price, the last of the alchemists [and] something of Priestley, the discoverer of oxygen'. It is possible that the chapters that follow may be of particular interest to the increasing number of present-day students of Price's prolific literary output, and to those who read modern newspaper articles and watch television programmes based on his writings.

I never met or corresponded with Price, which some might regard as an advantage to the critic, since no question of personal feelings, either conscious or unconscious, can be brought into question. Much valuable information, however, has been made available to me by those who knew him well over long periods of time, as will be evident from the chapters that follow. I have, I think, read nearly everything that Price published, together with an immense mass of press-cuttings about himself that he assiduously collected over forty years of his life. I have seen a good deal of his unpublished correspondence.

This book does not pretend to replace Tabori's biography of Price *in toto*. It is a series of essays on the many and varied

---

[1] Lambert included a long eulogy of Price in his autobiography *Ariel and All his Quality* (London, 1940), which Price reproduced *in extenso* on pp. 297–300 of his own autobiography, *Search for Truth* (London, 1942). Lambert collaborated with Price in the book, *The Haunting of Cashen's Gap* (London, 1936) about 'Gef', the alleged 'talking mongoose' on the Isle of Man.

aspects of Price's life and activities, in which I differ from
Tabori either in regard to the facts themselves or in their
interpretation. It follows that while the chapters are roughly in
chronological order, they are not entirely so. When one of
Price's particular interests persisted over a number of years, it
seemed desirable to discuss it in the compass of a single essay
for the sake of clarity. An obvious example is Archdeacon
C. O. Ellison's admirable study of Price's activities in numismatics (Chapter X) which commenced around the turn of the
century, and therefore logically follows my examination
(Chapter IX) of Price's first alleged psychical experience while
still a schoolboy in 1896 or 1898, according to his differing
stories of the incident. Price's intermittent interest in coin-
collecting continued until 1923, and Archdeacon Ellison's
essay properly covers the whole of this period. Price did many
other things before 1923, however, so that his exploits in
archaeology, which started in 1909, and his career as a book-
collector, of which we first hear in 1920, logically fall into
place, it may be thought, in Chapters XI and XII. Another
example of appropriate overlapping in time is Chapter XV,
which discusses Price's association with the Schneider brothers,
Willi and Rudi, which started in Munich in 1922 and continued for a whole decade. Chapter XVI, however, is devoted
to what I consider to have been the two outstanding examples
of contrived publicity-hunting on Price's part, Joanna
Southcott's box and the ridiculous Brocken affair, between
which there are so many significant parallels that they cannot
adequately be considered apart. In consequence, the events in
this essay start in 1927, the year in which Price received the
supposed Southcott box in such mysterious circumstances and
opened it in a blaze of publicity, and finish in 1932 with the
'magical experiment' in the Harz Mountains in which a goat
was supposed to change into a beautiful youth (which attracted
some 800 press reports in over a dozen countries), coincidently
with the penultimate year of the Schneider affair.

   Although this book is about a man who made his reputation
from his involvement in psychical research, it is not primarily
concerned with that controversial subject. Indeed, only the
Introduction and six of the twenty chapters that make up the
book discuss so-called psychical phenomena at all. My opinion

of Price's best known case, that of the notorious Borley Rectory, has been available in print for twenty years. No useful purpose would be served, therefore, by my pretending to be other than a convinced sceptic in my examination of the palpable frauds perpetrated by Price on the readers of his two Borley books in the matters of Kate Boreham and the French medals, discussed with other cases in Chapters XVII and XIX. In the other four essays that involve psychical research, I think it true to say that my primary aim has been to subject Price's presentation of his material to critical scrutiny, rather than the material itself. Can we believe a word he wrote on the subject of the supernatural, for example, after reading his two thrilling but entirely conflicting tales about the same supposed incident discussed in Chapter XVII? That is the principal question I have posed in the present work, against the background of an examination of Price's behaviour in regard to the more prosaic subjects in which he became involved, behaviour which can be scrutinised in relation to factual information as opposed to opinion or belief. It is of interest to reflect that a similar doubt was expressed over forty years ago by Lord Charles Hope in a criticism of Price's conduct in connexion with the Austrian medium Rudi Schneider. I discovered it in an old volume of the *Proceedings* of the Society for Psychical Research (xli, 1932–3) which I found in the Leeds Library. Lord Charles wrote:

What weight is now to be attached to any report, whether positive or negative in its conclusions, or any phenomena, produced under Mr Price's direction or control or recorded by him?

In view of the extraordinary respect and admiration with which Price's writings are regarded by many persons today, it is perhaps appropriate that the question should be repeated.

It remains my pleasant duty gratefully to acknowledge the considerable assistance I have received in the preparation of this book. My appreciation of much advice generously given in regard to particular incidents and problems is recorded throughout the text. The work could scarcely have been completed in its present form, however, without the continuous interest and help of Peter A. Bond, A.R.I.B.A., who has been my right hand in the historical inquiries in London, Anthony M. Carr, the Local History Librarian of Shropshire County Council, Dr Eric J. Dingwall, Archdeacon Charles O. Ellison, Professor C. E. M. Hansel, John C. T. Oates, F.B.A., Herbert E. Pratt, C. Wilfrid Scott-Giles, O.B.E. and Lord Wade.

My very special thanks are given to Alan H. Wesencraft, the Reference Librarian of the University of London, who has been unsparing in his kindness in supplying me with every piece of information for which I asked from the Harry Price Library, which is under his care, and for arranging for me to have permission from the University to quote unpublished documents, press-cuttings and other material preserved in the collection. I include in this expression of gratitude my appreciation of the permission of the University of London for me to quote from Price's published work. The University became the owner of the copyright on 1 September, 1977. In retrospect, I am also grateful to Mr Peter Underwood, Price's former literary executor, for his similar written permission. Mr Underwood and I are at amiable variance in our respective opinions of some of Price's cases, especially Borley Rectory, but we agreed that quotation, as opposed to paraphrasing, is fair to the reader, to Price and to all concerned. I am also indebted to Mr Underwood for clearing up the slight difficulty that arose through the failure of the Athenaeum Press to respond to my letter seeking permission to quote a few paragraphs from Tabori's biography of Price. I am very appreciative of the kind enthusiasm of my former secretary, Mrs Susan Spriggs, who left my service following her marriage, but has nevertheless insisted on preparing the typescript with her invariable skill and care.

Selby, North Yorkshire   T.H.H.

Contents

Illustrations

Introduction

If Percy H. Muir had not invited me to contribute to *The Book Collector* an essay on the career as a bibliophile of the late Harry Price (1881–1948), it is highly probable that the present volume would have remained unwritten. The accident of the circumstances that caused the inquiry on which the book is based to be undertaken is described in the first chapter. Once started, the investigation of Price's background and many activities became of such compelling interest that the urge to complete it was irresistible.

Since this book is a critical study of a man described on the dust-jacket of his autobiography as 'one of the most outstanding personalities of our day', it is only proper that at the outset I should quote some of the tributes paid to him. Price's autobiography, *Search for Truth: My Life for Psychical Research*, was published in 1942, and a good second-hand copy today commands a price of £9. On the rear flap of the dust-jacket, under the heading 'THE AUTHOR' is a list of press comments about Price, including the following:

'Mr Price has won a unique place as an investigator of paranormal phenomena'.   *Daily Telegraph*

'Mr Harry Price, the most eminent of psychical investigators . . . no one is better qualified to speak on the phenomena of spiritualism than he is'.   *Church Times*

'He is one of the liveliest as he is also the most industrious of writers upon psychical research'.   *Birmingham Post*
'He is the ideal investigator, sceptical, shrewd, anxious only to get at the truth'.   *Reynolds News*

'Mr Price's knowledge of spiritualism in all its forms is unrivalled'.
                                                      Yorkshire Observer

'Mr Harry Price, whose name is a by-word now whenever talk turns upon spiritualism, ghosts and manifestations'.   *Truth*

'This brave and skilful pioneer is a first-rate investigator'.

John o'London's Weekly

An unsigned obituary of Price was published in *The Times* of 30 March, 1948, in which he was described as the only son of Edward Ditcher Price of Shrewsbury, with some other personal details. An account of his early interest in psychical research was given, the wonder of which, it was said, 'remained with him all his life, and such was his transparent sincerity that he very nearly at one time persuaded the University of London to add psychical research to the curriculum and was in fact offered what amounted to a chair by Bonn University'. It was remarked that Price's investigation of the Borley Rectory phenomena 'led him to the conclusion that they could not be accounted for except as supernatural manifestations', and that his later books, including his autobiography *Search for Truth*, 'sum up the conclusions of a singularly honest and clear mind on a subject that by its very nature lends itself to all manner of trickery and chicanery'. I do not know who was responsible for the obituary, but it may be thought that it could scarcely have been more complimentary. No man could wish for more admirable moral qualities to be attributed to him than singular honesty and transparent sincerity and clarity of mind.

During his long career as the foremost psychic journalist of his generation, Price became the centre of many controversies, some of which continue today, nearly thirty years after his death. An obvious example is the notorious case of Borley Rectory, supposedly 'the most haunted house in England', which Price publicised in two highly successful books in 1940 and 1946, and in scores of contributions to newspapers, magazines and radio programmes. The first of these two books on Borley, *The Most Haunted House in England* was widely reviewed, and created something of a sensation. Martin Tindal, in *Time and Tide*, said that 'Mr Price's book about the haunting of Borley Rectory is among the events of the year 1940', and *Notes and Queries* observed that 'This record of ten years' investigation of Borley Rectory is a model of what such a record should be'. It was described as 'The most excitingly rich case in psychic annals in this country' in the *Glasgow Herald*, and the *Church Times* said that the book would 'remain among the most remarkable contributions ever made to the study of the paranormal'.

Twenty years ago Dr E. J. Dingwall, Mrs K. M. Goldney and I published the result of a five-year investigation of the Borley affair. I think it can be said that the reaction of responsible literary reviewers to our *The Haunting of Borley Rectory: A Critical Survey of the Evidence* (London, 1956) was consistently favourable, and it seemed at the time that the ghosts and poltergeists of Borley might have been laid forever. Godfrey Smith, in the *Sunday Times*, said that the Borley legend had been demolished 'with clinical thoroughness and aseptic objectivity', while Professor A. G. N. Flew in the *Spectator* wrote that the report was 'a shattering and fascinating document, offering satisfaction at last to all who have been curious to know what really was the truth about Borley [and] gripping the reader as a true story of detection'. Professor Flew concluded his review by saying that Borley had been a house of cards built by the late Harry Price out of little more than a pack of lies. Dr Letitia Fairfield, in the *New Statesman*, wrote that the dissolution of the Borley ghost had not been unexpected, and that it was difficult to see any answer to the evidence and conclusions of the report. The *Times Literary Supplement* said that the report was 'from every point of view a remarkable document—clear, succinct, judicious and, it seems, entirely conclusive', and that the evidence of Price's 'culpable negligence, adroit evasion or actual bad faith with which the report abounds is overwhelming'. The *Observer* remarked that 'not one brick in the whole extraordinary fabric of suggestion, muddle-mindedness, gullibility and publicity-hunting remains on another'.

Today the situation is totally transformed, and Borley's reputation as the most haunted place in the world seems to be completely restored. Three years after our report was published Mr Harvey Crane, in an article 'Can the Ghost of Borley be Buried?' in the *News Chronicle* of 11 April, 1959, referred to my collaborators and myself as 'the scoffers who accused Harry Price, the greatest of ghost-seekers, of rigging the whole legend'. On Sunday, 11 February, 1962, Borley was featured in the Independent Television programme, 'About Religion'. In an article on the telecast it was said:

Borley Rectory, near Sudbury, Suffolk, has been partially re-built
in the studio for tonight's 'About Religion'. Some of the most
puzzling, frightening and inexplicable events which made this
'the most haunted house in England' (so named during the Harry
Price and *Daily Mirror* investigations) will be repeated for viewers'
consideration.[1]

In its announcement of the programme the *T.V. Times* said:

Tonight, in the studio, is reproduced the Blue Room—as it might
have been—of Borley Rectory, called 'the most haunted house in
England' before it was mysteriously burnt down 23 years ago.
Some of the apparitions and hauntings there are described and
re-enacted.[2]

Since this appearance of a rehabilitated Borley on televison,
many sensational accounts of it have appeared in the popular
illustrated press, and without exception these have all reverted
to the original assessment of it as the unassailable record of all
time of a genuine haunting. Because of eager popular demand
by library users, both Price's books on Borley have been re-
printed. In 1973 *The Ghosts of Borley: Annals of the Haunted
Rectory* was published. This substantial volume was written by
the late Dr Paul Tabori, formerly a Vice-President of the
Ghost Club, and Mr Peter Underwood, the present President
of the same organisation. It was 'Dedicated to the memory of
Harry Price, the man who put Borley on the map', which is
perhaps sufficient indication of its theme and contents.

As a result of all this, history is almost repeating itself. On

[1] *The T.V. Guide*, Edinburgh, 8 February, 1962.
[2] The unfortunate impression gained by the informed viewer was that
those responsible for the script had not taken the trouble to read even
Price's account of Borley with any demonstrable care. The Blue Room was
depicted as a ground floor sitting room, whereas it was one of the bedrooms.
The apparition of the 'nun' was shewn gliding through the 'Blue Room' in
the programme, although even Price had emphasised, in italics, that the
'Nun haunted the grounds and *never* the house'. It was said that the Rev.
and Mrs Foyster used a planchette to communicate with the nun, which is
suggested nowhere in Price's books or anywhere else, so far as I am aware.
There have been several later television programmes on Borley, one within
the last twelve months.

17 June, 1929, nearly half a century ago, in the fifth of a series of sensational articles about Borley in the *Daily Mirror* over a period of seven days, it was reported :

The Rectory continues to receive the unwelcome attention of hundreds of curious people, and at night the headlights of their cars may be seen for miles around. One 'enterprising' firm even ran a motor coach to the Rectory, inviting the public 'to come and see the Borley Ghost', while cases of rowdyism were frequent.

In *Business Travel World*, March, 1975 we read:

DO YOU WANT TO TRY SOMETHING DIFFERENT? How about visiting the site of Borley Rectory—the most haunted spot in Britain? This is part of an eight-day Psychic Research Tour organised by Enjoy Britain and the World, Ltd., at a cost of £145 per person.

Today, even the Automobile Association has become infected. In one of its publications for the sight-seeing motorist, *Haunts and Hauntings* (London, 1974), there is a long section on Borley in which it is stated, without the slightest foundation in fact, that Harry Price 'experimented under conditions of the strictest security which allowed no possible room for trickery'. The present Rector, the Rev. Keith Finnimore, in his leaflet *Brief Historical Notes on Borley Parish Church*, has found it necessary to include an observation that although 'to most visitors Borley is famous for having ghosts' he personally has 'never had the vaguest ghostly experience there', and that he deprecates the 'sensation hunters [who] leave their mark on the place in the form of litter scattered just outside the church gateway'.

It may be urged that today there is no real controversy over Harry Price's popular and enthralling account of Borley, since the legend has successfully emerged from its temporary disrepute in 1956 and is now universally accepted on the basis of the book written by his disciples, Dr Tabori and Mr Underwood. We have, moreover, now seen it on television, so that it must be true! More seriously, it is worth considering the cause of the resurgence of popular belief in Borley today in the face of a sober and factual report that destroyed it twenty years ago. Interestingly enough, what has happened was actually forecast in 1956 by the reviewer of the report in *The Economist:*

> The record of cumulative suggestion, embroidery, misinterpretation, practical joking and downright fraud, painstakingly analysed by the authors of this book, is as good in its way as the ghost story itself. The Borley ghosts were, on the most favourable interpretation, poor creatures . . . But the build-up of the legend and the psychology of the witnesses is a much more interesting affair; and the authors' level-headed and patient unravelling of incident after incident, discrepancy after discrepancy, does the subject full justice.
>
> Entertaining as their book is, it leaves a slightly nasty taste in the mouth. Not because the late Harry Price emerges unmistakably as a rogue, a falsifier and manufacturer of evidence . . . but because the whole long Borley episode at once constituted and demonstrated a debasement of popular opinion and thought. Everything that was shoddy, muzzy, slipshod and anti-rational in the public mind responded to, and throve on, the Borley sensation. It will take more than this antidote to counter so massive and thoroughly assimilated a dose of dope.

The words were prophetic, as we have seen.

Another consideration to be taken into account in the revival of Borley is that the attitude towards occultism in all its forms in our country today is regrettably very different from what it was twenty years ago. The spiritual vacuum resulting from the decline in organised religion has caused belief in the tales told by psychic journalists like Price and those who have followed in his footsteps to become widespread in our increasingly permissive, materialistic and apprehensive society. I was told in Cambridge in 1975 that there is now a definite Price 'cult'. It is certainly true that original editions of his books now command exceedingly high prices, and that a number are being reprinted. An example is Price's *Stella C. An Account of some original Experiments in Psychical Research,* originally published in 1925 by Hurst & Blackett, Ltd. It was re-issued by the Souvenir Press in 1973.

The rear of the dust-wrapper of this later edition tells us that the book was one of a series, 'Frontiers of the Unknown. A Library of Psychic Knowledge. Edited by Dr Paul Tabori'. The list of contributors included the late Paul Tabori (2 books),

Peter Underwood (2 books), Peter Haining and the late George Medhurst. The following is the first half of the 'blurb', presumably calculated by the Editor to sell this kind of material in the prevailing climate of opinion:

Never before in our country has interest in psychical research, in the vast field of the occult, been at such a peak. Nor has this interest been as all-embracing—every country, every class and every age-group shares it. The rebellious youth of today explores with zest and never-flagging curiosity magic and witchcraft, mysticism and the borderland philosophies of the East. At the same time psychical research is achieving more and more academic recognition while for the general public faith in reason, in logical processes has been increasingly weakening. The irrational has become a haven from the bankruptcy of logic and order. If the natural and reasonable are forsaken, the supernatural and the extra-rational must flourish.

This is a series of books devoted to this inexhaustible material. It is edited by Dr Paul Tabori, literary executor of the late Harry Price, whose books about parapsychological subjects have included the biography of the great British ghost-hunter, *Companions of the Unseen* (a study of eight mediums) and *My Occult Diary.*

For those who (like me) find the construction of the last sentence obscure, it may be helpful if I mention that Tabori was the author of *Harry Price: The Biography of a Ghost-Hunter* (London, 1950) and *Companions of the Unseen* and *My Occult Diary.* The first of these three titles will be discussed in the present work, and I hope that the presentation of the documented facts will enable the reader to form his own opinion of Dr Tabori's reliability as a writer and competence as a biographer. It may be thought that the revival in recent years of widespread belief (without any new evidence to support it)[1]

[1] Such new evidence as has been published during the intervening years, indeed, supports a normal explanation for the events at Borley. A concrete example is contained in Sir William Crocker's *Far from Humdrum: A Laywer's Life* (London, 1967). A considerable amount of nonsense (by Price and others) has been written suggesting that Borley Rectory, which was severely damaged by fire during the night of 27 February, 1939, was burnt down by poltergeists. The facts of the matter have now been published by Sir William Crocker, the distinguished lawyer, who with the adjuster Colonel Cuthbert Buckle, investigated on behalf of the insurers the fire claim made by the owner, the late William Hart Gregson, whose name is featured in

in a case like that of Borley Rectory, is a useful example of the kind of symptom that has dictated the theme of the relevant chapters of Mr James Webb's *The Flight from Reason. Volume 1 of The Age of the Irrational* (London, 1971).

Psychical research is an emotive subject. It is therefore appropriate, perhaps, that although this book is about Harry Price, whose name above all others is synonymous with the sensational aspects of the subject in the public mind, the chapters that follow are not primarily concerned with parapsychology, as some prefer to call it today. Price was nearly forty when he joined the Society for Psychical Research, and at last found the vocation[1] that was to be the satisfying outlet for his immense energy, personal ambitions and thirst for publicity during the remainder of his life. This book is mainly, but not wholly, devoted to the study of Price's early life, family background and many activities before 1920. I found that an examination of his involvement in such unemotional subjects as numismatics, archaeology and book-collecting, to quote three examples of fields of activity in which logic and order prevail as opposed to the irrational (to quote Dr Tabori in reverse) throw a flood of light on Price's extraordinary personality.

For those readers who are not familiar with Price's career as a psychical researcher, and may wish to know something of this background, I am fortunate in being able to publish for the first time a document of great interest, written over twenty-five years ago by Dr Eric J. Dingwall, who knew Price well from 1920 until his death in 1948. When the late Paul Tabori was preparing his *Harry Price: The Biography of a Ghost-Hunter* (London, 1950) he invited contributions from Price's acquain-

---

Price's books. Of his claim Sir William wrote, "On his Borley property—bought for £500—and on his personal belongings—worth at most £100—Gregson managed to effect insurances for over £10,000. We repudiated his impudent claim for 'accidental loss by fire', £7,356, pleading bluntly that he had fired the place himself". Although Sir William's book had been available for six years when *The Ghosts of Borley: Annals of the Haunted Rectory* was published in 1973, no mention is made in the latter book or its index of *Far from Humdrum*, or its author. The original account of the fire, indeed, as told by Price, is repeated on pp. 114–17, with Gregson quoted as a witness.

[1] Price described himself as 'Psychist' in his entries in *Who's Who*.

tances. The essay that follows was not included in the biography on the grounds, as Dr Tabori wrote to Dr Dingwall, that 'Tabori proposes, Mrs Price disposes'.[1]

I first met Harry Price towards the end of 1920. He had been elected to the Society for Psychical Research in June of that year, and as for some time he had been keenly interested in the methods used by fraudulent physical mediums we found a great deal in common and discussed not only the actual methods used by fakers but the duplication of such effects ourselves.

At that time Mr Price was engaged in collecting books on conjuring which were later to form the nucleus of the Harry Price collection in the University of London, but which were then housed in the premises of the Society for Psychical Research where Mr Price arranged that they should be available to members.

Although Mr Price claimed to have been actively engaged in psychical research for twenty years he did not then seem to me to know very much about the scientific side of the subject, although his knowledge of fraudulent methods led him to propose co-operating with me in editing and reprinting a famous American book entitled *Revelations of a Spirit Medium*. It was during this time that I spent several hours almost every day with Harry Price. He was a man of immense energy, with an exceptionally keen and ingenious mind, and I soon came to the conclusion that were he to have opportunities of observing genuine physical phenomena (if such exist) he might develop into a psychical researcher of great ability. Accordingly, at the end of May 1922 I invited Mr Price to accompany me to the series of sittings with the medium Willi Schneider which Dr Schrenk-Notzing had asked me, as Research Officer of the Society for Psychical Research, to attend in Munich. The results that we observed were of so striking a nature that they impelled Mr Price to continue his studies, interest in which had been heightened by his experiment with the Crewe circle earlier in the same year.

On returning home Mr Price used to visit the rooms of the Society nearly every day. Many were the discussions that we had and the plans that we made for what we would do if ever we were lucky enough to come across a physical medium like Willi Schneider.

---

[1] I have sometimes wondered, as I think the reader may wonder in due course, whether the biography was ever submitted to the late Mrs Price for approval before publication, for there is much in it that she would have known was untrue. As an example, the whole of the information about Price's father on p. 20 of Tabori's book is contradicted in the entry of the marriage of Harry Price and his wife in 1908.

One day in 1923 Mr Price told me that he had accidently met a lady in a train who seemed to be a physical medium of remarkable powers and with whom he hoped to have a series of sittings. I well remember my excitement at hearing this news and I asked him impatiently when we should start and what room we should use for the investigation. To my great astonishment he told me that the sittings had already been arranged, that they were to be held in the office of the London Spiritualist Alliance, and that if I liked I should be a welcome member of the circle.

Relations between the Society for Psychical Research and the spiritualist organizations were at that time exceedingly strained. The Society was not a propagandist body and since spiritualists controlled the majority of the mediums, subjects for scientific investigation were difficult to obtain as it was well known that the Society was averse from publicity of any kind. Nevertheless, whilst deeply regretting the course Mr Price had taken, I saw Stella C., and the phenomena she presented were of such a nature that, if genuine, Mr Price's attitude towards them seemed to me difficult to explain. For it was clear that Mr Price must have known whether the manifestations were genuine or fraudulent. If genuine, how was it possible that a man of Mr Price's knowledge should not have taken the opportunity of conducting a properly controlled series of experiments instead of the kind of demonstrations that he was holding? If fraudulent, Mr Price himself *must* have been in the fraud. There seemed no escape from the dilemma and it was not till many years later that I realized that there was another explanation for his behaviour that avoided either of these alternatives. It was, of course, that Mr Price's real interest was not in science but in publicity. By contacting the spiritualists and at the same time keeping in touch with the critical psychical researchers he would have the best of both worlds. The spiritualists would not refuse him many mediums because there was always the chance that through his investigations publicity might be obtained and their propaganda furthered. By posing as a critical psychical researcher, fully informed as to the fraudulent aspects of mediumship, he could always attract numbers of persons who wanted to have an opportunity to be present at sensational events and who did not dislike seeing their names in the papers.

Two results followed from this decision on the part of Harry Price. On the one hand, through his immense energy, enthusiasm and general ability, he outstripped all other investigators in the variety and sensational quality of his work. On the other, the reports of his inquiries began to form the nucleus of a new kind of psychic journalism. When I first knew him he showed no signs of the ability to present psychic material in a way which appealed not only to the popular press but to the intelligent general reader who wanted to know what was being done in this field. At the end of his life he was by far the greatest master of this type of narrative. The most trivial incident or haphazard meeting could be made into an enthralling tale through the imaginative pen of Harry Price.

It is only by realizing Harry Price's excusable love of the lime-light and of personal adulation that we can understand his work in psychical research. For, apart from a very few serious studies which were done not by him alone but in association with his organizations, he never, in my opinion, advanced our real knowledge of the super-normal in any way whatsoever. The unequalled opportunities that came his way were used, not for the purposes of scientific research, but in order to forward the personal interests and ambitions that dominated his life. For this purpose he made use of numbers of prominent people who, in their turn, made use of him as a means whereby they could satisfy their curiosity about occult matters. The more sober investigators who, on account of the almost inevitable publicity, refused to be associated with Harry Price, began to credit the stories that were circulated about the way some of his investigations were conducted. A few, who wished to see what actually went on, soon dropped out and lost all interest in psychical research since they had never had any opportunity of seeing how serious work was carried on. On the other hand, through Mr Price's numerous articles and books the general public learnt a great deal about mediums, haunted houses and poltergeists, and the fact that the great prevalence of fraud was never under-emphasized lent a weight to Mr Price's efforts in this direction that otherwise they would never have possessed.

Although from the days of Stella C. my own way and that of Mr Price ran in different directions, our relations remained generally friendly. He was one of the very few men in England who was acquainted both with the problems of psychical research and with the relationship of conjuring to the art of the fraudulent medium. Although he never succeeded in persuading the University of London to form a Department for Psychical Research during his lifetime he bequeathed his magnificent library to the University in the hopes that one day it might become part of such a Department. Had he been able to resist the lure of publicity it is possible that his ambition to found a university department might have been achieved. Scientific men, I think, knew that sustained co-operation with Harry Price was impossible. Perhaps he himself realized, before his death, that the desire for publicity which had been the mainspring of his activities may have rendered impossible the achievement of that academic recognition that had been one of his dearest ambitions.

E. J. DINGWALL

Price's psychological make-up is worth examination, and I am exceedingly fortunate to have had the opportunity of discussing it with my friend Professor Mark Hansel of University College, Swansea. Price's pre-occupation with ancient manorhouses (including the published lie that his grandfather was born in one), the spurious heraldic honours displayed on some of his book-plates, the story of his 'old Shropshire family' and the inherited industrial wealth can all, I think, be explained by the squalid history of Price's parents, which was simply the subject of violent over-compensation in his autobiographical asides. In the atmosphere today of adulation of 'the common man', Price's efforts to create the impression that he was of gentle birth in affluent circumstances may seem as unnecessary as his determination to own a Rolls-Royce car, an ambition which he realised as one of the results of his extremely advantageous marriage, and his almost desperate attempts to obtain a degree *honoris causa* from either an English or foreign university, which failed.

Less easy to understand as part of Price's psychological structure (to me at least) was his quality of extreme recklessness in his published work, which was frequently so dishonest in its presentation as to lay him wide open to devastating exposure by the careful reader, it may be thought. A curious example of this is documented in the chapter in this book in which Price's two entirely different published stories of his 'psychic child' and 'dear old Nigger', based on a single alleged experience in his bedroom in Pulborough, are examined. Professor Hansel has suggested that although Price was probably badly shaken when at the age of thirty he was firmly exposed in the field of archaeology, he was shrewd enough to know ten years later, when he decided to devote the rest of his life to writing about the occult, that his audience would be largely composed of uncritical and gullible persons with a built-in resistance to anything that represented the rational view-point. In this connexion it is of interest to recall that little or no notice was taken of a letter published in the *Church Times* of 19 October, 1945 (a date between the publication of Price's two books on Borley) from Mrs Mabel Smith, the widow of the penultimate Rector of Borley, to whose incumbency five chapters of *The Most Haunted House in England* had been devoted. Mrs Smith wrote that she wished 'to state definitely that neither my husband nor myself believed the house haunted by anything but rats and local superstition. We left the rectory because of its broken-down condition, but certainly found nothing to fear there'. This did not prevent Price publishing *The End of Borley Rectory* in the following year with 18 entries in the index for Mr and Mrs Smith, but with no mention of the latter's letter.

Another friend whose opinion I value has suggested that if if I could bring myself to appreciate that Price was simply a none-too-scrupulous journalist, who could tell a very good story, this and similar problems would be solved. This may well be true, but I am nevertheless of the opinion that what Price did was unforgivable as well as foolish in view of the subject matter about which he wrote, and on which his reputation was entirely based. This is made clear, to me at least, by the example I have quoted in the previous paragraph. Price declared that the 'psychic child' version of the Pulborough tale could be an example of spirit return, while the implication behind his moving alternative story of the invisible pattering footsteps in his bedroom involving his dead retriever, 'dear old Nigger', could play upon the emotions of bereaved dog-lovers. The wholly inaccurate picture he presented of Borley, which he claimed contained the proof of survival, convinced many sincerely religious persons, some of whom contributed to his second book on the subject, *The End of Borley Rectory*. Others were being similarly urged to write sections of his third book on Borley, on which he was engaged at the time of his sudden death.

On the same theme of recklessness, the fact that he left behind so much damning correspondence in his files at the University of London Library at first sight may seem surprising. The Borley Rectory exposure, for example, could not have been so devastatingly documented if Price's own letters and the original testimony of his observers and other witnesses had not been available for comparison with the quite blatantly doctored versions he published in his books. Mr James Turner, on page 9 of the Introduction to the 1973 re-issue of Price's *Stella C. An Account of some Original Experiments in Psychical Research*, in which he describes his meeting with Price in 1947, tells us that Price knew that he might die at any moment from his heart condition, and that he gave the impression that he knew 'that the answers to the questions he had been so long searching for, were not far off'. I do not think that there is any truth in this. In the report of his death in the *Evening News* of 30 March, 1948, an interview with the late Mrs Price was described:

Mr Price made no preparations in the event of his death; it is doubtful if he left a will; there is no faithful disciple to carry on his work. His death—it is thought from heart failure—came completely unexpectedly yesterday afternoon. He was engaged on the opening chapters of his third book on the haunted Borley Rectory, the supernatural mystery that most absorbed him.

There is to be a post-mortem.[1] His widow told me today he had not consulted a doctor—and had, indeed, refused to see one despite the pain he occasionally felt over his heart. Neither she nor her brother, who lives next door, knows of any 'literary executor'.

'I myself have no interest in,[2] and could not carry on his work', Mrs Price said. 'In the past I've had too much to do about the house'.

[1] The fact that there was a post-mortem is proof enough that death was unexpected. I have taken out a certified copy of Price's death entry, and the circumstances are fully discussed in later pages.

[2] There is plenty of evidence to show that Mrs Price did not share her husband's interests. Her name does not appear in the index of his autobiography. *Bulletin VI* of Price's National Laboratory of Psychical Research, *Official Science and Psychical Research* (London, 1933) is an account of a dinner given by Price on 18 October, 1933 to honour M. René Sudre, at which 90 guests were entertained. The photograph forming the folding frontispiece of the booklet shows that ladies were present in strength, but they did not include Mrs Price. Mrs Clarice Richards helped Price to receive his guests. His former secretary, Miss Lucie Kaye, (as she frequently incorrectly called herself, both as to forename and surname) was also present at the dinner. Lucy Violet Kay contributed her memories of Price to Tabori's biography (pp. 300–4) in which she described how she accompanied him on most of his psychical research expeditions both at home and

On the first page of his biography Tabori said that Price's death was 'sudden and unexpected'.

Later in this book I shall describe how Price, with the lease of his London premises running out, persuaded the University of London to accept his library, complete with its files and equipment on 'permanent loan' at the end of 1936. It was stored and insured by the University for two years until the new Senate House was completed in 1938 and the collection could be moved there. Then came the war, which Price spent in Pulborough writing *The Most Haunted House in England* (London, 1940), his autobiography *Search for Truth* (London, 1942), *Poltergeist over England* (London, 1945) and *The End of Borley Rectory* (London, 1946). These publications were his first real successes, especially the two on Borley,[1] which is certainly the reason why he was engaged on Borley III when he died. I believe that in the excitement of all this congenial and financially rewarding activity, and at the age of only 67, Price had no thought of death all at. If he recalled that there was some compromising correspondence in those files of his in London, which in any event nobody could see without his express permission,[2] then I fancy that he decided there was plenty of time in the future when he could spend a day or so running through them, but certainly not until Borley III was completed and in the hands of the publisher.

The quality of audacity in Price's literary work appears to have reached its zenith in his later years. Indeed, in the section of Tabori's biography (pp. 267–70) outlining what Price had

---

abroad. She mentioned by name Borley, Oslo, Copenhagen and Paris in her account, and a photograph of them together in the latter capital is in the files at the University of London. It is reproduced as Plate 1 in the present work.

[1] Tabori wrote on p. 17 of the biography, 'His early books found only a limited public, but the later ones were immensely popular and brought him fame. In a poll taken among libraries in three English counties, late in 1948, on the most popular books, Harry Price was the only author with *two* books—the two volumes on Borley Rectory'.

[2] One of the eight conditions imposed by Price in regard to the 'permanent loan' was that only 'up to twenty-four friends' nominated by him, were to have access to the collection (*Report of the Library Committee, University of London, Senate Minutes*, 1936, p. 90).

seriously intended to include in Borley III, there are some episodes that cause one to wonder whether he might not have risked literary suicide had he lived to publish the book. One was the knitting needle that was alleged to have suddenly and inexplicably 'burst into five pieces' in a Hendon suburban home during a radio programme on Borley in 1947. Tabori said that Price had preserved the remnants of the needle and intended to write up the incident in detail in his book. Another example was the anonymous tale sent to the *Suffolk Free Press* by a woman who claimed to have seen a coach at Borley, complete with occupants in period dress, rise like a cloud into the air and disintegrate, 'the various limbs, wheels, etc. falling in all directions'. On the basis of his examination of Price's papers, Tabori declared of this ridiculous hoax that 'Harry Price intended to analyse it in great detail' in Borley III, speaking of it as 'another Versailles vision'.

The seeds of all this, however, existed over forty years before, when Price was in his early twenties, as is made evident by the admirable chapter on his numismatic activities just after the turn of the century contributed to this book by my friend Archdeacon C. O. Ellison. The developing pattern is duplicated, moreover, in the story of Price's pose as 'the well-known Sussex archaeologist' during his first years of residence in that county following his marriage in 1908. In 1920 he began the publication of articles on his latest interest, the history, bibliography and collection of old conjuring books, these essays betraying all the now familiar symptoms. In particular, it was in this year that Price boasted in print of his ownership of the unique Burmese manuscript on conjuring, the publicised jewel of his collection, presenting a mystery that has fallen to my lot to try to solve after over half a century.

Price's silent suppression of his exhibitionism from 1911 to 1920 has, we may think, a fairly obvious explanation. He had been exposed as a boaster and a liar for the first time. As will be seen, his claim to archaeological distinction was fatally and publicly punctured from an impeccable source, and so far as I have been able to discover, Price chose prudently to remain in obscurity for nearly a decade. Thirty years after this single unfortunate exposure, however, doubtless relying on the fact that Sir Charles Read, the former President of the Society of Antiquaries, had died in 1929 and that memories are short, Price re-told the story of his archaeological adventures in his autobiography in 1942 in a modified form. It was copied and embellished by Tabori in his biography of Price eight years later.

In the study of Price's early life and family background, essential to any real understanding of his character and the ambitions that obsessed him, it has not been possible to avoid some comment on the work of those writers who have preceded me, and who seem to have been content to copy from Price and from each other in book after book over a period of many years, apparently swallowing everything and checking nothing. The practical and well-established methods of historical inquiry used in the present work involve a little time and effort, and some expense, but are basically simple enough and available to anybody. Had they been used by Dr Tabori and those who have followed him, the perpetuation of a mass of inaccurate information first put about deliberately by Price would have been avoided, and its correction would not have been necessary.

I

Discovery of a Document

The circumstances in which the life of the late Harry Price came under scrutiny are not without interest and should, I think, be recorded. They demonstrate, among other matters, how a number of writers (otherwise presumably sensible and responsible persons) have allowed themselves to be deceived by fanciful stories blandly presented as facts in Price's autobiography, confirmed as they appeared to be in some details by his entries in *Who's Who* and his obituary in *The Times*, and more especially in a biography published two years after his death. I am sensitive in regard to my own admitted vulnerability (for a short time and thankfully not in print) to this barrage of suggestion and wilful deception, since I was one of the three writers who, twenty years ago, prepared a published report on Price's best-known case, the notorious Borley Rectory, allegedly 'the most haunted house in England'. I knew, therefore, from the experience of the five years' investigation upon which our book was based, that Price was a devious writer and a manipulator of evidence. What I did not know was that his biographer and literary executor, the late Paul Tabori, when writing *Harry Price: The Biography of a Ghost-hunter*, had accepted the tales Price had told about himself in his autobiography *Search for Truth: My Life for Psychical Research* without checking any of the essential ingredients, although he had the immense mass of Price's papers and press-cuttings at his disposal.

The combination of events that led to the present inquiry being undertaken began to take shape in the latter months of 1974, when I was staying with my friend and co-author Percy H. Muir and his wife at their home in Blakeney on the Norfolk coast. Percy Muir is the Chairman of the editorial board of *The Book Collector*. He was kind enough to suggest that I might care to contribute to that admirable quarterly journal an essay on the immense collection of books on conjuring and psychical research assembled by Harry Price, now in the possession of the University of London Library. I confess that this proposal pleased me very much. I have written fairly extensively during the last twenty years about old conjuring books and their importance to the bibliographer and the historian, including two books that librarians and antiquarian booksellers have accepted as the standard works of reference.[1] The opportunity to discuss in the pages of *The Book Collector* the curious history of the Price collection and the many rare and valuable items it contained was therefore an attractive prospect. Accordingly, during the winter of 1974/5 I wrote the essay and sent it to Mr Nicolas Barker, the Editor of *The Book Collector*.

I had concerned myself solely with the library and the more important and interesting books on its shelves. Nicolas Barker, however, suggested that one or two additional introductory paragraphs about Price himself, his background and the source of the money he had spent on the formation of the collection would be of great interest. The essay was returned to me so that this biographical material could be added. I naturally turned to my own bookshelves and to Dr Tabori's biography of Price, where on pages 20–2, for example, it is stated:

Harry Price was born on January 17, 1881, in Shrewsbury. In his autobiography he remarks that it was a record 'cold spell'; in places the mercury fell to 4 degrees Fahrenheit. So it was a chilly welcome for the Shropshire lad. His father was Edward Ditcher Price, a well-known paper manufacturer . . . [Harry Price] wanted to become a mechanical engineer. Besides magic, his greatest interest lay in gadgets and mechanics. Already articles of agreement were drawn up between his father and a well-known firm of engineers, but at the last moment Mr Price changed his mind. His paper-manufacturing business was lucrative and he wanted his son to have a share in it. Thus there began a connection with this branch of industry which lasted to the end of Price's life. He retained an interest in paper-manufacture even when he was a

---

[1] *A Bibliography of Books on Conjuring in English from 1580 to 1850* (Minneapolis, 1957) and *Old Conjuring Books: A Bibliographical and Historical Study* (London, 1972 and New York, 1973).

famous psychical expert, though in the last ten years of his life he devoted only a day or two a week to it and he seldom discussed his business activities. Few people knew of them. He preferred to keep the two divisions of his life in separate compartments, especially as his childhood hobby demanded more and more time and pushed his business interests into the background.

On page 23 Tabori added that when Price was in his 'teens the family 'moved to Brockley, Kent', an assertion presumably copied from Price's own quite untrue remark on page 16 of *Search for Truth* that in his 'early youth' his parents 'resided at Brockley (almost a rural suburb)'.

It is fair to point out, I think (although it does not exonerate Tabori from the charge of incompetence as a biographer), that there are many comments and asides in Price's books and other sources, for all of which he was responsible, that support this pretty story. In 1925, for example, he was appointed Foreign Research Officer to the American Society for Psychical Research, and in August of that year an article about him, 'Our Foreign Research Officer', was published in the Society's *Journal*.[1] It was unsigned, and may therefore be presumed to have been written by the Editor, but it would be idle to imagine, we may think, that the biographical details, written in New York, were not supplied from England by Price. The sentence relevant to our immediate purpose reads:

Educated at London and Shrewsbury for a career as a mechanical engineer, he was actually articled to a large firm of engine manu-facturers; but his father finding him necessary in his own business of paper-making, he joined this industry, in which he is still interested.

On page 16 of *Search for Truth* Price said that his father decided that he should enter the paper trade, 'with which he was intimately connected. I was disappointed, but I was still able to amuse myself amongst machinery, and nothing, I think, is more interesting than paper making and its allied processes'. On page 27 of the same book Price gave a vivid account of an incident that he claimed had occurred during his 'happy school

[1] *Journal*, A.S.P.R. xix, No. 8, August, 1925, pp. 417–19.

days' when he was 'at Shrewsbury', and which he declared on page 152 of the same book had been accurately described to him many years later by a 12-year old Silesian clairvoyant in Warsaw. On page 15 of his *Confessions of a Ghost-hunter* (London, 1936), Price described himself as 'a member of an old Shropshire family'.

It is of interest to reflect that Tabori's book has been available for over a quarter of a century, and that the article 'Our Foreign Research Officer' has been in print for over fifty years, and that neither has been challenged until now. Indeed, four years after the publication of the biography in 1950 Price's Shropshire birth and his father's local standing as an industrialist were apparently confirmed by a writer in that county. Mr Kenneth G. Kinrade contributed a long two-part article, 'The Life Story of Harry Price, the Shropshire-born Ghost Hunter', to the issues of the *Shropshire Magazine* of September and October, 1954. Mr Kinrade describes Price as 'This Shropshire-born businessman' and continues:

Harry Price devoted his life to the objective investigation of allegedly supernatural phenomena. He also devoted to it considerable sums of his own private income. This point must be stressed at the outset, because there have been some who doubted his sincerity and considered him a charlatan whose only aim was to make money for himself. Price was never, in the strictest sense of the term, a *professional* investigator. He inherited from his father, Edward Ditcher Price of Shrewsbury, a share in a paper-manufacturing business which enabled him to pursue psychical research, first as a hobby, then later as an almost full-time occupation.

Again, although it does not entirely excuse Mr Kinrade, it is fair to point out that in the penultimate paragraph of his long essay he expresses his obligation to what he calls Tabori's 'official life' of Price, and to the latter's *Search for Truth*. Indeed, in correspondence with me Mr Kinrade has said that he relied entirely on the *bona fides* of Price and Tabori, which he felt he had no reason to doubt.

That this kind of distortion of history can continue to feed upon itself for decade after decade, unless it is challenged and corrected, is demonstrated by several quite recent publications.

On p. 67 of his *Rare Books and Royal Collectors* (London and New York, 1967) the late Maurice Ettinghausen wrote:

A remarkable and unusual customer was Mr. Harry Price (1881–1948), the author of a number of best-sellers on haunted rectories and other occult subjects. A wealthy industrialist, he was keenly interested in magic and psychical phenomena and managed to amass one of the best-known collections on conjuring, stage illusions, mesmerism, spiritualism and all forms of occult activities.

In 1973 Price's *Stella C. An Account of some Original Experiments in Psychical Research*, first published in 1925, was re-issued by the Souvenir Press with a long new Introduction by James Turner, a well-known writer whose *Rivers of East Anglia* (London, 1954) is still one of my favourite bedside books. Mr Turner says that his Introduction, which he calls a 'sketch' of Price's life (p. 6) limited to what he describes as 'a few facts' (p. 8) can be extended by the serious student's reading of Price's *Search for Truth* and what Mr Turner calls 'that excellent biography by Dr. Paul Tabori' (p. 8). However, Mr Turner does tell his readers of Price's birth in Shrewsbury on that bitterly cold morning of 17 January, 1881, and of Edward Ditcher Price, that 'well known paper manufacturer' of whose important business Harry Price 'remained a director for the rest of his life' (p. 7). Mr Turner repeats Price's claim in *Search for Truth*, copied by Tabori, that both Price's grand-fathers (of whom something will be said in the present work) were 'very critical men', from whom Price had doubtless inherited much of his own sceptical nature. 'It is this scepticism', writes Mr Turner, 'that makes the truth of his work the more impressive'. One very useful paragraph of Mr Turner's (particularly to persons like myself, who never met Price) is the first-hand description of him as he was in 1947, the year before his death (p. 8). 'He was, then, bald-headed, short and stocky and still, as I've said, with much energy. The feature which struck you most was his eyes. They tended to look through you; they tended, at first, to be suspicious of you, as if he were uncertain whether you were a mocker or a believer'. The book received an excellent notice in the *Times Literary Supplement* of 28 September, 1973, the anonymous reviewer calling it 'a factual and fascinating volume'. Not much needs to be said, I think, of Harvey Day's *Occult Illustrated Dictionary* (London, 1975), except to notice that on page 102 Price is described as the son of a wealthy British paper manufacturer, 'whose mills he inherited, thus enabling him to give almost his entire attention to psychical research'.

As I confessed earlier in this chapter, it is possible that I might have been convinced by all this, and so made the alterations to my essay for *The Book Collector* with a minimum of time and effort, but for two interacting events in the spring of 1975. My old friend and colleague of nearly thirty years, Dr Eric J. Dingwall, had decided to sell his country home at Crowhurst near Battle, and he and his wife were about to move to a flat on the Sussex coast. My first wife and I had enjoyed stays at Pine Hill at least once a year for nearly twenty years, and it was therefore natural that I should be invited to spend a final week in May, 1975 in a house full of memories of happy days, and of evenings spent in the discussion of investigations and the planning of books in collaboration. When I left Pine Hill for the last time my car boot was filled with files of correspondence and parcels of papers covering part of the period of our many years of work together, which Dr Dingwall had asked me to accept. Amongst this mass of material was a complete set of all the documents concerned with the Borley Rectory inquiry we had carried out together, which I was very glad indeed to have, for more than one reason, over and above the fact that unknown to me the large Borley parcel contained the essential piece of paper that sparked off the present inquiry. Peripheral in its importance to the original central investigation as it had been, I had forgotten its existence for nearly twenty years. After our book on the so-called 'most haunted house in England' had been published in 1956 and its critical conclusions accepted by all responsible reviewers, I had turned my attention to other work and disposed of my own set of Borley papers except those dealing with the occupation of the Rectory by the late Rev. Lionel Algernon Foyster and his wife Marianne, in whom I had a continuing interest.

The complementary event in those early months of 1975 that helped to prompt the present inquiry was that I read for the first time *The Ghosts of Borley: Annals of the Haunted Rectory*

(Newton Abbot, 1973), written by the late Paul Tabori in collaboration with Peter Underwood (neither of whom I have ever met) and, as we have noted, 'Dedicated to the memory of Harry Price, the man who put Borley on the map'. It was an attempt to rescue the Borley legend from disrepute, and to restore Price's reputation as a credible psychical researcher. The book made such an unfortunate impression upon me that any regard I might previously have entertained for Tabori as a responsible writer was much reduced.

On my return to Yorkshire I began, as time permitted, to arrange the Borley documents in separate folders devoted to each witness. Price had died suddenly in the study of his home, Arun Bank in Pulborough in West Sussex, on 29 March, 1948, the cause of death being certified as 'occlusion of coronary arteries by very advanced atheroma', followed by a post-mortem but no inquest. He was in full literary activity at the time, writing his third book on Borley, obviously as a result of the very considerable success enjoyed by Price's *The End of Borley Rectory*, published only two years previously. The new book was to contain a high percentage of contributions from other writers and correspondents, and Price was especially eager to incorporate a piece of work from an acquaintance who was somewhat hesitant in agreeing to the proposal, for reasons now understandable. As will be recalled, there was a serious paper shortage in the years immediately following the war. Anxious to assure his not very willing contributor (whose work has remained unpublished to this day, so far as I am aware) that the third Borley book would definitely be published, Price declared that through the influence of Richard Dimbleby of the B.B.C. he had managed to secure the supply of a sufficient quantity of paper to enable a reasonable edition of the book to be published. As can be imagined, as soon as I came across Eric Dingwall's copy of the document recording this incident, an exceedingly pertinent question presented itself. If Price had inherited from his father, Edward Ditcher Price, allegedly a well-known paper manufacturer, a share in his lucrative business of sufficient magnitude to give Price a life of comfortable financial independence, why did he need the influence of the late Richard Dimbleby to obtain a supply of the very commodity from which his wealth was supposed to be derived?

II

Edward Ditcher Price

In his entries in *Who's Who* and elsewhere, Price had consistently described himself as the only son of Edward Ditcher Price of Shrewsbury and Emma Randall Meech. A preliminary suspicion that there was possibly something not quite as it should be was aroused by the fact that Kelly's enormous directory of the paper trade of the relevant period showed no trace of Edward Ditcher Price in Shrewsbury nor, indeed, did it list any firm of paper-manufacturers in the county town of Shropshire. However, Price's date of birth, 17 January, 1881, was firmly recorded both by Tabori and himself. It seemed to me, therefore, that a certified copy of the entry would be easy to obtain locally, and that it should provide some information about Price's father. Accordingly, I wrote to the Superintendent Registrar of Births, Deaths and Marriages for the Shrewsbury Registration District of Shropshire County Council. Mr A. G. T. Hadley replied that he was unable to trace any record of such a birth, which was surprising.

I recognised the possibility that Price might have been born away from the town of Shrewsbury itself, and I therefore wrote to Mr Anthony M. Carr, the Local History Librarian of Shropshire County Council at Shrewsbury Public Library, to ask if the local directories of the period contained an entry for Edward Ditcher Price. Mr Carr, who has most kindly afforded me every help in the investigation, replied:

> I regret to say that we have found no proof that either Harry Price or Edward Ditcher Price had any connexion with Shrewsbury. An examination of the county and town directories for the 1880s and 1890s failed to produce any trace of E. D. Price.

Mr Carr became very interested in the whole problem, as is

demonstrated, indeed, by the fact that it was he who most thoughtfully and spontaneously sent me xeroxes of Kenneth Kinrade's 'The Life of Harry Price, the Shropshire-Born Ghost Hunter' from the *Shropshire Magazine*, which I would most probably never have seen otherwise. Mr Carr ultimately checked the whole of the fourteen directories for both town and county covering the years 1879 to 1908 (that is to say, from the period around Price's birth to the date of his marriage as recorded in *Who's Who* and *Search for Truth*) without finding any trace whatever of either father or son within the boundaries of Shropshire. As an indication of the thoroughness of the search, in which the staff of the County Record Office most kindly assisted, I may say that an 'Edward Price' was traced in the voters' list of 1886 for Waters Upton, a village about five miles from Wellington. This gentleman, however, proved to have been the Assistant Overseer and Tax Collector for the parishes of Wrockwardine and Wrockwardine Wood, working from 28 Foundry Lane, Wellington from 1885 to 1905.

After the totally negative results of the Shropshire inquiries, it became clear that the next step must be to find the entry for Price's birth at the General Register Office in London. This task was undertaken for me by Lady (Pauline) Joy, who is an experienced and very able researcher and has done previous work for me. The certified copy of the entry was sent to me in due course, and was an exceedingly surprising document. The date of birth, 17 January, 1881, was confirmed. Harry Price, the son of Edward Ditcher Price and Emma Randall Price, formerly Meech, was born at 37 Red Lion Square, London in the Registration District of Holborn Western and the Sub-District of St. George the Martyr and St. Andrew.[1] Edward Ditcher Price, a commercial traveller, gave 37 Red Lion Square as his place of residence. I must say now that 37 Red Lion Square, to be discussed later in more detail, provided a small

[1] 17 January, 1881 was a cold day in London as well as in Shrewsbury. *The Times* of that date reported that 'The severe frost which has prevailed over the United Kingdom during the past few days showed no sign of abatement this morning'. On 18 January *The Times* said, 'On Sunday night and yesterday morning the very low reading of 20 degrees of frost was again recorded at the Royal Humane Society's Receiving House, Hyde Park.'

preliminary mystery in itself, which was later solved. Most fortunately, I had available to me the willing assistance of a Cambridge friend, John C. T. Oates, F.B.A., the Deputy University Librarian and Reader in Historical Bibliography in the University, who in a copyright library has at his disposal a splendid run of London directories. There was no such address as 37 Red Lion Square listed in the directory for 1881. Subsequent investigation showed that No. 37 had existed in the directories from 1856 to 1877, but not as a house. It was, indeed, occupied continuously during that long period as the business premises of James Perry & Co., Patent Pen and Ink Makers. After 1877, however, both the firm and No. 37 disappeared simultaneously from the directories.

The most surprising part of the whole very odd certificate, of course, was the description of Edward Ditcher Price as a commercial traveller in 1881. We were already a long way removed from the pretty story of Price, 'the Shropshire lad', and his chilly welcome on that bitterly cold morning in Shrewsbury, but what about the share in the lucrative paper-manufacturing business that he was supposed to have inherited from his wealthy father? It was clear that every effort must be made to find out more about the life and financial position of Edward Ditcher Price. If he had travelled for a paper-making firm as early as 1881 and had proved himself to be particularly efficient, it was just conceivably possible that after many years of service he might ultimately have been invited to join the Board, perhaps as Sales Director.

Pages 306–12 of Price's autobiography *Search for Truth* are devoted to 'My Lifeline. A Chronological Record of Principal Events'. The entry for his marriage on page 307 is brief and uninformative. '1908. Married. (Aug. 1.)' Neither the place of the marriage nor Mrs Price's name is mentioned in the text of *Search for Truth*; nor, as we have noted, does she appear in the index. From Price's entries in *Who's Who*, however, we know that her maiden name was Constance Mary Knight, which made the obtaining of a certified copy of the marriage entry a comparatively simple matter.

The ceremony took place at the Parish Church of Pulborough in West Sussex, where Price was to live for the remaining forty years of his life He was declared on the certificate to be a bachelor of 26 (he was actually 27, having been born in January, 1881) and a commercial traveller. His father was Edward Ditcher Price, deceased, also a commercial traveller. Constance Mary Knight was a spinster of 26, of no occupation, and her father was Robert Hastings Knight, deceased, gentleman. Both bride and bridegroom gave their address as Riverside, Pulborough, which was otherwise ascertained to be the home of the bride's mother. All three witnesses who signed the register were members of the Knight family. The principal importance of the discovery of this entry was that it showed that Edward Ditcher Price was a commercial traveller at the end of his life, an occupation also stated to be followed by Harry Price until his marriage.

The knowledge that Price's father was dead by 1908 enabled the indexes at the General Register Office to be searched backwards for the record of his death. Edward Ditcher Price, described for the first time (according to the order in which the entries were discovered) as a paper merchant's traveller, died on 7 July, 1906 at 32 St Donatts Road, New Cross in South London. The cause of death was certified as 'Fatty degeneration of the heart. Heart failure'. He was declared to be 71 years old. The informant was his son, Harry Price, of the same address.

The discovery of the death enabled a copy of the entry in the Probate Register to be obtained, which offered additional information, throwing a flood of light on the financial background of the Price family. Edward Ditcher Price was a widower, and died intestate. Letters of administration were granted to Harry Price of 32 St. Donatts Road, New Cross, commercial traveller, and Anne Adams of 141 Waller Road, Hatcham, the wife of Alfred James Adams. Harry Price and his married sister Anne were described as 'the natural son and daughter and only next of kin'. The total gross value of Edward Ditcher Price's estate was declared to be £189.18s.0d.

These surprising facts disposed of the tales first put about by Harry Price over fifty years ago and eagerly swallowed and copied by Tabori and other writers, of the supposed paper-manufacturing business for which Price gave up his training as a mechanical engineer and of which he became a director, the inherited wealth (presumably £94.19s.0d.) and the private income, on which so much print has been wasted. The revelation on the death certificate that Edward Ditcher Price was a traveller for a paper merchant seems to point fairly clearly to the inspiration for the lies Price told about himself. With some of the facts ascertained, it is of interest to recall Tabori's remarks on the subject of Price's business interests, already quoted in a different context in the previous chapter:

> He retained an interest in paper-manufacture even when he was a famous psychical expert, though in the last ten years of his life he devoted only a day or two a week to it and he seldom discussed his business activities. Few people knew of them.

It is fair to point out that on page 141 of his book, *Beyond the Senses* (London, 1971) Tabori, who was a Vice-Chairman of the Ghost Club, said that he met Price on several occasions, which does not suggest that he knew him well. Tabori was, moreover, very much a third choice as Price's literary executor and biographer after both the late Sidney H. Glanville and Mrs C. C. Baines had declined. If Tabori made any inquiries about Price's supposed business interests at all, it is perhaps scarcely surprising that he was told that Price kept his alleged directorship of his late father's paper-manufacturing firm very much to himself. As both Tabori and Mrs Price are now dead, we shall never know whether she was questioned on the subject and if so, what answer she gave.

The fact that Edward Ditcher Price was declared to be 71 in 1906 meant, unfortunately, that he was born in 1835 at latest, which was too early for his birth to be registered. However, there were other clues capable of being followed up at the General Register Office, including the death of his wife and his marriage. In the former connexion there was, for example, the possibility that Price might have inherited money from his mother, who we know predeceased her husband. The indexes at the General Register Office were accordingly searched backwards from 1906 until the death of Emma Randall Price was found and a copy of the entry obtained. She died on 18 August, 1902 in St. Thomas's Home in Lambeth, the cause of death being 'Carcinoma of uterus operation. Cardiac failure'. She was described as 'the wife of Edward

Ditcher Price, commercial traveller, of New Cross', the latter being the informant and giving 32 St. Donatts Road, New Cross, as his address. Emma Randall Price was declared to be 42 years old. The Probate Register was searched for five years following the death without finding any entry for Emma Randall Price. She therefore died intestate (which is not perhaps surprising in view of her comparative youth and her probably unexpected death from heart failure following an operation) and left no estate.

Another interesting fact that emerged from Emma's death entry was the considerable difference in age between husband and wife. If Emma had lived on until 1906 she would only have been 46 in that year, when Edward Ditcher Price was declared to be 71 years old. Subsequent inquiry in other fields, indeed, has shown that he was within a matter of days of his 72nd birthday when he died. He was, therefore, some 26 years older than his wife, which was unusual. How out of the ordinary the marriage was, the next stage of the investigation amply demonstrated.

III

Scandal in Holborn

Since Harry Price was born in January, 1881, the search backwards in the indexes at the General Register Office for the entry of the marriage of Edward Ditcher Price and Emma Randall Meech commenced in that year. On the basis of the declaration by her husband that Emma was 42 when she died in 1902, she was evidently born in 1860 and was either 20 or 21 when she gave birth to her son. It was therefore rather startling to find that the marriage took place as early as 11 January, 1876, when Emma was certainly no more than 16, and Edward Ditcher Price was at least 41. The bridegroom was described as a bachelor, his age being merely given as 'Full', and his occupation that of a grocer at 70 Theobald's Road, Holborn in London. His father was declared to be John Price, deceased, a licensed victualler. Emma Randall Meech, a spinster, was simply stated to be a 'Minor' of no occupation. It was declared that she lived at 63 Gray's Inn Road, and that her father was Henry Augustus Meech, deceased, a solicitor. The marriage took place at the Parish Church of St. Andrew in Holborn, and the ceremony was performed by the curate, H. W. Blunt. Archdeacon Charles O. Ellison has drawn my attention to the significance of the fact that the marriage was 'By Licence', involving the payment of a fee but obviating the duty of calling banns. No members of either family signed the register. The witnesses were Thomas Challenger, whom the directories showed to be the church sexton, and Emma Dunnett, the latter lady making a second shadowy appearance in a different capacity three months later in the story of this inquiry.

A number of curious matters disclosed by the marriage entry obviously called for closer examination. It was clearly of great interest that Edward Ditcher Price, described by Harry Price and other writers for over half a century as a wealthy paper manufacturer, had been a grocer before he became a commercial traveller for the rest of his life. An examination of London directories revealed that Edward Ditcher Price had been self-employed in the grocery trade in London since 1861 at least, when he was about 26 years old. He had occupied a succession of small shops at 29 Tottenham Court Road, 7 Theobald's Road (on the opposite side to the later shop at No. 70) and 3 Commercial Street, Shoreditch, finally moving to 70 Theobald's Road, where he was last shown in the directory published in 1879. He was a grocer on his own account in a small way of business in London, therefore, for at least 18 years. After this long period, he then changed his occupation completely to that of an employee, a commercial traveller (not even in the grocery trade) in which his lack of success may reasonably be judged by the fact that his total estate at his death was less than £200, and that his wife left nothing at all. It may be thought that the fact that this total transformation in Edward Ditcher Price's way of earning his living occurred only a year or two after his marriage can scarcely be a coincidence, and that the results of the next stages of the inquiry leave the connexion between the two events in little doubt.

An oddity about the entry also attracting immediate curiosity was the marriage of Edward Ditcher Price at the mature age of 41 at least to a girl of certainly no more than 16, easily young enough to be his daughter. A simple if discreditable explanation for this unusual union that naturally springs to mind could not have involved Emma's pregnancy with Harry Price, who we recall was born rather less than five years after the marriage. There was, however, the daughter Anne to be considered, whose existence had come to light for the first time from the particulars of Edward Ditcher Price's intestacy. The indexes were searched from the date of the marriage, 11 January, 1876 for the birth of Anne until the entry was found, a matter of only three months later. She was born at 70 Theobald's Road, which was evidently a house and shop, on 23 April, 1876. Emma had been nearly six months pregnant at the time of the marriage. The informant was not the father, as might normally have been expected, but Emma Dunnett, described as 'Present at the birth, of Crown Street, Ipswich,

Suffolk', and who we recall was one of the two witnesses at the wedding three months previously. What position Emma Dunnett held in this unusual household is a matter for conjecture. In parenthesis, it is of interest to record as a matter of minor importance that the Reference Librarian in Ipswich states that nobody named Dunnett is listed at all in Crown Street in the relevant directories of the county town of East Suffolk at that time.

Writing on page 13 of his autobiography *Search for Truth* about what he was pleased to call his 'critical faculty', Harry Price declared:

I think I must have inherited a good deal of that scepticism that has landed me in hot water so many times. My maternal grandfather was a solicitor and my father's father was an amateur of the law. Both were very critical men.

The last sentence was clearly hearsay at best, since both Price's grandfathers were dead at the time of his parents' marriage, as we have seen. If, moreover, he had seen a copy of his mother's birth certificate (to anticipate a little) as we may reasonably assume, especially in the case of a man writing his autobiography, then Price was lying and knew that he was lying, just as his mother and father had lied 66 years previously. Tabori, as we might now come to expect, simply repeated all this on page 20 of his biography of Price, virtually word for word.

I cannot understand Price's description of his paternal grandfather, John Price, a licensed victualler, as 'an amateur of the law'. I am frank to say that I do not pretend to know what the phrase is supposed to mean, and I have found no assistance from either standard dictionaries or dictionaries of quotations. I have been a magistrate since 1959, enjoying a fairly wide acquaintance among solicitors, and have never once heard the expression used. Price's statement that his maternal grandfather, Henry Augustus Meech, was a solicitor, apparently confirmed by the declaration in the marriage entry, was, however, capable of being checked. In dealing with the affairs of this very odd family, moreover, it seemed to me essential that it should be checked. The name of my colleague, Lord Wade, one of Yorkshire's most distinguished solicitors, opened the necessary doors for me, and the Records Department of the Law Society in London made a very thorough check of both the list of all deceased solicitors, and of the Law Lists prior to 1876. The Chief Executive Officer, Mr P. Ryan, wrote to me on 13 January, 1976 to say that the Law Society could find no trace whatever of Henry Augustus Meech. The address of 63 Gray's Inn Road declared to be Emma's home, moreover, was shown in the London directories of 1876, 1877 and 1878 as occupied by Robert Underhill, a Cut Glass Maker. If it is urged that Emma might have been employed as a servant at this address, and therefore did live there, then one can only point to the marriage entry, in which it was declared that Emma followed no occupation.

It was clear that there was at least one step that could be taken towards the disentanglement, in part at least, of the imbroglio of the marriage entry. A search for Emma Randall Meech's birth entry was made, and a certified copy obtained. It was an astonishing document, when compared with the marriage entry and with those related events for which the dates and particulars had already been established. Emma Randall Meech was born on 7 August, 1860 at 2 Lacey Terrace, Newington, a district lying between Lambeth, where she was to die 42 years later, and Bermondsey. The directories for that period, however, show the occupier of 2 Lacey Terrace as George Patterson, machinest, from which we must assume that Emma's parents were lodgers, or that the address was false. Her mother was declared to be Emma Meech, formerly Steggall, and it was she, oddly enough, who registered the birth on 12 September, 1860, five weeks after its occurrence. One wonders why her husband could not have performed this duty.

Emma Randall Meech's father was declared to be Henry Meech, a newspaper reporter, which made it clear that his supposed profession as a solicitor and the additional and impressive forename of Augustus in the marriage entry were both spurious. I was dealing with a family of liars, from whom Harry Price had inherited something very different from his alleged 'critical faculty'. As I have remarked, if he had seen a copy of his mother's birth certificate, he was fully aware that his maternal grandfather was not a solicitor. From another point of view, indeed, it was of great interest to discover that Henry Meech was a newspaper reporter. Twenty years ago, my co-authors and I wrote on page xi of our book on Borley Rectory that Price 'was one of the best known and most prolific psychic journalists of his generation'. We knew nothing of his curious antecedents at that time. Our description of him was based on our positive knowledge of his ability to fill his books and articles with enthralling accounts of his alleged adventures in the occult, a high percentage of which were partly or wholly fictitious.

Returning to Price's mother, the date of birth of 7 August, 1860 meant that Emma was only 15 years old when she married Edward Ditcher Price on 11 January, 1876 and when her daughter Anne was born on 23 April of the same year. Since Anne was presumably conceived in July, 1875, it would appear that Edward Ditcher Price had enjoyed sexual intercourse with Emma when she was 14 years old and he was a man of 40 at least. These sorry details, and the previous matters revealed by the inquiry, are not uplifting. It is, however, necessary to consider them against the background of the repeatedly published stories, continuing to the present day, of Harry Price's inherited wealth and his share in a large family industrial concern, together with his claim, later to be examined, of descent from an ancient, distinguished and armigerous family.

Edward Ditcher Price's conduct was disgraceful by any standards, it may be thought, but it was not a crime. Under the provisions of the *Offences against the Person Act* of 1861 it was not a criminal offence for a man to have sexual intercourse with a child unless she was under the age of 12. If this liaison had occurred ten years later, Edward Ditcher Price would presumably have gone to prison, for in 1885 the relevant age was raised to 16. If we assume, not unreasonably, that in the latter half of the nineteenth century law-making followed in the wake of public opinion, then we may think that in the 1870s and 1880s ordinary English men and women were becoming increasingly critical, and rightly so, in their attitude to sexual offences against children. In the case of Edward Ditcher Price, the fact that he was a middle-aged man would doubtless make his seduction of the fatherless 14-year old-Emma seem more disgraceful, as would the fact that he did not condescend to marry her until she was well advanced in what one imagines would be visible pregnancy. Local disapproval in the neighbourhood of the grocer's shop at 70 Theobald's Road, on which Edward Ditcher Price depended for his livelihood would, it may be thought, be inevitable. It is not hard to imagine that the effect on the grocery business at the shop and house, where Emma went to live and where the baby was born, would be disastrous. Price wrote on page 302 of *Search for Truth* that his father was a 'High Churchman, [with] family prayers, and the *Church Times* every Friday'. This may have been pure invention, but if it was true that Edward Ditcher Price was ostentatiously (and sanctimoniously) a pillar of the Church, it may be thought that the local scandal resulting from his seduction of a fourteen-year-old girl would be increased.

It would seem that if anything was left of the trade and good will by 1879 it was sold to Henry Harrod, another grocer, who is shown as the new occupier of what had been No. 70 Theobald's Road in the directories in 1880. Mr Peter Bond, A.R.I.B.A., who has investigated the history of the locality with considerable professional skill and ingenuity, has discovered that the numbers in this part of Theobald's Road were changed by the local authority with effect from 15 November, 1878, when No. 70 became No. 92, which in its turn has led him to believe that Edward Ditcher Price could have moved from his shop in that year. The point is not a critical one in our consideration of this curious series of events which occurred a century ago. We know, moreover, that by January, 1881, when Harry Price was born at 37 Red Lion Square, Edward Ditcher Price had already become a commercial traveller.

IV

A Shropshire Inquiry

As we have seen, Harry Price was born at 37 Red Lion Square on 17 January, 1881, and his father, Edward Ditcher Price, who was the informant of the birth, gave the same address as his place of residence.[1] At first sight it seems odd that No. 37 is missing from the directories after 1877, when James Perry & Co. relinquished their occupation after a stay of over twenty years. We may think, however, that there is a reasonable explanation that fits all the established facts. In the Preface to Kelly's Directory for 1881 it is stated:

The names for the Directories are selected with great care by experienced agents, but the publishers cannot undertake in any case to give any reason or explanation why a particular name has not been included.

This passage makes it clear that it was perfectly possible for Edward Ditcher Price to have lived at 37 Red Lion Square for a year or two both before and after 1881 without being listed in the directories.

In parenthesis, it is of interest to notice that by an odd coincidence this remark by the publishers is very applicable to one aspect of the much later entry for 32 St. Donatts Road, New Cross, where, as will be seen, the directories show Edward Ditcher Price as the occupier from 1894 to 1906. In the directories for 1907 and 1908, however, No. 32 is not listed at all, the numbers skipping without comment from No. 30 to No. 34. A likely explanation would seem to be that after his father's

---

[1] It is well known that the giving of untrue particulars to a Registrar results in prosecution. As an extra precaution, however, the list of 'Midwives' and their addresses in the directory for 1881 was checked. 37 Red Lion Square was not included.

death Harry Price did not continue the tenancy of No. 32,[1]
and that after his departure the circumstances of the occupancy
of the property (possibly by more than one family, for example)
were such that it was not listed as a private residence in the
directory. It seems very probable, from the facts ascertained
from local authority records by Mr Peter Bond, that a somewhat
similar fate overtook 37 Red Lion Square after it was vacated
by James Perry & Co.

Some time before 1888 Nos. 37 and 38 Red Lion Square,
presumably old-fashioned and decaying properties, were demolished and replaced by a residential block named St.
George's Mansions. The existence of this new building was
first noticed in the directories for 1888, but without any listing
of occupants. There was, therefore, a period from 1877 to the
year of demolition when No. 37 had no long-term future as a
building. It is reasonable to suppose that the owner, Mr David
Roper, would wish to extract some temporary revenue from it
by letting it off in rooms to tenants whose names would not
appear in the directories, rather than leave it empty. That this
is more than mere speculation is supported by the fact that we
already know that Edward Ditcher Price and his family,
probably in financial straits for reasons that have been discussed,
left the house and shop at 70 Theobald's Road in 1878 or 1879,
and were certainly living at 37 Red Lion Square in 1881. How
long did they live there after the birth of Harry Price, and to
where did they move?

We already know from the details of the death of Emma
Randall Price that the family was living at 32 St. Donatts Road,
New Cross as early as 1902. Tabori recorded the name of

---

[1] He was to marry in 1908, and live in West Sussex for the rest of his
life. My guess is that after his father's death he lodged with a Mrs. Hills.
Peter Bond has discovered in the Harry Price Library an old envelope used
as a receptacle for press cuttings, addressed to Price 'c/o Mrs. Hills, 22
Harefield Road, Brockley' with an unreadable date stamp. The house is
an end terrace dwelling, about half a mile north of Adelaide Road, the
home of his future wife, Constance Mary Knight. Another possibility is that
he may have lived for a time with his married sister Anne Adams in nearby
Hatcham. I therefore think it is almost certainly pure coincidence that for
one year, 1908, the London directories show 'Harry Price' as the occupier
of 91 Coleraine Road, Blackheath, preceded in 1907 by the Rev. Arthur C.
Evans and followed in 1909 by William Henry Price.

Price's school on page 21 of his book; and I therefore wrote to Mr F. A. Clewley, the present headmaster of Haberdashers' Aske's Hatcham Boys' School, Pepys Road, New Cross, S.E. 14, who most kindly sent me Price's school record. He entered the school in January, 1892 at the age of 11 (from a previous school unfortunately not recorded),[1] his address being 6 Amersham Road, New Cross. Mr Clewley added that 'a change of address to 32 St. Donatts Road is recorded, though no date for the move is given'. A glance at the map of South London shows that both these addresses in New Cross were within easy walking distance of Price's day-school. Mr Clewley told me that there are no records at the school of Price's academic performance after 1894, and that the Leavers' Register for the relevant period was unfortunately lost when the school suffered damage from enemy action during the 1939–45 War.

In parenthesis, I may say that Mr Clewley told me that Price's school record includes the information that Edward Ditcher Price was a commercial traveller, a fact which Tabori, who must have been provided with the same details, did not disclose in his biography. Indeed, his assertion that Price's father was 'a well known paper-manufacturer' is on page 20, immediately opposite to page 21, on which Price's school career is described in Tabori's book.

The address of 6 Amersham Road was entirely new to me, and provided most welcome additional information on which to work. The directories showed that Edward Ditcher Price was living there as early as 1887 (possibly in 1885 but not in 1884) and as late as 1892, which we already know from the school records. He was shown as the occupier of 32 St. Donatts Road from 1894 to 1906, the year of his death, and presumably moved there in 1893.

The history of Edward Ditcher Price's life in London has been gradually built up on the basis of this inquiry to a period of 45 years. It shows us that after some 18 years of self-employ-

---

[1] As Edward Ditcher Price was living at 6 Amersham Road for at least five years before Harry Price entered the Hatcham School, it seems certain that the latter would attend a junior day-school in the vicinity. His name is not included in the directory of former pupils (*c.* 1929) from 1870 to 1900 of the Adams Grammar School in Newport, Shropshire, also associated with the Haberdashers' Company.

ment as a grocer in a succession of small shops from 1861 to
1878 or 1879, two or three years after his marriage he left his
last shop at 70 Theobald's Road, ending his connexion with
the grocery trade forever, and moved to accommodation of
some sort at 37 Red Lion Square, Holborn. Some time before
January, 1881 he obtained employment as a commercial
traveller. More particularly, during the later years of his life at
least, on the evidence of his death certificate, we know that he
was a traveller for a firm of paper merchants. At some date
between 1884 and 1887 he moved from Holborn to New Cross,
where he was to live until his death in 1906, first in Amersham
Road and then in St. Donatts Road.

We now know, from the examination of the life of Edward
Ditcher Price, that Harry Price's claim on page 16 of *Search
for Truth* that in his 'early youth' his parents 'resided at
Brockley (almost a rural suburb)' is untrue. If this fiction had
its origin in the fact that his wife's parents had lived at what
was 10 Adelaide Road, Brockley (a house that no longer exists
today) one wonders if it was the latter residence that Price
speciously described as his parents' home on page 28 of *Search
for Truth*.

We recall that he claimed that there was 'a large coach-
house', in which was kept the family 'phaëton' or four-wheeled
open carriage for one or two horses. There was also a stable
for the accommodation of young Harry's 'dear old mare' named
Sallie, on whose back he 'used to ride into the country two or
three times a week'. These colourful tales in Price's autobiography propped up, it may be thought, the fiction of the
supposedly comfortable financial circumstances of Edward
Ditcher Price, a wealthy paper-manufacturer and a descendant
of a distinguished family.

Although Harry Price's pretence to birth and early childhood
in Shropshire is proven false, three pieces of evidence led me to
believe that his father might have had some early connexion
with that county. First, my friend the late Hartley Thwaite,
F.S.A., kindly ascertained for me from the Society of Genealogists
that the name Ditcher is quite rare. It is found occasionally in
Middlesex, and in isolated instances in Suffolk and Somerset,
but the greatest concentration of the name is in Shropshire. On
the other hand, a search of *Boyd's Marriage Index* from 1776 to

1837, in all counties and miscellaneous indexes, showed no trace of a Ditcher-Price marriage.

Secondly, in Price's first album of press-cuttings there are a few items, almost wholly from the *Wellington Journal*, recording events in Shropshire in the early 1900s. Thus I found, for example, cuttings taken from the issues of this newspaper of 23 April, 1904, 13 May, 1905 and 11 November, 1905 recording respectively the wedding at Tibberton, near Newport, of a Mr Topham and a Miss Lander, an account of an otter-hunt at Wood Eaton, near Newport and the 'Suicide near Wellington' by drowning of a Mrs Helen Amelia Turner of Poynton. The name Price was not mentioned in these reports, but they nevertheless gave the impression that whoever had collected them had been interested in that part of England, and had possibly been acquainted with the families concerned. As Harry Price was neither born nor brought up in Shropshire it seemed unlikely that he had any nostalgic interest in that county. Edward Ditcher Price, however, came into a different category, for I had no idea where he was born. All I knew was that he had settled in London in 1861 at latest, and had spent the remainder of his life there. It was therefore possible for him to have been born in Shropshire, and to have been interested in these news items from the *Wellington Journal* to which, in company with the *Kentish Mercury*, his son doubtless subscribed (or was sent free copies) as a result of his serial articles on numismatics at that period, to be discussed in a later chapter. A typed slip in the front of the album, moreover, stated that the cuttings were not in date order, which was true, coupled with an explanation that some had been removed from another album. This circumstance makes it feasible that all the cuttings had not necessarily been assembled by Harry Price, and that Edward Ditcher Price might have been the original collector of some of them.

The third piece of evidence pointing to an early family connexion with Shropshire seemed to me to be supplied by two other items in the album. The first was a printed handbill announcing a 'Grand Gramophone Recital' by 'Mr. Harry Price (of London)' on 10 August, 1899 at Withington, a village about five miles from Wellington. The second was a cutting from the *Wellington Journal* of 18 April, 1903 reporting another gramophone recital given by Mr Harry Price 'of London' at Tibberton, near Newport. For Price to be invited to come from London to give these entertainments suggested the presence in these Shropshire villages of relatives or friends who would make the necessary recommendations.

The picture that was emerging from these facts and the inferences to be drawn from them was that Edward Ditcher Price might have been born in the Wellington and Newport area of Shropshire, moving to London some time before 1861 to enter the grocery trade and to spend the remainder of his life in the capital. The problem was the tracing of his birth, since it was too early, as I have previously remarked, for it to be registered at Somerset House. His baptism would be entered somewhere in a parish register, but the unfortunate historian needs to know the identity of the parish before he can consult the register (if it has been published), or write to the incumbent to ask for a copy of the entry. In other words, the investigator has to know the answer before he can ask the question.

The clues available were first that Edward Ditcher Price's father was stated to be John Price (unfortunately a very common name) described as a licensed victualler,[1] and declared to be deceased at the time of his son's marriage in 1876, as we have seen. In parenthesis, one could only hope that this declaration in Edward Ditcher Price's marriage entry was of a different calibre from that in regard to 'Henry Augustus Meech, deceased, solicitor'. Secondly, the approximate area of interest around Wellington and Newport (not Shrewsbury, we may note in passing) seemed to be reasonbly defined by the few examples available. Thirdly, the assumption of the presence of relatives still living in the district at the turn of the century suggested that Edward Ditcher Price may have been a member of a fair-sized family.

The Census Returns are of practical use to the historian only if he knows the approximate district in which to search, with the additional qualification that it was not until the census of 1841 (the fourth) that the names of all persons present in the

---

[1] The relevant editions of *Kelly's Directory of Shropshire* listed publicans named John Price at Bridgnorth, Newport, Whitchurch, Gobowen and Rodington.

household when the census was taken were recorded, together
with their approximate ages. In the 1841 return for the small
village of Rodington, situated on the River Roden, 4½ miles
north west of Wellington, the following family was listed:

John Price	50	Publican
Ann	45	
Ann	25	
Elizabeth	23	
George	20	
Edward	6	

The Shropshire directories of 1856 and 1863 both showed John
Price, publican, as the licensee of the Bull's Head at Rodington.
H. Walcot and G. F. Carter, in their *Historical notes on the parish
of Rodington* (1952), tell us that the Bull's Head is a very old
public house, known to have been a resort of cock-fighting
miners in bygone years. The Rodington parish register recorded
the baptism on 27 July, 1834 of Edward Ditcher, son of John
Price, innkeeper and his wife Ann.[1] This dating means that
when Edward Ditcher Price made the 14-year-old Emma
pregnant in July, 1875 he was 41 years old.

The 1851 Census Return showed more accurate ages, and
the place of origin of the head of the family. John Price, stated
to be aged 63, was born in Dudley, Worcestershire. This clue
enabled the inquiry to be extended to the latter county, and I
an indebted to Miss Margaret Henderson, the Senior Assistant
Archivist in the County Record Office at Worcester, who kindly

---

[1] Since only Edward was given the second forename of Ditcher, and no
Ditcher-Price marriage is recorded, we may wonder about the provenance
of the name. John Price married Ann Hulse, and it is therefore of interest
to notice that Ann Ditcher was a witness at the wedding of Joseph Hulse
and Elizabeth Bentley in Rodington. In the Register at Berrington, another
village in the vicinity, are 23 entries for Edward Ditcher (3 individuals)
and 16 entries for Ann Ditcher (3 individuals). The Ditchers of Berrington
were butchers, with an early entry in 1759 of the marriage of Edward
Ditcher with Ann Hardy. At least two Ann Ditchers were daughters of
different Edward Ditchers. In any event, it is not difficult to imagine that
John Price and an Edward Ditcher of about the same age, baptised on
27 June, 1792 in Berrington, and the son of Edward and Martha Ditcher,
could have been close friends.

looked at the parish registers of Dudley St. Thomas for me. John Price, the son of John and Lucy Price of Dudley, was born on 10 July, 1787 and baptised on 8 February, 1788. Interestingly enough, his elder brother James, born on 24 April, 1785, was baptised on the same day as John. Price's 'old Shropshire family' had therefore moved in three generations from Worcestershire to London, with only Edward Ditcher Price's birth in Shropshire *en route*.

Edward Ditcher Price was not listed as a member of the Rodington household in the Census Return of 1851, which suggests that by the age of 17 he had left Shropshire to learn the grocery trade in London where, as we know, he was to open his first shop about ten years later. His exodus from a small village like Rodington in order to make a living in London would be very natural, it would seem, in view of the size of the Price family. This was ascertained from the Census Returns of 1841, 1851, 1861 and 1871, and the relevant parish registers, which combine to give us an outline of the history of John Price and his wife and nine children.

John Price, as we have seen, was born in 1787. By 1810, when he was 23, he was described as a publican in the village of Oakengates in the parish of Wombridge near Wellington, when on 22 May of that year he married Ann Hulse. Their first child, Mary Hulse, was baptised on 4 August, 1811 at Oakengates, and was buried in Rodington on 31 October, 1835 at the age of 24.[1] A second daughter, Ann, was born in Oakengates in 1813, to be followed by the birth of twins, Lucy Longford and Elizabeth, in 1817, and the first son, George, in 1821. Susanna Jane was born in 1826, and the second son, Joseph Henry, in 1829. All these births took place in Oaken-

---

[1] If Mary had lived for the normal span of seventy years she would have become Harry Price's aunt. It may be regarded as surprising, therefore, that in his tale of his adventures in the haunted Shropshire manor house of 'Parton Magna' (to be examined in a later chapter) Price said that 'a girl named Mary Hulse had died at the Manor under suspicious circumstances' without any comment (*Confessions of a Ghost-Hunter*, p. 17). It was reported in the *Salopian Journal* of 11 November, 1835, that the death occurred on 23 October, 'after a long and painful illness, [of] Mary Hulse, eldest daughter of Mr Price of Rodington, whose amiable disposition will long be cherished by her family and friends'.

gates, but by 1831, when Rhoda Hulse was born in Rodington, the move had been made to the Bull's Head. It was in this small public-house, which I have visited, that Edward Ditcher Price, the ninth child and third son, was born in 1834, as we have seen.

It was of interest to see that at the time of the 1861 Census, John Price, by then a widower of 74, was still working as a publican at Rodington and that living with him were his unmarried daughters Ann, Lucy and Rhoda. Two years later the directory of 1863 confirmed that the 'amateur of the law' was still the licensee of the Bull's Head. The printed Rodington register ends in 1837, but through the kindness of Mr Anthony Carr, the Local History Librarian, I was able to obtain from the County Record Office the entry for the burial of John Price at Rodington on 18 November, 1868 from the original register. He was 81, and his address at his death was given simply as The Lees.

This was a farm-house (not in Rodington) occupied at the relevant time by John Price's second son, Joseph Henry Price. The tracing of its location, and the importance of its discovery to this inquiry, properly belong to a later chapter largely devoted to The Lees and to certain events that are alleged to have occurred there. In the present account of the family of John Price, however, it is of interest to record that in the Census Return of 1871 one of the persons living at The Lees with Joseph Henry Price was his niece, Priscilla Price. It is clear that this young lady could only have been the daughter of George Price, and it is therefore of interest that her place of birth was given in the Census Return as Ironbridge. This was the heart of what was the industrial area of Shropshire, where in 1709 Abraham Derby first smelted iron ore with coke instead of charcoal, and in 1779 Abraham Derby III built the first iron bridge in the world. This suggests that George Price, like his brother Edward Ditcher Price, had to seek a living away from Rodington. Only Joseph Henry Price remained near home, in a village a few miles distant. It is reasonable to assume that he was there as early as 1868, when his father died at The Lees, and he is shown there in *Kelly's Directory of Shropshire* in both 1870 and 1879, but not in 1885 or thereafter.

The occupation of The Lees by Joseph Henry Price is of

importance, as will be seen, in the examination in a later chapter of the story told by Price in three of his books and in at least two articles, of what he asserted was his first psychical experience. He wrote in 1926 that it was this thrilling adventure (variously dated by him as having occurred in 1896 and 1898)[1] that was the direct cause of his intense and sustained interest in occult phenomena.

[1] Compare, for example, the *Journal* of the American Society for Psychical Research, February, 1926, p. 78 and *Search for Truth*, p. 28.

V

Early Years in New Cross

Harry Price probably left school about 1897 or 1898, and married in 1908. Neither Price nor Tabori are of much help to us in solving the problem of how Price earned his living during the intervening ten years. He was committed in print as early as 1925 to the tale of his articles to a large firm of engine manufacturers, which had to be abandoned to enable him to join his father's allegedly well-known and lucrative paper-manufacturing business and to amuse himself amongst the machinery. We know that this was pure invention, and that it would therefore be foolish to expect to find any facts about this period of Price's life in the pages of *Search for Truth*. Tabori wrote (p. 30) with perhaps a hint of unease:

> The years before the dawn of the new century and the First World War were happy and busy ones for Harry Price. He had his work in the business of which his father was part-owner. But it could not have been a full-time occupation, for it left him plenty of leisure. Or perhaps he had a greater capacity for doing a job than most of his contemporaries.

I fancy that as Tabori went through Price's papers he may have been puzzled at what he found in regard to Price's activities during this period.

One thing seems certain. Judged by Edward Ditcher Price's financial position as disclosed by his probate entry, we may think that his son would need to earn a living of some sort up to the time of his marriage in 1908. We know that in that year Harry Price declared that he was a commercial traveller, according to the certified copy of his marriage entry. This is a wide term, however, and it is unfortunate that everything that Price wrote must be regarded as suspect. However, I wondered for a time, since Edward Ditcher Price was a traveller for a firm of paper merchants, whether his son managed to obtain a job with his father's employers, and that this connexion continued up to and after Harry Price's marriage. This would be a very different state of affairs from the totally untrue story of the directorship of his wealthy father's paper manufacturing business, but there were some precedents to suggest that such a blown-up distortion of the truth of the matter might be typical of Price. I must say now, however, that an examination of such evidence as is available suggests that this is not so. Whether the reader agrees with this view depends to a large extent on his or her opinion of the evidence in regard to the identity of the firm for whom Edward Ditcher Price worked.

Rather oddly, I have been unable to find any notice of the death of Edward Ditcher Price in Harry Price's first album of press-cuttings, which extended to 1924.[1] A report of his mother's death in the *Kentish Mercury* of 22 August, 1902, however, is pasted unobtrusively on the rear of a hinged slip of paper, to the front of which is pasted one of the instalments of Price's serial on Kentish trade tokens printed in the same newspaper at this period. In announcing his wife's death Edward Ditcher Price gave himself the distinction of two London addresses. The first was St. Donatts Road, New Cross, and the second was 'Little Sutton-street, E.C.', which does not exist in London gazetteers and directories today. In 1902 it was occupied by commercial premises, including those of a firm of box manufacturers, two firms of printers and one (only) firm of paper merchants, A. J. Brown, Brough & Co. It may be thought reasonable to suppose that in giving himself two London locations Edward Ditcher Price had used his employers' address. It was interesting to find that in 1881, the year when Edward Ditcher Price described himself as a commercial traveller on the certified copy of his son's birth at 37 Red Lion Square, the firm of paper merchants concerned, A. J. Brown & Co. (as it was at that time) was established at 11 Newgate Street, approximately one mile distant. The firm of A. J. Brown,

---

[1] This album is lettered on the spine 'Harry Price. Press Cuttings. (1896–1924)', and clearly must be regarded as the first on the evidence of dates. It is not numbered. Price confused the matter by numbering the next album of cuttings as Vol. 1 (1921–1925).

Brough & Co. Ltd., exists today at 3 Dufferin Street, London, E.C., dealing in the sale of paper, polythene and twine, with branches in Liverpool and Leicester. The Chairman and Managing Director, Mr H. J. C. Brough, has been kind enough to give such information as he can to Mr Peter Bond and myself, negative though it is.

Understandably, after two World Wars and several changes of address, the firm's records of seventy years ago no longer exist, and the period around the turn of the century is beyond living memory.[1] Edward Ditcher Price, therefore, might or might not have been employed as a traveller by the firm at that time. What is certain, however, is that during the last twenty years of his life, a period for which the firm's records do exist, Harry Price had no connexion whatsoever with the firm of A. J. Brown, Brough & Co.

During the period from the end of his schooldays and his marriage ten years later, Price spent many evenings giving gramophone entertainments at variety concerts around New Cross, Deptford, Walworth and Greenwich, and as far afield as Shropshire, as is shown by a multiplicity of cuttings and printed programmes pasted into his first album. Tabori declared (p. 24) that Price 'was in great demand for concerts, social evenings and similar functions all over the country'. From 1902 to 1904 he devoted much time to numismatic journalism, an activity that will be examined in a separate chapter. Suffice it to say that he contributed some fifty articles to two provincial papers, albeit not original with him. The *Kentish Mercury* of 9 October, 1903, under the heading 'Foot-Rot and its Cure', announced the invention of 'a remedy that has lately been placed upon the market by Mr Harry Price of 32 St. Donatts Road, New Cross'. The advertisement continued:

This specific, which has been termed the acme of veterinary science as regards this complaint, absolutely cures both the contagious and non-contagious forms of foot-rot. Besides being a pre-

---

[1] I encountered a similar difficulty when I was writing the history of a financial institution, founded in 1864, with which I have been associated for over forty years. The first Minute Book recording details of staff was only started in 1912. (Trevor H. Hall, *The Early Years of the Huddersfield Building Society*, Huddersfield, 1974, p. 101.)

ventive of the disease, it has the advantage of being inexpensive,
economical and exceedingly simple in its use. It is the outcome of
painstaking experiments conducted with a view to permanently
curing the sheep, and eliminating all traces of the infection.

At an unknown date during this period Price also seems to have
been in some sort of partnership as 'Price and Creasy', operating
from 32 St. Donatts Road, New Cross. In the press-cutting
album there is a printed, undated hand-bill (of the size to push
through letter-boxes) advertising 'Wholesale and Retail' what
were described as the firm's 'Quexol China Cement', 'Quexol
Chemical Glue' and 'Quexol Chemical Paste Powder'. Messrs.
Price and Creasy claimed to be the 'Sole Proprietors and
Makers' of these various adhesives.

Price was also employed, presumably for financial reward,
in the photography of grocers' shop fronts in the neighbourhood
of New Cross for advertisement purposes. In his cuttings book
are preserved photographs of shops with the proprietors
standing at the door, with names such as Rolfe & Sons of
Lewisham, Digsen & Co. of Deptford and F. Keeble of Brock-
well. Each is in juxtaposition with a cutting of the resultant
printed and published advertisement, with a manuscript note,
'From a photo by HP'.

The impression one gains from this curious collection of
evidence is that Price had no regular employment during this
period, and that he scratched a living as best he could from
these various activities of his. His father was a total failure as
a business man, as we have seen, and it may be that Price
inherited this incapacity. It is not easy to imagine that his cure
for foot-rot revolutionised veterinary medicine. If Price distributed his hand-bills and peddled his 'Quexol' products around
New Cross and the surrounding areas of South London, he
may have regarded the description 'commercial traveller' on
his marriage entry as a respectable euphemism. The simple
truth of the matter is that Price's deceit in regard to every
aspect of his life makes it impossible to be certain about some
matters, and forces the historian into balancing one probability
against another. I would say that the documentary evidence
for Price's varied activities, preserved in his cuttings book, is
incontrovertible, and that it is difficult to understand why he

should have found it necessary to dabble in all these various occupations if he was in regular employment, or to comprehend how he found time for them if his days were otherwise gainfully employed. I find it astounding that Tabori, with all the evidence available to him, made no comment whatsoever on this curious state of affairs, and persisted in the tale, already quoted, that Price 'had his work in the business of which his father was part owner'.

It is true that in later life Price became a prolific and successful writer on occult subjects, and that in his death entry he was described simply as an 'author', with no reference whatsoever to his supposed connexion with the paper-manu-facturing industry, but his first book (which was in collabora-tion) was not published until 1922. Even Tabori (page 17) conceded that Price's 'early books found only a limited public'. The fact remains, however, that from the time of his marriage in 1908 Price became a man of independent means and apparently unlimited leisure, with ample money at his disposal to spend freely upon his hobbies. How then, we may ask, can this sudden transformation of his financial fortunes be explained? The evidence for the financial vacuum is solid so far as any inherited money is concerned. How was it filled?

VI

Marriage and the Knight Family

An interesting sidelight on Price's determination to record the best possible picture of himself is the fact that although every single reference in official documents and directories to Edward Ditcher Price's two addresses in Amersham Road and St. Donatts Road places these streets firmly in New Cross, this district of South London does not appear at all in the index of *Search for Truth*. Throughout that book (pages 16, 30, 45, etc.) Price consistently declared that during his young manhood, following his Shropshire upbringing, his parents lived in Brockley, which lies to the south of New Cross. London friends inform me that Brockley is a superior residential district to New Cross. Price's future wife, Constance Mary Knight, lived with her parents at 10 Adelaide Road, Brockley, where her father, Robert Hastings Knight, gentleman, died on 2 February, 1906, five months before the death of Price's father on 7 July of the same year. Mr Knight's widow, Mary Ann Knight, moved to Riverside, Pulborough in West Sussex, the scene of Price's marriage on 1 August, 1908. It is of interest to see that in the reports of the wedding in the *Kentish Mercury* of 7 August, 1908 and elsewhere, the distinction between Brockley and New Cross is confirmed. Price was described as the 'son of the late Edward Ditcher Price of New Cross', and his bride was stated to be the 'daughter of the late R. H. Knight, of 10 Adelaide Road, Brockley, and Mrs Knight, of Riverside, Pulborough'. It was a singularly appropriate correction, it may be thought, of Price's pretence 34 years later in *Search for Truth* that he and his parents had lived in Brockley. There was another difference, moreover, between the two families, even more easily defined than the relative salubrity and respectability of Brockley and New Cross. It concerned money, which is a subject we can all understand.

Robert Henry Knight, a perfumer, of 47 Bishopsgate, in the City of London, died at the age of 68 on 21 August, 1879. In his long and complicated will he made various specific bequests, including sums of money to his Trustees and Executors, and provided for the equal division of his personal estate between his son, Robert Hastings Knight, and his two daughters. This 'personal estate' included his 'plate, furniture, china, linen, glass, wines and other household effects'. It was the only part of his estate that ranked for probate, and was valued at 'under £5000', a not inconsiderable sum in 1879.

The main part of the will dealt with the bulk of the estate, which was bequeathed to his Trustees upon trust, and was described as 'all my other estate and effects whatsoever and wheresoever both real and personal'. The will contained specific instructions to the Trustees, 'who shall continue the same residuary estate in the same state of investment as the same may be at the time of my decease, and to receive the rents, interest and annual income thereof, and after payment thereout of all taxes, rates, insurance, repairs and other outgoings and incidental expenses relating thereto to pay and divide the net residue of such rents, interest and annual income unto and equally among my said three children Emma Thomazine Knight, Amelia Mary Knight and Robert Hastings Knight during their respective lives'.

There can be no doubt from the foregoing that property was involved in the Trust, and that this was considerable is suggested by the giving of power to the Trustees at their discretion 'to demise and lease any part of my residuary estate for any term of years which they may deem advisable, and on such term with or without a premium as they may think fit, but nevertheless any premium paid for any lease shall form part of the capital of my estate and be invested in or upon government or real or leasehold security and the income applied as hereinbefore declared respecting the rents, interest and other annual income from my residuary estate'. A premium under a lease (usually of commercial property) is a capital sum agreed between the landlord and the tenant and paid at the beginning of the term by the tenant in return for a reduction in the market rent by an amount equal to the annual value of the premium spread over the term of the lease. The fact that Robert Henry

Knight was at pains to instruct his trustees that such premiums must be regarded as capital to be invested either in government securities or additional property suggests that the premiums would be substantial sums of money, and that the rents upon which the premiums would be calculated would be equally high. The substantial nature and value of Robert Henry Knight's trust property and investments is also indicated by the fact that his son, Robert Hastings Knight, is described in various subsequent documents simply as 'Gentleman'.

Robert Hastings Knight, gentleman, of 10 Adelaide Road, Brockley in the county of Kent, died on 2 February, 1906 of a tumour on the brain. In the interim his sister Emma Thomazine had died, and the trust income was divided between his surviving sister Amelia Mary and himself. In his will dated 30 June, 1905 he appointed Trustees, being his son Robert Henry and his wife Mary Ann, for which he had 'general power of appointment . . . by virtue of the will dated the fourth day of July 1879 of my late father Robert Henry Knight or which shall devolve on me as the heir at law or next of kin of my said father'. The precise instructions as to the handling of the 'trust property' were similar to those of the will of his father, except that any capital sums coming into the hands of the trustees from conversions and premiums were to be invested 'in any of the securities for the time being authorised by law for the investment of trustee funds'. The will is as complicated as the previous one, but it is again obvious that substantial amounts of property were involved, as well as government securities, both of which produced 'the income arising from the said property and investments and securities, hereinafter called my trust property'. Again, a small 'personal estate' only ranked for probate, and the trust property was exempt. The heirs to it were 'my said son Robert Henry Knight and my only daughter Constance Mary Knight as tenants in common the share of such daughter to be for her sole and separate use'.

1   Harry Price and Lucy Violet Kay at the Third International Congress of Psychical Research, Paris, 26 September – 2 October 1927 (see p. 15). Reproduced by permission of the University of London Library

2   "Sequah" (William Henry Hartley), Aberdeen, October 1888 (see p. 58)

VII

The Great Sequah

This chapter and those which follow are concerned with two stories told by Price of incidents in his early life, which he claimed were of the highest importance in the subsequent development of his talents. The first was described in the opening chapter of his autobiography, *Search for Truth*. He declared that the incident was probably 'entirely responsible for shaping much of my life's work [and] occurred a week or so before my eighth birthday'. Thirteen years earlier, in a shorter account included in the Preface to the published *Short-Title Catalogue* of his library, Price said 'I was exactly eight years old'. On the basis of these assertions, we can at least date the event as occurring in January, 1889, since we know that Price was born on 17 January, 1881. He said:

One cold January morning the 'Great Sequah', with his brass bands, gilded chariots, and troop of 'boosters' in the garb of Mohawk Indians, pitched his tent—so to speak—in Shrewsbury's principal square.

The performance consisted of the drawing of a tooth from a small boy, the sale of quack medicines and more importantly, a conjuring performance including the production of doves, flags, bags of sweets and small toys from a borrowed and apparently empty hat. Price wrote:

During the whole of this eventful morning I stood, cold but happy, open-mouthed at this display of credulity, self-deception, auto-suggestion, faith-healing, beautiful showmanship, super-charlatanism, and 'magic'. The miracles of the market-place left me spellbound.

Price continued by saying that 'on my arrival home I demanded from my astonished parents an explanation of how it was that an empty hat had contained two doves, and would they please show me exactly how it was done'. He said that 'after several days' pestering on my part' his father finally succumbed, and as one of his son's birthday gifts, presented him with a copy of 'Professor Hoffman's' *Modern Magic*, which Price said was the first item he owned in the collection of 17,000 volumes on magic of all kinds which he subsequently assembled. At the bottom of page 12 of *Search for Truth*, linked to 'Professor Hoffman's' (which is in quotation marks in the text) is a footnote, 'i.e. Angelo John Lewis, M.A., a mathematician and author of many works on conjuring'. It is surprising, in view of the importance that Price properly attached to his first acquisition as a book-collector, that it was too much trouble to spell the author's pseudonym, 'Hoffmann', correctly. *Modern Magic*, first published in 1876, is open at the title-page before me as I write. Price made the same mistake in 1929 on pages 218–20 of his printed *Short-Title Catalogue* of his library, in which he listed his ownership of over fifty items by Professor Hoffmann, including fourteen editions of *Modern Magic*, so that the error persisted for thirteen years. Angelo Lewis was a barrister-at-law, not a mathematician.

Price's first account in 1929 of his experience in what he called 'Shrewsbury's principal square'[1] differs in some details from the later story in *Search for Truth*, but the essential sentences which are of particular interest are very similar:

> The miracles of the market-place left me spell-bound. I was exactly eight years old. On my arrival home I demanded from my astonished parents an explanation as to how it was that an 'empty' hat contained two doves and would they please show me exactly how it was done.

The first distinct impression we gain from Price's account is that he was alone as he stood, 'cold but happy', watching the conjuring performance, 'during the whole of this eventful

---

[1] 'The Square', as it is actually named, is in the centre of Shrewsbury, and contains the market hall, built in 1595, and Baron Marochetti's fine statue of Lord Clive. I chose a fine, sunlit April afternoon to stand in it, and was warm but puzzled, rather than 'cold but happy'.

morning'. His father and mother were clearly not with him, since it was not until his 'arrival home' that he was able to confront his parents and to demand an explanation of the secrets of magic. He was either 'exactly eight years old', or alternatively 'a week or so' short of achieving that age. He was therefore in any event a small child, from which it is reasonable to assume that home was not far away. The second impression we gain from the story, therefore, is that in January 1889 Price's home was in Shrewsbury.

The impressions thus imposed upon us by Price are contradicted by the fact, as we already know, that the London directories of the period show that as early as 1887 and as late as 1892 Edward Ditcher Price and his family were living at 6 Amersham Road, New Cross in South London, which Price was careful not to mention. If it be urged that the Price family might have been staying with their Shropshire relatives on holiday, there are one or two facts to be taken into consideration which would seem to militate against such a possibility. First, Price said that he returned *home*, which usually means what it says. Secondly, the study of John Price's family, as we have seen, did not include any relatives living in Shrewsbury, or nearer to the county town than villages like Rodington and Withington, at least six miles away. Thirdly, we may think that January, following closely upon the Christmas vacation, is not a usual or attractive month to take two young children away on holiday, when they should have been at school in any event.

Herbert E. Pratt, for many years the Hon. Librarian of the Magic Circle and a formidable collector of memorabilia of entertainment and allied subjects, has most kindly sent me a number of cuttings relating to 'Sequah' (never, in a single instance, described as the 'Great Sequah') which are of considerable interest. All are taken from *The World's Fair*, a weekly journal which is still extant. These cuttings, a dozen in all, combine to tell us that Sequah 'was Hartley, an American who ran a Medicine Show in the U.S.A., and brought an American Medicine Wagon to this country where he employed real Indians and a brass band to entertain the great crowds. He pulled teeth and massaged stiff joints with a balm that can still be purchased in this country'.

In a cutting recalling Sequah's visit to Middlesbrough it was said, 'He used to stand six nights a week on the Victoria Square, a large piece of land next to the fine Municipal Buildings, drawing big crowds nightly. His Prairie Flower (stomach mixture) and an embrocation for rheumatism also had good sales in chemists' shops. A great feature was the rubbing with the embrocation oil of rheumatic victims, several of whom said they felt cured when they left the band wagon'. Not one of these cuttings mentions conjuring.

Through the kindness of Professor Edwin A. Dawes, a distinguished member of the Magic Circle, I have obtained, with additional published accounts of Sequah, a near full-size photographic reproduction of a whole-page advertisement by Sequah on page 18 of *The Northern Figaro*, Aberdeen. It is dated 6 October, 1888, some three months previous to the date of Price's alleged experience in Shrewsbury. Again, there is no mention whatever of conjuring, nor does the advertiser lay claim to the title of 'The Great Sequah', all of which is of considerable interest in view of the closeness of the dates.[1]

The advertisement is illustrated by a head and shoulders picture of Sequah, dressed as a cowboy, and is entirely devoted to the advertisement of the 'peerless remedies' prepared by the 'Sequah Indian Medicine Firm', guaranteed to cure 'Indigestion, Biliousness, and all diseases of the Stomach, Liver and Bowels, Kidney Troubles, Lumbago, Sciatica and Chronic Rheumatism in all its forms, and exceedingly useful in almost all Chronic Diseases'. The two specifics advertised in very large lettering were 'Sequah's Prairie Flower' and 'Sequah's Oil' at 2/- per bottle. We may notice the coincidence that in his story of the 'Great Sequah' in *Search for Truth* (p. 11) Price precisely mentions by name both 'Sequah's Oil' and 'Prairie Flower', which could suggest one of two things. If an exceptional memory on Price's part is assumed, capable of recalling the small details of an incident experienced at eight years of age, then some may believe that this confirms the truth of the account. To others, recalling Price's familiarity with the history of charlatanism in all its aspects, it may suggest precisely the opposite. If it be suspected that the thrilling story of Price's

[1] See Plate 2.

adventure in Shrewsbury at the age of eight (or nearly eight) was invented, then the provenance of his precise naming of 'Prairie Flower' and 'Sequah's Oil' is not hard to imagine.

It is of great interest that no mention whatever of conjuring is included in the advertisement, nor in any of the dozen and more published accounts of Sequah's activities sent to me by Professor Dawes and Mr Pratt. Sequah's name, moreover, does not appear in S. W. Clarke's monumental and exhaustive *The Annals of Conjuring* (London, 1929), which includes the histories of even drawing-room performers and some amateurs. My own doubts in regard to this romantic tale of Price's childhood are mainly based on the solid fact that he was living in New Cross in 1889, and the suspicious smoothness with which the whole story fits into the legend that Price was the son of Edward Ditcher Price of Shrewsbury (which we recall he used in his entry in *Who's Who*) with all its accompanying invented details which have persisted and been copied over a period of many years.

VIII

The Sceptic

On page 28 of *Search for Truth* Price wrote:

When I was aged 15 years and 9 months I founded the Carlton Dramatic Society. I did it for a special purpose. A few weeks previously, when spending my school vacation in Shropshire, I had investigated a story of haunting in an old Salopian manor house. It was my first haunted house, and my first introduction to *Poltergeister*. This case so impressed me that, when I returned home, I decided to dramatise my experiences in the form of a three-act play. Knowing that I should not find a manager or company to produce it for me, I made up my mind to form my own company and be my own manager.

Since Price was born on 17 January, 1881, it is clear that he was claiming that the Carlton Dramatic Society was founded about the middle of October, 1896,[1] and that his experience in Shropshire of his first haunted house took place 'a few weeks previously', during the last weeks of his school holiday in September of that year. On pages 28–30 of the same book Price described the early performances of the Society between 1896 and 1898, including 'musical evenings' and plays (all written by Price) with titles such as *Snowed Up*, *Miss Angelica's Séance* and *Half-Hours with the Mediums*, and a musical comedy, *Claude Duval*, which Price both wrote and in which he played

---

[1] On p. 156 of Price's first press-cutting book is pasted a printed ticket for a musical entertainment on Friday, 18 November, 1898. At the top is printed, 'The Carlton Dramatic Society. Founded 1895'. In the office of the Archives and History Group, The Manor House, Old Road, London, S.E. 13 is a 234-page manuscript (*c.* 1940) *Fifty Years on the Amateur Stage*, by Harry Golding. It is a history of the amateur dramatic societies in South London over a period of half a century from about 1880. The Carlton Dramatic Society and Harry Price are not mentioned.

the principal part of the gallant highwayman. Finally, on page 30 of *Search for Truth*, he wrote:

Having founded the Carlton Dramatic Society for a specific purpose, I set about—rather tardily, I am afraid—writing my ghost play. I called it *The Sceptic* and, as I have said, the plot was based on my experiences with a Shropshire Poltergeist. The play was ready at last and we performed it at the Amersham Hall, New Cross, on Friday, December 2, 1898. We had a packed house and it proved a great success.

On the same page of *Search for Truth* Price underlined his assertion that *The Sceptic* was a dramatisation of his first encounter with psychic phenomena:

I will not give the reader an outline of the plot, as I am going to relate to him my actual experiences in the haunted house on which the play was based.

It is unfortunate that the text of *The Sceptic* is not now present in the Harry Price collection in the University of London Library. The available evidence consists of what Tabori described on page 22 of the biography as 'a yellowed playbill' advertising the performance of *The Sceptic* on 2 December, 1898, and a short report of the event in the *South London Press* of 10 December.[1] Mr Alan Wesencraft has most kindly sent me xeroxes of these two documents.

Tabori's 'playbill' is actually a programme of an evening's entertainment, of which *The Sceptic* was the last of twenty-two items of songs, recitations, musical sketches and the like. Tabori failed to copy correctly the cast of the play, reversing the parts of Sid Palfery and Alf Smith. More seriously, however, in his reproduction of the programme on pages 22–3 of his book, Tabori omitted the essential line that gives us our first indication of the true flavour of the play. I have put the suppressed line in square brackets:

---

[1] The notice in the *South London Press* is not now present in Price's press-cutting albums. Mr Wesencraft thoughtfully obtained a copy for me from the Brixton Public Library.

[A Farcical Comedy in Three Acts, entitled:—]

'THE SCEPTIC'

By Harry Price.

Cast—

Bert Holloway	*Undergraduates at*	Mr. SID PALFERY
Will Clancy	*King's College,*	Mr. HARRY PRICE
Ted Newnham	*Cambridge.*	Mr. PERCY PALFERY
Briggs	*Scout to Will Clancy*	Mr. ALF SMITH

ACT I. Will Clancy's Room at King's College.
ACT II. Reading Room at King's College.
ACT III. THE BEDROOM SCENE. The haunted chamber
in the ruined wing of 'Castleford Chase',
Sir George Newnham's Estate, in Wiltshire.

Two months supposed to elapse between Acts 2 and 3.

Five minutes Interval between 1st and 2nd Acts, and
ten minutes between 2nd and 3rd Acts.

The short report in the *South London Press* confirmed that *The Sceptic* was 'an original farcical comedy in three acts by Harry Price'. We also learn a little more of the theme of the play:

It told in a sufficiently amusing fashion of the adventures of three Cambridge undergraduates. The incidental details of college pranks, impecuniosity, haunted chambers, ghosts and various evolutions through conservatory windows, suggested many old friends in a new dress.

The unavailability of the text of the play is unfortunate, but the programme and the press report combine to give us a reasonably clear picture of a farce, two-thirds of which takes place in a Cambridge college. The final scene in the ruined wing of a mansion in Wiltshire presumably involves some comings and goings of 'ghosts' through conservatory windows. I fancy that there is sufficient evidence to enable us to form an opinion of the truth of Price's claim that he founded the Carlton Dramatic Society in October, 1896[1] for the 'special purpose' of

[1] Or 1895, according to the ticket in the press-cutting book.

dramatising his first psychical experience, that had so greatly impressed him,[1] in Shropshire during the previous month.

On pages 31–5 of *Search for Truth* Price told the thrilling story of his adventure in September, 1896:

And now for my experiences with my first *Poltergeist*. I used to spend many of my school holidays in a little Shropshire village a few miles from Shrewsbury. In the village was—and still is—an old manor house. It had remained empty for some time but, just previous to my visit, it had been leased by a retired Canon of the Church of England, and his wife. The man was in failing health. The house had a reputation for being haunted, and very soon after the Canon's settling down in the place, strange occurrences were reported.

The manifestations were said to have started in the farm-buildings attached to the house. Animals were discovered un-tethered and wandering, and pans of milk in the dairy were found overturned. Suddenly, however, the phenomena outside the house ceased, and the ghost (or poltergeist) transferred its attention to the inside of the house. A noise like the pattering of a child's feet was heard on the landing. Fires in the various rooms would be raked out during the night by unseen entities, the burning embers being scattered over the floors. The Canon's wife had to arrange for water to be poured on the fires before retiring to rest.[2] Price wrote on page 32 of *Search for Truth*:

[1] As we shall see, in his first account of the case in the *Journal* of the American S.P.R. in 1926, Price claimed that the impression made upon him was such that it was 'an experience from which he dates his intense and sustained interest in psychic phenomena'.

[2] These details of the 'phenomena' compare oddly with Price's short account of the case on p. 296 of his *Fifty Years of Psychical Research* (London, 1939). There is no doubt whatever that he was referring to 'Parton Magna', because in a footnote he gives the correct reference to pp. 15–24 of *Confessions of a Ghost-Hunter*. He wrote, 'In particular, I consider that the genuineness of many *Poltergeist* cases has been established. As a lad, I was deeply impressed and absolutely convinced of the manifestations for which the Germans have given us a most appropriate term. The house in question was in Shropshire and the typical stone-throwing, window-rattling and door-slamming "ghost" made a great impression on my adolescent and receptive mind, and from then onwards I decided to become an investigator'.

It can be imagined that the events at the Manor House[2] did not improve the Canon's health, and his wife finally persuaded him to leave the place, at least for a short period. This was in the early autumn, just before I arrived in the village for my usual few days' vacation.

Price said that what had finally driven the family out of the house was a nocturnal noise as if someone was stamping about the house in heavy boots, making sleep impossible. He asserted that he had no difficulty in persuading the wife of the Canon's cowman to hand over the key, so that Price and a boy friend could spend a night in the house.

I must confess that I had little idea what I was going to do in the house, or how I was going to do it. But I had a small tripod camera with me, so I decided—hopefully—that I would photograph the ghost, if possible!

Price said that he knew that he would have to photograph the ghost by flashlight, so he cycled into Shrewsbury and bought some magnesium powder, a couple of batteries with which to fire it, a coil of flex and a switch. He proposed to mix the smokeless powder from some sporting cartridges with the magnesium powder in order to ensure its ignition by means of a piece of platinum wire connected by flex to the batteries and the switch. The ghost made a habit of stamping loudly down the staircase into the large hall, off which was the door to the morning-room. A pair of kitchen steps were set up in the hall. Price continued (pp. 33–4):

I placed my camera on one of the lower treads of the steps, and then proceeded to focus on the centre of the stairs. On the top of the steps I placed an eggcupful of the flash mixture in an old Waterbury watch case that I had with me. The platinum wire was inserted in the powder, and the flex, batteries and switch were taken into the morning-room. I extinguished the stable lantern and, after withdrawing the shutter of the dark-slide and uncapping the lens, we crept into the morning-room, the door of which we softly closed. We lay down on the floor.

[2] The location of which Price concealed under the name of 'Parton Magna'.

The time was 11.30 p.m. After a vigil of a further hour, Price and his friend heard the noise of someone walking heavily in clogs from a room overhead. The ghost came stamping down the stairs, and was heard to pause in the hall for a few minutes, before starting to stamp up the stairs once more. When Price estimated that the ghost was half-way on its upward journey, he pressed the switch. There was a violent explosion and flash, the latter being visible to Price and his friend under the morning-room door. Simultaneously, whatever it was that was ascending the stairs distinctly *stumbled*, and there was a noise of some object clattering down the stairs.

We bravely marched into the hall, and made a tour of inspection. We found that the steps had moved slightly, but there was no sign of the ghost or of the Waterbury watch-case. This we found later on the stairs. The force of the explosion had projected the case up the stairs, and it had rolled down again. That was the clattering noise we heard. I had used too much gunpowder.

Price said that he and his friend searched the house, tidied up and left the haunted Manor House in the small hours of the morning. When the plate was developed there was nothing on the negative except an over-exposed picture of a staircase. 'But the trip,' wrote Price (p. 34), 'had been worth while as— very definitely—we had contacted a real ghost in a real haunted house. The experience was thrilling and made a great impression on me'.

Price concluded his story of his first experience of a haunted house on page 35 of *Search for Truth*:

Some years later I was destined to visit the house many times, as it was then in the possession of a friend. Neither he nor I, nor his family, experienced any untoward incident in the Manor. I wish I could give the reader the exact location of the place,[1] but it is now—I believe—in the occupation of a well-known London business man and he might object. I hope to call upon him one day.

[1] In his first account of the case, published in the *Journal* of the American S.P.R., to be considered in detail in the next chapter, Price asserted that 'for the sake of historical accuracy, the real name of the mansion has been supplied to the Editor of this *Journal*, to be placed in the archives of the Society'. Miss Rhea A. White, the Director of Information of the A.S.P.R.,

The account of Price's first psychic adventure occupied four pages of *Search for Truth*. He had published a much longer account six years previously in the first chapter of his *Confessions of a Ghost-Hunter* ('The Ghost that Stumbled', pp. 15–24), and this enlarged version was included *verbatim* with the omission of one paragraph of no significance probably missed in copying,[1] in his *Poltergeist over England* ('The Poltergeist that Stumbled', pp. 213–19) published three years after *Search for Truth*. There were minor discrepancies between the longer account and the shortened version, doubtless due to carelessness rather than design. In the former, for example, it was stated that the Canon had purchased the house, as opposed to taking a lease of it. Price also confessed in the more detailed story that he had given the village a fictitious name:

As a member of an old Shropshire family, I spent nearly all my holidays and school vacations in a little village—in fact, a hamlet—which I will call Parton Magna. In Parton Magna is the old Manor House, *circa* A.D. 1600. It had been purchased by a retired canon of the Church of England, and his wife.[2]

Without any intervening reference to his domestic and scholastic circumstances in September, 1896, Price wrote later in the same account:

On my way back to school for the Michaelmas term I broke my journey at Parton Magna in order to stay a few days with our friends, who then made me acquainted with the state of affairs at the Manor House; in fact, it was the principal topic of conversation.

---

in reply to an enquiry by Dr Dingwall, says that a careful search of the Society's archives and indexes has produced no trace of such a letter from Price.

[1] The omitted paragraph (*Confessions of a Ghost-Hunter*, p. 18) was, 'Permission to spend a night in the Manor was easily obtained from the woman (who lived in a cottage near the house) who was looking after the place, and doubtless she regarded us as a couple of mad schoolboys who would have been much better in bed.' In the two longer accounts Price omitted the reference to Shrewsbury, and said, 'On the morning of the adventure I cycled into the nearest town . . .' The nearest town to 'Parton Magna' was in fact Wellington, as I was subsequently to discover.

[2] *Confessions of a Ghost-Hunter*, p. 15, and *Poltergeist over England*, p. 213.

He added that 'by a lucky chance I had with me a delicate chemical balance which I was taking back to school', and that the purchase of the magnesium powder, flex and batteries resulted in 'a big hole [being made] in my term's pocket money'.[1] Bearing in mind that in 1896 Price was living in St. Donatts Road, New Cross, and was attending a day school within walking distance in Pepys Road, New Cross, these later topographical details could be confusing to the reader.

Because Price's description of the *fons et origo* of the haunting proved to be of importance to the investigation I undertook, I paraphrase or quote the more detailed version from the two longer accounts. Price said that at the period of his story the history of the manor house at Parton Magna was the subject of excited discussion by the villagers. The house had been built by a rich recluse who, because of 'an unfortunate *affaire de coeur*', as Price called it, had elected to retire from the world and its disappointments. A niece looked after him and managed his servants. One night the recluse went to the young woman's apartment, and strangled her in bed.

After this most unavuncular act the old man left the house, spent the night in the neighbouring woods and at daybreak threw himself into the river that runs through the fields near the house. The legend, like the *Poltergeist*, also runs true to type. Like most traditions, there is a grain of truth in the story, the fact being that many years previously a girl named Mary Hulse had died at the Manor under suspicious circumstances.[2]

As I have remarked in a previous chapter, it is very surprising that Price did not see fit to mention the astonishing coincidence that Mary Hulse were the forenames of his grandfather's first child, who died of natural causes in 1835.

As we have seen in *Search for Truth*, Price said that he was destined in later years to visit the house many times as it was then in the possession of a friend. In the longer account, this story became more romantic:

[1] *Confessions of a Ghost-Hunter*, pp. 17–18, and *Poltergeist over England*, p. 215.
[2] *Op cit.*, p. 17, and *op cit.*, p. 214. If there is a word of truth in this story, the reader may wonder how anyone could know how the recluse spent his time between the murder and the discovery of his body in the river.

Fate decreed that some years later I should spend many happy weeks in the house. If sometimes during that period my heart beat faster than its accustomed rate, the cause was *not* a supernatural one! Suffice it to say that I did not see or hear anything of the alleged spirit of Mary Hulse, though I will candidly admit that I was not looking for her—my interest in the diaphanous maiden having been transferred by that time to one of a much more objective nature![1]

Price's unreliability as a writer apart, it was clear that the case presented difficult problems for the investigator. The alleged happenings had occurred in the late nineteenth century, virtually beyond living memory, in a location concealed by Price under the name 'Parton Magna'. Indeed, the only clues (if they could be relied upon at all) seemed to be that 'Parton Magna' was within cycling distance of Shrewsbury and that a river flowed through the fields near the house, which had been purchased (or leased) by a retired clergyman in failing health shortly before September, 1896. For some time it seemed to me that the difficulties of an inquiry into such a story might well prove to be insuperable.

Mr Anthony Carr, the Local History Librarian of Salop County Council, most kindly sent me the details of old manor houses contained in the Shropshire *Provisional List of Buildings of Architectural and Historic interest for consideration in connexion with the provisions of Section 30 of the Town and Country Planning Act, 1947,* but unfortunately no property of this kind, '*circa* A.D. 1600', fitted the requirements of close proximity to a river for convenient suicide, and at the same time to be within cycling distance of Shrewsbury. Upton Magna, for example (with its tempting similarity of name to 'Parton Magna') is close to the county town, and is not a long way from the river Severn, but has no seventeenth-century manor-house. Mr Carr also spoke with Miss Jean Hughes of Shrewsbury, the author of two books on Shropshire hauntings and folklore and a well-known lecturer on these subjects, to find that she has no knowledge of any story of a local haunted house with the smallest resemblance to that told by Price, nor of the tale of the death in suspicious circumstances in bygone years of any girl named Mary Hulse. It was

[1] *Confessions of a Ghost-Hunter,* p. 24, and *Poltergeist over England,* p. 219.

Miss Hughes who most kindly looked up for us the newspaper accounts of the period, recording the death of Mary Hulse Price from natural causes in 1835.

In Tabori's biography of Price (pp. 306–11) is a list of articles contributed by the latter to periodicals, and I thought it worth while to ask Mr Alan Wesencraft of the University of London if I might have xeroxes of two of these, which from their titles appeared to be earlier accounts of the case than those published in Price's books. With his invariable kindness, Mr Wesencraft supplied me with copies of the articles concerned, which proved to be of the greatest possible interest.

'I Hunt a Ghost in a Haunted Manor' was published in the *Indian National Herald*, Bombay, on 12 April, 1928. It contained several surprises.[1] First, Price said that 'these strange happenings took place while I was *on a visit* [my italics] to an old manor house in a village I will call Parton Magna'. Secondly, he said that 'a flashlight photograph was taken at the exact second the mysterious unseen visitor was in the act of entering the hall'. Thirdly, and most oddly of all, throughout the whole of the article he omitted any reference whatever to the unnamed friend who in the later accounts he declared had shared his adventure. He wrote, for example:

At about half-past eleven I was beginning to get very sleepy, when suddenly I heard a noise in the room overhead—the traditional apartment of the unfortunate Mary Hulse . . . Just before midnight I again heard a noise in the upper room; it was as if a heavy person was stamping about in clogs . . . Keenly excited, I decided to investigate the stairs and Mary Hulse's room . . . By the time I had fixed the camera to my satisfaction it was about half-past one . . . Then I lay down upon the carpet near the door of the morning-room and commenced my vigil . . . I left the manor about 3.30 a.m. and developed the plate the same morning.

[1] Perhaps the most astonishing statement made by Price that is entirely confined to the *Indian National Herald* account is the following, 'There was another pause in the hall, and again the footfalls commenced their upward journey. Determined to have a look at the ghost, I flung open the door. The footsteps came to a sudden stop with the turning of the key in the lock. There was nothing to be seen. I then decided to make an attempt at a flashlight picture if the poltergeist descended the stairs again.' It is precisely this kind of glaring discrepancy in Price's tales of his adventures in the occult that forces the reader into doubting the truth of any of them.

In this version of the tale, wholly in the first person singular, Price appears as a solitary and therefore much more intrepid investigator than in the later accounts. It is fair to say, however, that he does not give the slightest indication of the date of the occurrence, and that the reader of this article in isolation would have no inkling that Price claimed elsewhere that he was a schoolboy of fifteen at the time, and that it was his first encounter with the occult, in company with a friend. These assertions had all been made, however, in a much longer article published two years previously, containing some details never re-published by Price, which opened up the possibility of an investigation at last, and eventually took me to Shropshire and 'Parton Magna'.

Price contributed 'A Strange Experience with a Shropshire Poltergeist' to the *Journal* of the American Society for Psychical Research of February, 1926 (pp. 77–87). He wrote in the opening paragraph that 'it was the writer's first psychic experience—an experience from which he dates his intense and sustained interest in psychic phenomena'. The curious tale of breaking his journey back to school in New Cross *via* Shropshire was not excluded, but receded into the background. He wrote:

At the period of which I am writing, my parents lived near London, and I was entrusted to the care of some very old friends who resided in the village, which I will call Parton Magna.

That Price was accompanied by a friend was conceded:

To say I was nervous at the idea of spending a night in the house would be a mild description of my feelings, but the novelty of the project eventually overcame my fears of the unknown and I persuaded a boy friend to accompany me in my adventure.

One of the most astonishing details of this first account by Price of the 'Parton Magna' affair is his dating of it, which is totally at variance with the stories told in his books, in which, as we have seen, he specifically placed the episode in September, 1896, a few weeks previous to his foundation of the Carlton Dramatic Society when he was 'aged 15 years and 9 months' (*Search for Truth*, p. 28). Instead, he wrote:

In the early part of the year 1898 the Manor House was, as I have stated, bought by a clergyman whose ill-health had compelled him to relinquish a strenuous living in the Midlands (p. 78) . . . It can be imagined that the Canon's health was suffering under the anxiety caused by the disturbing events I have recorded above, and he was persuaded to leave the house for at least a short period. This was in the autumn of the year 1898. On my way back to school for the Michaelmas term I broke my journey at Parton Magna [from where, one wonders?] in order to stay a few days with our friends, who then made me acquainted with the state of affairs at the Manor House (p. 81).

If the date of the affair was really the autumn of 1898,[1] on the assumption that a first account with the date twice stated is likely to be more reliable than subsequent versions, how can we possibly reconcile it with Price's story, quoted earlier in this chapter, of the foundation and early history of the Carlton Dramatic Society? We recall that Price recorded in *Search for Truth*:

(1) That he founded the Carlton Dramatic Society when he was aged 15 years and 9 months, i.e. in October, 1896.

(2) That he founded the Society for a specific purpose, i.e. because 'a few weeks previously' he had investigated his first haunting 'in an old Salopian manor house', which had so impressed him that he wanted to write a play based on the experience. He decided, however, that for this purpose he must first establish his own company and become his own manager.

(3) That between 1896 and 1898, before writing his play *The Sceptic* based on his 'Parton Magna' experience, he wrote three plays and a musical comedy, all of which were performed with great success by the Carlton Dramatic Society.

(4) That finally, 'rather tardily' in 1898, Price 'set about' writing *The Sceptic* and when 'the play was ready at last' it was performed at the Amersham Hall, New Cross on 2 December, 1898.

Obviously nothing fits when the dates of 1896 and 1898 are

---

[1] Hereward Carrington and Nandor Fodor accepted the date of 1898 in their record of the case on p. 51 of *The Story of the Poltergeist down the Centuries* (London, 1953).

compared, and we are in even greater difficulty when we read
Price's account in 1926 of how *The Sceptic* came to be written,
with which we are regaled in the penultimate paragraph of
'A Strange Experience with a Shropshire Poltergeist', an
account that is completely at variance with the tale told in
Search for Truth. He rounded off his story of his adventure in
the last weeks of the school summer holidays in 1898 with the
following:

> Soon after the beginning of term I returned home from school
> owing to illness and in my leisure time wove the essential features
> of the above narrative into a three-act 'psychic comedy' called
> 'The Sceptic', which was publicly performed before an audience of
> more than 500, at an entertainment I gave at the Amersham Hall,
> South London, on Friday, 2 December, 1898. It was my first—and
> last—attempt at a psychic play (p. 87).

It may be thought that on the basis of this early version of
the story of Price's 'first—and last—attempt at a psychic play',
his earlier successes with his *Miss Angelica's Séance* and *Half-
Hours with the Mediums*, and indeed the very existence of the
Carlton Dramatic Society, had been entirely forgotten, for in
1926 he mentioned none of these events. If his memory was
faulty at the time, it appears to have been restored in 1942,
when *Search for Truth* was published. On pages 28–9 of his
autobiography, after describing the two first ventures of the
Carlton Dramatic Society, two 'musical evenings' staged on
15 October and 27 November, 1896, Price continued:

> There is a hiatus in my first press-cutting book, and I have no
> more programmes of the Carlton Dramatic Society until 1898,
> when I staged my ghost play. But we gave a number of entertain-
> ments and concerts—all for charity—at various places. I also wrote
> a number of playlets, including *Snowed Up*, 'a honeymoon episode
> in one act'; and, later *Miss Angelica's Séance* (in which many magical
> effects were employed).

After all this, as we have seen, he wrote ('rather tardily') *The
Sceptic* in 1898.

These startling contradictions in dates between 1896 and
1898, the alternately forgotten and remembered incidents of

the earlier productions described in *Search for Truth* but not in 1926 (and unfortunately unrecorded because of the 'hiatus' in Price's first press-cutting book) and the entirely different stories of how *The Sceptic* came to be written, are exceedingly puzzling and, it may be thought, somewhat suspicious. When we try to date *Miss Angelica's Séance* and *Half-Hours with the Mediums*, moreover, we encounter additional problems. The only reference to them I have been able to find, apart from Price's account in *Search for Truth*, is on page 313 of the first printed catalogue of his collection. There is one entry for the text of *Miss Angelica's Séance*:

[Price, Harry] Miss Angelica's Séance; or, Cupid and the Medium. A Magical Playlet [Typescript.] [London, 1922].

There is no entry for any text of *Half-Hours with the Mediums*, and the single reference to this production is on the same page of the catalogue:

[Price, Harry] [Programme of entertainment, "Half Hours with the Mediums, or, Behind the Scenes in the Spirit World"]. Horsham, 1920.

The latter entry fits partly, but only partly, with Price's comment on pages 29–30 of *Search for Truth*, immediately following the sentences in which he described how *Miss Angelica's Séance* and *Snowed Up*[1] were written and produced by him for the Carlton Dramatic Society before the advent of *The Sceptic* in 1898:

About this time I also wrote the first edition of *Half-Hours with the Mediums*, a two hours' entertainment consisting entirely of 'miracles' as staged by the fake mediums, with whose tricks I was becoming thoroughly acquainted, *young as I was*. [My italics.] This entertainment was brought up to date from time to time, even as late as 1920. I also wrote the 'book' for an ambitious musical comedy called *Claude Duval*.[2] I forget who supplied the musical score, but it was very successful. I took the part of Claude. Where

---

[1] This production is not recorded in the catalogue.
[2] This item is also omitted from the catalogue.

are all these friends *of my schooldays?* [My italics.] They passed completely out of my life when the Carlton Dramatic Society rang down its curtain for the last time, somewhere about 1902.

The two phrases I have placed in italics make it clear beyond doubt that Price was claiming that both *Miss Angelica's Séance* and *Half-Hours with the Mediums* were first written and produced over twenty years before the only dates for them recorded in his catalogue. He was thirty-nine in 1920 and forty-one in 1922.

There may have been 'first editions' of *Miss Angelica's Séance* and *Half-Hours with the Mediums*, written and produced by Price before 1898. Anything, it is popularly supposed, is possible. The 'hiatus' in the first press-cutting book, however, and the absence of any record of these supposed early productions in Price's catalogue of his collection, combine to give the critic a feeling of unease about them. The internal evidence of the single text available to us, moreover, that of *Miss Angelica's Séance*, demonstrates that it could not possibly have been written before the early nineteen-twenties.

The typescript of this one-act play is in the Price Collection in the University of London Library. Its 23 typed pages are pasted into covers of what appears to be decorated wrapping paper. The full title is *Miss Angelica's Séance; or, Cupid and the Medium*, by Harry Price. The rather puerile plot concerns the efforts of Miss Angelica Flyturtle ('a lady of uncertain age— and means') to persuade Professor Boreham-Baddeley, F.R.S. ('a wealthy widower, highbrow and sceptic') to marry her, despite his promise to his late wife Laura that he would always remain a widower in the event of her death. Miss Angelica pays a professional spirit medium, Madame Sikotriks, to produce a message ostensibly from Laura, releasing the Professor from his undertaking:

'Go straight ahead, John; she's a bit ancient, but not a bad sort. Cheerio! Laura.'

The Professor becomes an enthusiastic convert to spiritualism, and at the end of the play the two principal characters embrace each other fondly.

Professor Boreham-Baddeley refers to 'Professor Einstein' no less than five times, on pages 3, 4, 6 and 20. Albert Einstein (1879–1955) was only nineteen years old in 1898, and was an engineer in the Swiss Patent Office until 1909, the year when he became a professor, first at Zürich and Prague, and finally at the Prussian Academy of Science. On page 8 of the type-script Miss Angelica is preparing the ground for the deception of Professor Boreham-Baddeley and his acceptance of the possibility of spirit communication with his dead wife. Miss Angelica picks up a newspaper and glances at it:

Only this morning I read of Sir [Arthur] Conan Doyle conversing with his mother at a séance. She was plainly visible—wrinkles and all (hands paper to PROF.).

We can clearly relate this passage to a statement by Doyle in his autobiography:

In the presence of Miss Besinnet as medium and of several witnesses I have seen my mother and my nephew, young Oscar Hurnung, as plainly as ever I saw them in life—so plainly that I could almost have counted the wrinkles of the one and the freckles of the other.[1]

On 14 March, 1922 Doyle wrote to the late Harry Houdini about the report on Miss Ada Besinnet prepared by the 'Psychic College':

If that had not been in the hands of really experienced and sympathetic people it would have seemed like a huge exposure, and yet it is clearly shown how honest the medium is, how true are her phenomena, and how, in trance, she is certainly at the mercy of her control who mixes the normal and the supernormal. After I had seen my mother in her presence I did not want any proof as to her powers.[2]

Doyle did not become an active propagandist in the cause of spiritualism until 1916,[3] and his mother, Mary Doyle, affec-

---

[1] Sir Arthur Conan Doyle, *Memories and Adventures* (London, 1924), p. 401.

[2] Bernard M. L. Ernst & Hereward Carrington, *Houdini and Conan Doyle. The Story of a Strange Friendship* (London, 1933), p. 133.

[3] As I try to show in the essay 'Conan Doyle and Spiritualism' in my *Sherlock Holmes and His Creator* (Duckworth, London, 1978).

tionately referred to in the family as 'the Ma'am', did not die until 1921.[1] These dates and facts would seem to place the writing of *Miss Angelica's Séance* firmly in the early nineteen-twenties, and any hypothetical unrecorded 'first edition' of it must have had an entirely different text.

To sum up, it seems to me that Price's tale in *Search for Truth* of his foundation of the Carlton Dramatic Society in 1896 and his motive for so doing is full of contradictions when it is examined. Such evidence as is available in regard to the theme of *The Sceptic*, moreover, offers no support for Price's story that it was compulsively written by him because of his determination to record for posterity the impressive experience 'from which he dates his intense and sustained interest in psychic pheno-mena', as he claimed in the *Journal* of the American S.P.R. in 1926. The experience itself was variously claimed by Price to have occurred in 1896 and 1898. According to him, the opportunity to spend a night in the house at 'Parton Magna' (either alone or with a friend) presented itself because of the accident of his breaking his journey back to school in Shropshire for the Michaelmas term, armed with a delicate chemical balance and a term's pocket-money. Since investigation has shown that in both 1896 and 1898 Price's home and his school were within walking distance of each other in New Cross in South London, we cannot avoid looking at this tale with reservations that amount to suspicion. This suspicion is not diminished by the curious story of 'Mary Hulse'. At the con-clusion of the next chapter, it is possible that the reader may share my view of the likely provenance of the tale of 'Parton Magna'.

The foregoing pages have been devoted to a documentary study of the related problems of 'Parton Magna', the Carlton Dramatic Society and the writing of *The Sceptic*. In the chapter that follows I hope that the reader will accompany me in imagination to Shropshire and to the field investigation that enabled at least the first of these mysteries to be solved after half a century of concealment by Price.

---

[1] John Dickson Carr, *The Life of Sir Arthur Conan Doyle* (London, 1949), p. 331.

IX

Search for 'Parton Magna'

As I have remarked in the previous chapter, Price's first account of the 'Parton Magna' haunting, published as 'A Strange Experience with a Shropshire Poltergeist' in 1926, contained some details which were never published again, so far as I am aware. Whether he thought afterwards with anxiety that the clues he had given might enable 'Parton Magna' to be located by an experienced investigator I do not know, but they were omitted completely from the article in the *Indian National Herald* two years later and suppressed in all three accounts in his books. It is true that some of Price's statements are exaggerations of the truth, and some others are palpable lies, as we shall see. I can say, however, that the 1926 article led me to Shropshire and, I believe, to 'Parton Magna'.

On page 78 of the 1926 account Price wrote:

In Parton Magna is the very old Manor House, *circa* A.D. 1600. This building had—and has—very intimate associations for me, as it was in this house that my grandfather was born, and in it my uncle resided for many years. At the time of which I am writing the house did not belong to my family, but naturally we were on friendly terms with the owner, a retired Canon of the Church of England, and his wife. Just previous to the Canon's taking up his residence there, the Manor House had been successively occupied by a number of families who, for various reasons, had relinquished their ownership. There were rumours that the place was haunted— but popular tradition provides a ghost for every old country house, especially if a tragedy has taken place within it. My father, who had been intimately acquainted with the Manor House all his life had, of course, heard the rumours but had never experienced anything that could not be accounted for by natural causes. My uncle resided in the house for many years, but no one ever remembered his complaining of having been disturbed by supernatural manifestations . . . (p. 79). The Manor House, Parton Magna, is an old building in the Jacobean style, and I believe it is the only triple-gabled house in Shropshire. Derwent Hall, Derbyshire, is a well-known, but very much finer example of the type of building erected at this period. The Manor is of stone, constructed from the easily worked Oolite which stretches in great beds right through the counties of Wiltshire, Gloucestershire, Oxfordshire, Shropshire, etc. Time and weather have given the house a soft grey tint enlivened by the partial incrustation of many-hued lichens. I would give the correct name and exact location of the house except for the fact that it is now in the occupation of a director of one of the great London stores who would, I am certain, be much annoyed were publicity directed towards his residence.

I have come to the conclusion that if any sense is to be made out of Price's stories, the ingredients have to be looked at individually, comprehending the curious psychological motives that inspired him to distort the truth and to lie, when this seemed necessary in order to support the fictitious background to his life and antecedents he appeared so desperately anxious to create. Thus, the story that his grandfather, John Price, the licensee of a small public house in the village of Rodington for most of his working life, was born in a Shropshire family manor house is palpably suspicious in its own right, even if we did not already know that he was born on 10 July, 1787 in the parish of Dudley St. Thomas, in Worcestershire. The flat lie in regard to the Shropshire birth was necessary, however, if the legend of Price's 'old Shropshire family' was to be supported. It can therefore be ignored as a clue to the identity of 'Parton Magna'. The claim that the property concerned is 'the only triple-gabled house in Shropshire' is absurd on the face of it, which can be confirmed by anyone within reach of a library by a glance at the illustration of Wilderhope Manor on page 86 of A. J. C. Hare's *Shropshire* (London, 1898). I found three other examples during a six-day stay in Shropshire, two being clearly visible on either side of the A49 between Shrewsbury and Whitchurch on the homeward journey to Yorkshire. Price's ignorance or exaggeration does not mean, however, that his uncle might not have lived in a house with three gables.

I visited Shropshire in April, 1976, for the first time in my life. I already knew, as we have seen, that Price's grandfather,

John Price, had been buried in Rodington in 1868, but that the parish register recorded the place of death as The Lees, without any amplification of the address. A scrutiny of 6-inch maps of the area showed, however, that The Lees was marked as a house at Walcot, Withington, a village less than two miles from Rodington. A fact of some significance, as will be seen, is that in the relevant issues of *Crockford's Clerical Directory*, Withington with Walcot is shown as a parish. The map showed that within 200 yards of The Lees is the confluence of the rivers Roden and Tern, the latter being a tributory of the Severn. The two smaller rivers flow past the side and the rear of the house, offering a choice to a demented murderer with an inclination towards suicide.

Through the kindness of Mr Anthony Carr, the Local History Librarian, whom it was a great pleasure to meet after our long correspondence, I was able to see the 1871 Census Return, which showed Joseph Henry Price, aged 42 and unmarried, as the head of the household at The Lees, Walcot. Living with him in the house were his two unmarried sisters, Lucy Longford Price and Ann Price, whom I already knew to be two of the daughters of John Price. Joseph Henry Price was therefore unquestionably the brother of Edward Ditcher Price and the uncle of Harry Price, and John Price had presumably spent his last years with his son. The issues of *Kelly's Directory of Shropshire* of 1870 and 1879 both showed, under 'Withington', Joseph Henry Price, farmer, living at 'Walcot Lees', but he was no longer there in 1885.

After a day in the Local History Library in Shrewsbury the time had come for field investigation, and the following day The Lees was visited. As my son-in-law's car approached it from the direction of Rodington, the first point we noticed was its three gables, which faced us.[1] It is a farm-house,[2] at present occupied by Mrs Alice Edwards and her son Gordon, who made us very welcome and showed us over the property. It has a large hall, with a morning-room opening off it, but the staircase is modern, having been installed during the ownership of the house by Mr Walter William Hollingsworth which, Mrs

---

[1] See Plate 3.
[2] In the telephone directory it is 'Lees Farm, Walcot'.

Edwards told us, preceded the later occupancies of The Lees by Mr A. Woolridge and finally herself. There are many agricultural buildings adjoining the house. It is not a manor house, but I fancy that Price's assertion that it was can be put down to his customary gilding of the lily where his family was concerned. A manor house sounds better than a farm-house. We shall encounter his taste for manor houses again later in this book when we examine the extraordinary (and spurious) book-plate of 'Robert Ditcher-Price, Norton Manor, Radnor' to be found in some of Price's books, and compare it with the splendidly indignant letter I received from the distinguished family who have lived at Norton Manor since the seventeenth-century. The interior of The Lees, in very general terms, fits Price's account of the haunted house.

W. W. Hollingsworth lived at The Lees for many years. He is listed as the occupier in *Kelly's Directory for Shropshire* from 1917 to 1941, so that he was certainly there in 1926, when Price published his first account in the *Journal* of the American Society for Psychical Research. It will be recalled that Price asserted that in 1926 the house at 'Parton Magna' was 'in the occupation of a director of one of the great London stores who would, I am certain, be much annoyed were publicity directed towards his residence'. In the directories of the period Hollingsworth is shown as 'farmer, Walcot Lees', but Mrs Edwards assured us that his farming was simply a hobby, and that Hollingsworth was engaged in retail business, which involved his travelling to London and Birmingham. To our intense interest she most kindly showed us an old photograph in her possession of one of Hollingsworth's original shops. The town was not indicated, nor the street, but the numbers on the fascia were 27 and 29, and the inscription was 'Bourne & Hollingsworth, Millinery Showrooms'. My daughter, Mrs Kathryn Liversedge, M.A., who some years ago was the Staff Trainer with Swan & Edgar, Ltd., in London, instantly remembered that Bourne & Hollingsworth of Oxford Street can indeed be described as 'one of the great London stores', of which Hollingsworth was one of the early directors. Most fortunately, one of Hollings-worth's farm workers, now in his eighties, lives near The Lees, and was able to confirm the facts given to us by Mrs Edwards. He had never heard any stories of haunting in connexion with the house. I shall return to some discrepancies in the exterior physical features of The Lees in a later paragraph, but suffice it to say that we left Walcot well satisfied with the results of our visit and delighted to possess a coloured picture of the house given to us by Mrs Edwards. We took some photographs of the house and its environs ourselves, and broke our drive back to Shrewsbury to have a glass of beer at the Bull's Head at Rodington. Mrs Edwards knew nothing of a Canon of the Church of England ever having lived at The Lees, and I was therefore naturally anxious to see what might be contained in the directories at the Local History Library on this point, now that I was convinced that I had actually located 'Parton Magna'.

It will be recalled that Price asserted that shortly before his visit (in 1896 or 1898) a retired Canon of the Church of England had bought (or leased) the house. He was in failing health, and had been forced to relinquish a strenuous living in the Midlands. At the actual date of Price's investigation (either alone or accompanied by a friend), the Canon had been forced to leave the house because of the activities of the poltergeist. The first directories I looked at were those of 1895 and 1900, which showed, under 'Withington', that the Rev. John Thomas Halke, LL.B. was living at 'Walcot Lees'. In each entry the vicar of Withington with Walcot was given as the Rev. William A. Meakin, which confirmed the notion that Halke was a retired clergyman. This fitted Price's story that the haunted house at 'Parton Magna' had been purchased (or leased) by a retired Canon of the Church of England shortly before Price's adventure in the house in 1896 or 1898. As usual, however, discrepancies began to develop between the tale told by Price and the facts, as the latter were ascertained.

The Rev. J. T. Halke was born in May, 1832, according to the section on 'Clergy' in *Mate's County Series. Shropshire. Historical, Descriptive and Biographical*, published in 1906. The son and grandson of clergymen, but a descendant on his mother's side from a family of Kentish lawyers, he read law at St. John's College, Cambridge, but ultimately decided to follow his father's vocation by taking Holy Orders. From this work of reference and *Crockford's Clerical Directory* we find that the Rev. J. T. Halke was ordained a Deacon in 1856 and became a

Priest in 1857. He was the curate of Atcham, a country parish about five miles south-west of Withington, from 1856 to 1859, this appointment being followed by the curacy of another small parish, that of Waters Upton about seven miles north-east of Withington. Halke was curate of Waters Upton from 1859 to 1867, after which he became the vicar of Withington-with-Walcot from 1867 to 1889, retiring in the latter year at the age of 57. The small size of these villages is indicated by their population figures in *Bartholomew's Survey Gazetteer of the British Isles* (Edinburgh, 1927), which then were Atcham, 358; Waters Upton, 191; and Withington-with-Walcot, 235. Halke had therefore spent the whole of his working life as a priest in three small villages in this corner of Shropshire, having married Lucy Meredith of Bishop's Castle, also in Shropshire. He seems to have been a typical country parson of sporting tastes possessed of private means, and it is stated in *Mate* (p. 90) that his chief interests were 'his gun and horticulture' and that he was 'an excellent shot'. This assumption is supported by his early retirement at 57 to pursue his outdoor activities.

Halke is shown as the vicar of Withington, living at the Vicarage, in the directories of 1870, 1879 and 1885, but on his retirement in 1889 he continued to live in the village (which Archdeacon C. O. Ellison tells me is unusual) having moved into The Lees, where he is shown as the occupier in subsequent years, being recorded, for example, at 'Walcot Lees' in 1900. His last entry in *Crockford* is in 1915, when he was still at Withington, having lived to the age of 83. There is no record in *Crockford* or elsewhere of his ever having been made a Canon, but from Price's point of view a Canon doubtless sounded better than a simple 'Reverend', just as a manor-house sounded better than a farm-house.

In my opinion there can be no reasonable doubt that The Lees is Price's 'haunted manor house' at 'Parton Magna'. This conviction is based on the coincidence of six principal points. First, Price's uncle lived there. Secondly, in 1896 (and 1898) a retired clergyman was living there. Thirdly, in 1926 a director of a large London store was living there. Fourthly, the house has three gables. Fifthly, two rivers, the Tern and the Roden, are in the immediate vicinity of the house. Sixthly, the interior of the house fits Price's description in very general terms. The contradictory facts that Price's grandfather was not born in the house, that The Lees is not a manor house, that Halke was not a Canon and that the house is mainly built of rendered brick and not stone[1] and is nearer to Wellington than Shrewsbury can all, I think, be ignored on the grounds of Price's inaccuracy, exaggeration and devious writing.

It will be recalled that on page 35 of *Search for Truth* Price said that in later years he visited the house many times, as it was then in the possession of a friend. As his autobiography, published in 1942, was presumably written in 1941 at latest when Hollingsworth was living The Lees, the latter gentleman cannot have been Price's friend since the two men had not met. We recall that in the same paragraph of *Search for Truth* Price wrote of 'the well-known London business man':

I hope to call upon him one day.

Was the friend the Rev. J. T. Halke, whom Price said was a Canon of the church in 1896 (or 1898) 'in failing health' as a result of his work in 'a strenuous living in the Midlands' and had retired to The Lees in 1896 (or 1898)? We know that there is no truth in any of this, since Halke was (a) not a Canon (b) had spent his entire working life as a country clergyman in three small Shropshire villages (c) had retired in 1889, not 1896 or 1898 and (d) was evidently a healthy and vigorous man, since he lived on for over a quarter of a century after his retirement, devoted to his gun and horticulture. Halke is, however, a faintly more possible candidate for the role of Price's 'friend' than Hollingsworth. We recall that Price wrote in 1926 that in 1898 (or 1896), 'naturally we were on friendly terms with the owner', although we notice that Price's account of Halke's health, history and circumstances was quite erroneous. The effort of trying to interpret Price's tales can be compared with an endeavour to follow the trail of a fish in water. Little or no reliance can be placed on the truth of any single statement made by him. All we can do is to try to make

---

[1] Neither my son-in-law, Christopher S. G. Liversedge, A.R.I.B.A., a member of the Council for the Preservation of Rural England, nor I (F.R.I.C.S. and F.S.A.) think that the house can be as old as '*c.* 1600'.

some sense, if possible, of a collection of half-truths and actual lies.

What are we to make, moreover, of Price's extraordinary enlargement of the tale of his subsequent stay in the house in *Confessions of a Ghost-Hunter* and *Poltergeist over England?* In those two books, it will be remembered, he said that he 'spent many happy weeks in the house', and that his 'heart beat faster than its accustomed rate', not on account of the alleged spirit of Mary Hulse, but because of the presence of a much more objective young lady. This romantic episode, we recall, is alleged by Price to have taken place in later years than 1898 (or 1896), and we have to remember that in 1908 Price married the wealthy Constance Mary Knight of Brockley. Tabori tells us (p. 30) that Price 'married a girl he had known since childhood'. Was the honeymoon spent in the house in which Price claimed he experienced his first encounter with the occult, as the guests for 'many happy weeks' of the Rev. J. T. Halke? It seems improbable, and we may be forgiven, perhaps, for tempering these questions with the suspicion that the entire tale may have been wholly or partly manufactured.

I have tried to avoid speculation in this book so far as possible, but the case of 'Parton Magna', now half a century old, leaves us little alternative if we wish to look beyond the established facts. The 'farcical comedy', *The Sceptic*, was certainly performed in 1898, but the available evidence suggests that it had no discernible connexion with the thrilling Shropshire ghost story first published by Price in 1926. His tale of the night spent in the supposedly haunted house in either 1896 or 1898, with or without a friend, as a result of a journey back to school broken in Shropshire *en route*, seems to be totally discredited by the established facts. It may be thought that his account of the startled 'ghost' that stumbled on the stairs because of the shock of the exploding flash-powder, requires no comment.

On the other hand, Price knew that the house had three gables and was close to a river, although his statements that it was the only triple-gabled house in Shropshire and that it was built of stone were both unfounded. He was aware that after his uncle's tenancy of The Lees came to an end it was occupied first by a retired clergyman (promoted in his story to a Canon) and then by a director of a London store. The explanation that seems to me most likely to fit this curious assortment of information and discrepancies is twofold.

I think it possible that Price may have had a vague childhood memory of the house, dating back to a visit with his parents during those few years in the early 1880s between his birth and his uncle's vacation of The Lees. I fancy that the rest of the tale may well have come from his father, Edward Ditcher Price, possibly coupled with some local legend of a Shropshire haunting. Price's remark on page 302 of *Search for Truth* that his father 'continually impressed me with the fact that the dead are all around us and have a profound influence upon the living' may suggest that Edward Ditcher Price believed in psychical phenomena, or may have been pure invention. I think that on this flimsy foundation Price concocted the thrilling tale of the stumbling poltergeist, linking it with the story, which I also believe to be untrue, that he founded the Carlton Dramatic Society solely so that he could dramatise the experience under the title of *The Sceptic*. We may recall in this connexion the remark of Dr Dingwall, who knew Price well for over a quarter of a century, 'The most trivial incident or haphazard meeting could be made into an enthralling tale through the imaginative pen of Harry Price.'

I have left until the last the matter of Mary Hulse and the legend of her tragic death at The Lees in the early seventeenth century. Price asserted on page 17 of *Confessions of a Ghost-Hunter*, we recall, that it was a fact 'that many years previously a girl named Mary Hulse had died at the Manor under suspicious circumstances'. It is unfortunate for this story that the Withington parish register, which starts in 1592, has no Hulse entry.

* * * * *

The identification by me of The Lees with the 'haunted manor house' at 'Parton Magna' was made in April, 1976, as the account of the inquiry has shown. On 28 March, 1977, when this book was complete, Alan Wesencraft wrote to tell me of a discovery he had just made while examining and cataloguing for the first time some of the photographs, negatives and lantern-slides and other small items in the Price collection. He enclosed an old, faded and discoloured photograph he had found, among many others, in an envelope marked 'Miscellaneous'. It is almost certainly nineteenth-century. It precisely resembles in its evidence of age the many photographs, using wet plates, taken by my great-grandfather, John Hall of Wakefield, in the preparation of his unique, extra-illustrated large-paper copy of W. S. Banks' *Walks in Yorkshire: Wakefield and its Neighbourhood* (London & Wakefield, 1871). The photograph now discovered in the University of London Library is of The Lees. It bears a note in Price's handwriting, 'The Lees, Walcot, Salop. See, "The Ghost that Stumbled", in *Confessions of a Ghost-Hunter*, by Harry Price, London, 1936'. The fact that Price initially spelt the name of the house as 'Leese' or 'Leeze', and then crossed it out and wrote 'Lees', suggests that he was not familiar with the house himself, and that the provenance of the tale may resemble that suggested earlier in this chapter.

Alan Wesencraft's completion in the summer of 1977 of the cataloguing of the small items in the Harry Price Library resulted in the discovery of another photograph reproduced as Plate 4. It will be seen that the picture itself, showing part of a room with a superimposed 'ghost', is totally at variance with Price's tale of the single flashlight photograph allegedly taken at 'Parton Magna' in 1896 or 1898. We recall (*Search for Truth*, p. 34) that Price asserted that there was nothing on the negative except an over-exposed picture of an empty staircase. It may be thought, too, that the caption, 'The Lees' Ghost. Taken at Midnight', is scarcely confirmed by the lights and shadows of the photograph. The label pasted on the back of the photograph, 'Bennett Museum. Catalogue No. 7', like the caption, appears to have been made with a home printing outfit, and presents another puzzle. A search for a Bennett Museum, kindly made for me by my friend C. Maynard Mitchell, F.S.A., Director of Leeds City Council Museums, in museum directories covering the last half-century has produced nothing but the Arnold Bennett House at Cobridge, Stoke-on-Trent, which possesses no material of this kind. Inquiry among organisations involved in psychical research and spiritualism has drawn a similar blank. There is no mention of a 'Lees' Ghost' in any of the literature on the subject known to me, including the late

3 Lees Farm, Walcot, Withington, 1976 (see p. 79)

4 "The Lees' Ghost" (see p. 86). Reproduced by permission of the University of
London Library

Sir Ernest Bennett's *Apparitions and Haunted Houses* (London, 1939). The provenance of the photograph, therefore, and the curious facts of Price's possession of it and his failure to mention it in any of his accounts of his supposed adventures at 'Parton Pagna' are mysteries I have been unable to solve.

X

The Numismatist

by the Venerable Charles Ottley Ellison

[I am proud to introduce this chapter on Price's numismatic activities, contributed to this book by my friend Charles Ellison, Archdeacon of Leeds from 1950 to 1969, and Emeritus since then. His brief mention of numismatics as his recreation in *Who's Who* is a model of understatement, for his distinction in the subject is proverbial among coin-collectors. His assembly of English silver crown pieces, including many patterns and proofs as well as standard issues, was considered before its dispersal in 1969 to be one of the finest and most comprehensive in the North of England. A Life-member of the British Numismatic Society, Archdeacon Ellison was President of the Yorkshire Numismatic Society in the years 1964 and 1965. In the latter year he received the Silver Medal of the Society, its most coveted award. His paper on Irish Ormonde Money, delivered in the same year at the National Numismatic Congress, formed part of his research on the Money of Necessity of the Civil War, and is well known.

I would add with gratitude that the discussions I have enjoyed with Archdeacon Ellison in regard to every chapter of this book have been of the highest benefit to me. T.H.H.]

The years 1897 and 1923 marked the beginning and ending of Harry Price's recorded interest in coins, though it was by no means maintained at fever heat throughout the intervening period. In the former year, according to his biographer Tabori, while still a schoolboy, he 'sold his first work on ancient coins for £200!'[1] This ambiguous statement is not confirmed by Price himself, and one feels he would not have failed to mention it if it had been true. Some time in 1923 he placed on exhibition in his village church at Pulborough, in Sussex, his 'fine and rare collection of the ancient gold coins of the Sussex princes

[1] Tabori, p. 21.

(most of them washed up at Selsey)', along with other items. On 26 September in the same year the gold coins disappeared from the church, where the exhibition had been left unattended and also, unknown to its owner, uninsured. They were never recovered. This story, too, is not without its difficulties, but Price states that the loss put an end to any further numismatic work, and even caused him to abandon his *Numismatic History of Sussex* upon which he had been engaged for twenty years, although, in his own words, the book was 'nearly completed' in 1923, and 'all the plates had been engraved'.[1]

It is true that by this time Price had long since turned his attention to other subjects, but the Pulborough theft, if such it was, gave him a dramatic excuse to bring down the curtain on what he called his 'endless work and research' into the history of the trade tokens of Kent and Shropshire issued in the seventeenth and eighteenth centuries. In 1942, when his *Search for Truth* was published, he claimed to have formed 'very complete collections' of these tokens some forty years earlier.[2] This claim will be examined later in the chapter.

His so-called research, to which we must now turn, was published in two provincial weekly papers, namely *The Kentish Mercury* and *The Wellington Journal* (of Shropshire). The former series, entitled 'Coins of Kent and Kentish Tokens', appeared between the years 1902 and 1904, and the second and much shorter series on 'Shropshire Tokens and Mints' was published 'during this same period', to quote Price's own words. All the articles are included in the first of forty large volumes of press-cuttings and other items covering the whole of Price's working life.

From an examination of the articles, written when Price was a young man in his early twenties, it seemed very probable that the precise and detailed numismatic descriptions of the various tokens were quoted verbatim from some standard book on the subject available to him at the time he was writing. One

---

[1] *Search for Truth*, p. 51. The gold coins were pre-Roman, and were therefore about 2000 years old. Fifteen coins were missing in all, valued by Price at £10 each. Also missing was a Roman silver ingot, found in a ploughed field near Pulborough, valued at £50, as well as other unspecified objects of a total value also of £50.

[2] *Ibid.*, pp. 50–1.

authoritative work at that date was George C. Williamson's revised edition of William Boyne's *Trade Tokens Issued in the Seventeenth Century in England, Wales and Ireland, by Corporations, Merchants, Tradesmen, Etc.*, in two volumes, London, 1889 and 1891 (hereinafter referred to as 'Williamson'). Boyne's original work had been published in 1858, and the revision was carefully carried out by Williamson, with the assistance of collaborators in the different counties.

The two volumes of Williamson are in the Leeds Library. On consulting them for the purpose of this inquiry, an extraordinary coincidence came to light. Inside the cover of each volume was Price's first spurious book-plate, described on page 126. This lucky find established that Williamson was indeed the work which had provided Price with the material for his articles on the seventeenth-century tokens, and here, actually to hand, were the very copies he had used throughout the series, without the formality of any acknowledgment, so far as the present writer has been able to discover. When he had no further use for them, having turned from numismatics to archaeology, and possibly needing the space on the shelves of his growing library, he sold the two volumes to Bernard Quaritch Ltd., the antiquarian booksellers, from whom the Leeds Library purchased them for £2.11s 2d. in 1913.

Williamson treats the counties in alphabetical order. Under each county, the towns and villages are listed also in alphabetical order, and under each place-name the issuing tradespeople appear likewise in alphabetical order. The tokens are numbered by counties; thus, under Shropshire, the numbers run from 1 to 107, the Shrewsbury tokens, for instance (29 in all), being nos. 66 to 94. The more numerous Kentish tokens are numbered 1 to 589.

Price's method, on the other hand, is to number the tokens separately under each place of issue, starting in every case at no. 1. Thus, for example, he numbers the Shrewsbury tokens 1–29. This different system of enumeration is his only departure from the method of cataloguing and describing the tokens employed by Williamson. It is much less convenient because it means that under each county there will be several coins bearing the same reference number, and for the purpose of identification the place of issue must also be quoted, whereas in Williamson the county reference number alone is sufficient to identify a particular token.

The Shropshire tokens are described in ten articles in *The Wellington Journal* during the period 10 May, 1902, to 1 November, 1902. The first three articles were concerned with eighteenth-century tokens (referred to later) and the remaining seven with those of the seventeenth century. It is only, of course, in regard to the last-named that Price's work can be compared with Williamson.

Price's Shrewsbury no. 1 is thus described:

O, "Thomas Achelley. 71"—A wheatsheaf "T.A." "1d."
R, "In Salop, 1670"—A fleur-de-loys. "T.A." (Octagonal shape).

In Williamson the same token (no. 66) is described:

O. THOMAS · ACHELLEY 71 = A wheatsheaf. T.A. 1^D.
R. IN · SALOP. 1670 = A fleur de lys. T.A. (Octagonal.)[1]

Although the two descriptions of the coin are superficially the same, there are important differences which betray Price's inexperience. His lavish display of inverted commas is a confusing intrusion into the numismatic picture. They are not to be found in Williamson, nor, of course, do they appear on the token itself. Price also mistakenly employs lower-case in recording the legends which are entirely in capital letters, as in Williamson. The purpose of the printed description is to give the reader an exact representation of the coin, and where the inclusion or omission of a single dot may be of vital importance, the strictest accuracy is essential. All Price had to do was to copy out his source correctly, but even this simple task was apparently beyond him, or its necessity unrecognised. These discrepancies strongly suggest that he did not, in fact,

[1] *O.* Obverse. *R.* Reverse. 71, abbreviation for 1671. T.A. Initials of issuing tradesman, Thomas Achelley (a baker), in this case found on both sides of the coin, but more usually on the reverse only. Fleur-de-loys, a misprint, correct in Williamson. In Williamson the sign = separates the legend on the perimeter of the coin from the centre of the field. Price uses a dash which is liable to be misconstrued.

have the actual tokens before him when he was writing his
articles.

Williamson's Shropshire no. 94 has a note attached, reading:
'This token is of brass with copper centre.' When Price comes
to the coin (Shropshire, Shrewsbury no. 29 in his case) the
corresponding note reads: 'This is a brass token with copper
centre.'

He quotes, still without acknowledgment, other sources
mentioned in Williamson, such as the Shrewsbury Rent Roll
of 1657, and reproduces some detailed notes on the Quaker
sect, but in this instance Price has allowed himself the liberty
of a slight paraphrase, which, whilst insufficient to disguise the
original, does nothing to improve its English style.

First, Williamson:

John Millington, if not a Quaker himself, was friendly to the
cause of this persecuted sect. Richard Davis, the Welshpool Quaker
(see Wales) says in his autobiography: 'A little while after this I
came to hear that some of the people that were called Quakers were
at Shrewsbury, in the county of Salop, being distant from my abode
about 18 miles. When the time called Christmas came, my master's
work being somewhat over for a while, I got leave to go so far. I
went first to the house of John Millington, where many friends
resorted'. In 1661 Davies [*sic*] was taken prisoner at Wem, with
about twenty-five more, and committed to Shrewsbury Gaol, where
they suffered much hardship; but after some days John Millington
interceded with the gaoler, who was prevailed upon to let them all
go, taking their word for their appearance at the next Assizes.[1]

Price recounts the same story, beginning with the words:
'John Millington was a Shrewsbury Quaker.' He then faithfully
repeats the extract from the autobiography of Richard Davis
('A little while after this . . . many friends resorted') and
continues: 'In 1661 Davis himself was imprisoned in Shrewsbury Gaol, with several others, and it was owing to the
intercession of John Millington that he (Davis) and the others
were ultimately released, giving their parole to appear at the
next Assizes.'

The numbered series of articles on 'The Coins of Kent

[1] Williamson, ii, p. 963, note to item no. 82.

and Kentish Tokens' appeared in *The Kentish Mercury* from 28 May, 1902, to 1 July, 1904, the first five being concerned with tokens of the eighteenth century, followed by thirty-five on seventeenth-century tokens. Up to, and including, Part XI of the seventeenth-century series, the articles were modestly signed at the foot with the initials H.P. From Part XII a heading replaces the initials: 'By Harry Price, Memb. Num. Soc. Lond. ETC'. At Part XIV (17 April, 1903) this had become: 'By Harry Price, M.R.A.S., M.N.S.Lond. ETC.'. (*The Kentish Mercury* of the same date announced in its personal column: 'Mr. Harry Price, of Cloverley, St. Donatt's Road, New Cross, Memb.Num.Soc.Lond. &c., has been elected a member of the Royal Asiatic Society').

From Part XX onwards, the words 'All Rights Reserved' were added to all the articles, while the heading of the last three parts is: 'By Harry Price, F.R.N.S., M.R.A.S., ETC.'.

The same reliance on Williamson in Price's descriptions of seventeenth-century Kentish tokens is exhibited as was evident in his articles on the Shropshire series. Two examples, typical of the rest, will suffice.

Twenty-nine Greenwich tokens are listed in Part I, the last one, no. 29, being described by Price as follows:

O. "JOHN · WARRELL · THE" A ship.
R. "TAVERNE · IN · GREENWICH."—I.A.W." (Farthing)[1]

"The Ship at Greenwich", Price adds, "is still familiar to most readers of *The Kentish Mercury*".

The same item in Williamson reads:

341. *O.* JOHN · WARRELL · THE = A ship
R. TAVERNE · IN · GREENWICH = I.A.W. $\frac{1}{4}$.

"The Ship is still one of the principal hotels in Greenwich."

In Part XX, Price describes the tokens issued in St. Mary Cray. He writes, 'Concerning the tokens of St. Mary Cray, we

---

[1] The superfluous inverted commas are still present as are the misleading dashes, though by now Price had learned to use capital letters where necessary.

only know that "The Black Boy" is still the leading hotel, the effigy of the boy holding the pipe clearly denoting the sign of the hostelry in those days.'

(1) *O.* —"ANN · MANING · IN · S"—A boy holding a pipe.
     R. —"MAREY · CRAY · IN · KENT"—"A.M. 1658"
     ($\frac{1}{2}$d.)

(2) As last, but "1665".

Williamson reads:

485. *O.* ANN · MANING · IN · S. = A boy holding a pipe.
      R. MAREY · CRAY · IN · KENT = A.M. 1658 ($\frac{1}{4}$)
486. A variety is dated 1665.
      "The Black Boy is the leading hotel in St. Mary Cray".

Price here makes a mistake about the value of the 1658 token, but leaves us in no doubt about the identity of St. Mary Cray's 'leading hotel'.

This last example comes from the first of Price's articles appearing under the words 'All Rights Reserved'. One wonders whose rights are to be reserved, and for what purpose? Perhaps would-be copiers are being warned off to prevent the discovery of Price's sources.

The thirty-five parts of the series on the seventeenth-century Kentish tokens, which, it will be remembered, had been preceded by five parts dealing with the eighteenth-century series, were followed by two articles on 'The Coins of the Kings of Kent', and two more on 'The Coins of the Archbishops of Canterbury'. At the very beginning of the first pair of these articles, Price writes, with unusual candour, 'In commencing a description of the coins of the Kings of Kent, I cannot do better than quote a portion of the introduction to the *Handbook of the Coins of Great Britain and Ireland*, issued by the British Museum authorities.' This he proceeds to do at great length. In the articles on the coins of the Archbishops of Canterbury he acknowledges his indebtedness to 'Hawkins'. These two splendid works provided a mine of information which Price quarried assiduously for the material in these last four articles.[1]

Before leaving the subject of the newspaper articles on the trade tokens of Shropshire and Kent, some consideration must be given to Price's eight contributions on the tokens of the eighteenth century, of which three dealt with the 25 issued in Shropshire and five with the 40 from Kent. The good fortune which revealed his sources for the seventeenth-century series, through the chance discovery of a book-plate, did not repeat itself with regard to his eighteenth-century sources. Nevertheless there is a very large area in which he clearly relied on the standard work available when he was writing, namely *The Tradesmen's Tokens of the Eighteenth Century* by James Atkins, published in London in 1892. The technical descriptions of the great majority of the tokens listed by Price are obviously copied from Atkins, allowing for Price's uncertainty with capital letters, and his addiction to inverted commas.

For example: *Shropshire. Coalbrookdale. Halfpenny.*

Price. *O.* view of a bridge; "Ironbridge at Coalbrookdale, 1779"

R. a man working a machine; "Inclined Plane/at Ketley/ 1789", in three lines under. The "1" in date inclines to right.

E. [edge] "Payable at Coalbrookdale and Ketley"; very rare; only a few impressions of this coin have been taken, the obverse die having broke".

Atkins. *O.* View of a bridge. IRON BRIDGE AT COAL-BROOK DALE 1779.

R. A man working a machine. INCLINED PLANE/AT KETLEY/1789. In three lines under. The 1 in date slopes to right.

E. PAYABLE AT COALBROOK-DALE AND KET-LEY. Very rare; the obverse die broke when only a few impressions had been taken.

---

[1] *Handbook of the Coins of Great Britain and Ireland in the British Museum*, Herbert A. Grueber, F.S.A., Assistant Keeper of Coins, London, 1889. *The Silver Coins of England*, Edward Hawkins, F.R.S., F.A.S., Keeper of Antiquities in British Museum, London, 1887.

Dudmaston. Penny.

Price.   *O.*   A Large Building. "Dudmaston, Shropshire". "Jacobs" in the exergue.   *R.*   A Globe between a Rose and Thistle, "British Penny 1797";   *E.*   "I promise to Pay on Demand the Bearer One Penny".

Atkins.   *O.*   A large building. DUDMASTON SHROPSHIRE. Ex: Jacobs.

           R.   A globe inscribed BRITAIN between a rose and thistle. BRITISH PENNY. EX: 1797.

           E.   I PROMISE TO PAY ON DEMAND THE BEARER ONE PENNY.

Kent. Appledore. Halfpenny.

Price.   (1)   *O.*   Man carrying a pack to a windmill, and part of a house within a beaded circle. "THE UNION OF APPLEDORE, KENT, 1794". A border o dots.   *R.*   A lion and lamb lying in standing corn, "PEACE, INNOCENCE AND PLENTY".   *E.* "PAYABLE AT W. PECKHAM'S APPLEDORE. XXX"

Atkins.   (2)   *O.*   A man carrying a sack to a windmill, and part of a house, in a beaded circle. THE UNION OF APPLEDORE KENT. 1794.

                    R.   A lion and lamb lying together in standing corn. PEACE INNOCENCE AND PLENTY

                    E.   PAYABLE AT W. PECKHAM'S APPLE-DORE · X · X · X ·

In his description of the Boscobel Halfpenny (Atkins no. 3) Price has interchanged the obverse and reverse. Where Atkins has *R.* An oak tree, Price has *O.* The Royal Oak. Otherwise the two descriptions are identical.

Price describes an Orpington coin at great length (11 July, 1902). It is not found in Atkins, and is not, in fact, a trades-man's token at all, but a large bronze piece struck as 'A mark of respect to the Rt. Hon. T. Skinner, Sir R. Glode, Kt., and Mr. W. Austin'.

Under Romney, Price has two tokens, Atkins only one.

It is difficult to account for the rare instances in which Price differs from Atkins except on the assumption that he had at his disposal some additional work, or works, of reference unknown to us. Atkins, in the introduction to his book, mentions four other works, printed a long time previously, which he hopes his own work will replace and bring up-to-date. It is possible that Price had access to one or more of these. What is certain is that just as Williamson was the standard work on seventeenth-century tokens when Price was writing his articles, Atkins matched it almost entirely with regard to the tokens of the eighteenth century. It only remains to add that where there is any variation between them, Atkins' version must be preferred.

The two numismatic series on the coins and tokens of Shropshire and Kent were rounded off with an index of Kentish place-names which is undated, but, by its position in the book of press-cuttings, would appear to have been printed around the middle of 1905, some six months after the appearance of the final article at the end of 1904.

Harry Price perhaps deserves credit for the immense and monotonous labour of copying out his material, extending over two-and-a-half years and covering many columns of closely-printed letterpress. But whatever reward he may have earned for perseverance with his set task was gained at the expense of any claim to be regarded as an original researcher in the field of numismatics.

It must be presumed that Price was paid, and possibly well-paid, for his efforts. The receipt of a fee would explain two points about his newspaper articles. First, it would account for the concealment of any of his sources of information until the whole series was about to be concluded, the veil only being partially lifted in his final four articles, and never lifted at all from the earlier and much more extensive series on the tokens. Secondly, his insistence on appending to his name as author all his pseudo-academic qualifications for the job in hand might well help him to raise his charges.

Although the articles would have a circulation limited more or less to the counties of Shropshire and Kent, they secured for Price an obscure appointment in far-off Ripon in Yorkshire, which, from the first, he misrepresented and exaggerated. In the book of press-cuttings to which reference has already been made, there is a letter dated 10 May, 1904, from the Honorary Secretary of the Ripon Naturalists' Club and Scientific and Literary Association, on notepaper bearing in minute letters

the address 'Museum, Park Street, Ripon'. The letter states
that after much consultation with the municipal authorities
'the transfer of our exhibits to the Town Hall is now an
accomplished fact, but we are continuing the Society which
will have some of its members co-opted on the municipal
committee. You were unanimously elected Curator of numismatics, and I have much pleasure in intimating the same to
you.' Price has added in his own hand: 'I am appointed
Curator of Numismatics, Ripon Museum.' He had, in fact,
been appointed Curator of Numismatics to the Ripon Naturalists' Club and Scientific and Literary Association, whose only
connection with Ripon Museum was that its meetings had
hitherto been held on the Museum's premises in Park Street.
When these were no longer available (at about the same time
as Price's appointment) the Association was granted the use of
a room at the Town Hall, and the Museum was transferred to
the Wakeman's House where it remains to this day. Writing a
year later in *The Askean*, the magazine of his old school, Price
takes a further step along the path of deception by calling
himself 'Hon. Curator, Coin Department, Ripon Museum'.
Yet a third permutation appears in *The Kentish Mercury* of
3 June, 1904, in which Price is described as 'Hon. Curator of
the Numismatic Department, Ripon Museum'. There is no record
that the duties involved in the post to which he had actually
been appointed ever required a visit to Ripon Town Hall.

The years 1902 to 1904 were the high spots in Price's career
as a numismatist. He had written in a general way on coins in
The Askean from June, 1902, at the age of 21 years, much to
the surprise of the editor, who remarked in the same number
'Whoever expected Price would break out in this manner?'
His newspaper articles on the tokens and coins of Shropshire
and Kent had begun a month earlier in May, 1902, and were
concluded in December, 1904. In January, 1903, he joined the
Numismatic Society of London, which, by a lucky chance not
perhaps unforeseen at the time, was granted a Royal Charter
in the following year, under the title of the Royal Numismatic
Society, conferring the rank of 'Fellow' on the existing members
of the parent body.[1] They acquired the right to append the

[1] I am indebted to Miss Marion M. Archibald, Hon. Secretary of the
Royal Numismatic Society, for the precise terms in which the then President

letters F.R.N.S. to their names, but only on appropriate numismatic publications, as no professional qualification was indicated by their use. Price, never a man to hide his light under a bushel, and undeterred by the official restriction, continued to add the letters F.R.N.S. to his name as author of several books on psychical subjects for the next twenty-five years. He remained on the list of Fellows up to 1932, after which his resignation from the Society was assumed.

In 1904 he joined the British Numismatic Society, and secured the appointment at Ripon—'a post I hold to this day' he boasted in 1942.[1] After *The Kentish Mercury* had printed the final index to his articles in 1905, the flame of Price's devotion to coins and tokens burned less steadily, until it was finally extinguished by the Pulborough affair in 1923. That something was saved from the past seems to be indicated by his will, signed on 5 April, 1943, in which he bequeathed his collection of coins (amongst other assets) to the University of London. By the date of his death in 1948, if *Search for Truth* is to be relied upon at all, the coins remaining in his possession were a sorry lot, consisting of 'those pieces struck by mediums, conjurers, etc., of which I have a large collection'.[2]

Through the good offices of Mr A. H. Wesencraft, Reference Librarian of the University of London, Miss Marion M. Archibald, of the Department of Coins and Medals at the British Museum, to whom reference has already been made,[3] has kindly inspected the contents of the coin cabinet which came into the University's possession on Harry Price's death, and has remained in its strongroom ever since. She reports that the cabinet contains two trays (about 80 pieces) of seventeenth- and eighteenth-century Sussex trade tokens, the remaining contents being described by Miss Archibald as 'miscellaneous junk'. Strangely enough, in spite of Price's description of the residue of his collection, it appears to contain only one coin that could be termed a conjurer's piece.

---

announced the change. 'We are no longer Members of the Numismatic Society of London,' he said, 'but through the deliberate act of His Majesty the King in Council, we have become Fellows of the Royal Numismatic Society.'

[1] *Search for Truth*, p. 51.   [2] *Ibid.*, p. 51.   [3] See note 1, p. 98.

Harry Price declared that the items placed on exhibition in Pulborough Church in 1923 included traders' tokens (presumably of Sussex origin as it was a Sussex exhibition), and Anglo-Saxon (silver) pieces struck at Sussex mints,[1] as well as the 'ancient gold coins of the Sussex princes',[2] but only the last-named had been taken from the church on 26 September, according to the telegram he received in London informing him of the loss, and only the gold coins were reported missing in contemporary accounts of the incident. The Sussex trade tokens remaining in Price's coin cabinet can be assumed to be survivors of the 1923 display in Pulborough Church.

We are therefore left with a final mystery. What had become of 'the very complete collections' of the trade tokens of Kent and Shropshire he claimed to have formed when he was specialising in the issues of these two counties? If the collections were indeed complete, not to say 'very complete', they would comprise, as we have seen, no fewer than 761 pieces and doubtless out-rival the British Museum. But they have vanished, and we are left to speculate as to what had become of them. Had they been sold, or given away, or lost, or—unworthy thought—can it be that the 'very complete collections' existed only in Harry Price's fertile imagination and, of course, on paper in the pages of his source books? We shall never know.

In numismatics, as in everything else, Harry·Price's geese were all swans. His collection of fifteen early British gold coins was a 'fine and rare' one. His collections of the trade tokens of Kent and Shropshire were 'very complete', and his newspaper articles on the subject were later dignified as 'books', though never published between covers. His modest appointment as Curator of numismatics to the Ripon Naturalists' Club and Scientific and Literary Association was transformed out of all recognition to 'Hon. Curator, Coin Department, Ripon Museum'. He had a medallion struck, depicting on the obverse his own head facing left, surrounded by the legend HARRY PRICE · NUMISMATA · REX · 1903 · (thus betraying the shortcomings of his classical education), and on the reverse the seated figure of Minerva, Goddess of Wisdom, with the legend PAYABLE · EVERYWHERE. Cards bearing a photograph

---

[1] *Search for Truth*, p. 51.   [2] See note 1, p. 89.

of this medallion were sent to his friends at Christmas, 1903, from Cloverley, St. Donatt's Road, New Cross, S.E., 'With the Compliments of the Season, from . . .'.

He joined various societies (the formality of paying his first subscription being invariably reported in the local press as an 'election') with the object of acquiring the appropriate initials or abbreviations to put after his name, whether authorized or not, 'ETC.' bringing up the rear to suggest omissions for lack of space. It was not until much later on in his life, when he had become well-known as a writer, that the words 'By Harry Price' were deemed sufficient to hold their own on the title-page, without further embellishment.

These and other extravagances could be more readily forgiven as personal idiosyncracies were it not for the contradictions and distortions of the truth which are evident throughout his life and written work. It is unsafe to rely on any statement made by Harry Price which lacks independent confirmation. The best we can say of him is that he was a man of boundless energy and many enthusiasms, a prolific writer and propagandist, with a passion for the limelight, and an endless capacity for self-deception, the guiding principle of whose career might well have been borrowed from Lewis Carroll's *Hunting of the Snark*, 'What I tell you three times is true', except that in Harry Price's case the three versions were more than likely to differ radically from each other.

His transient, but while it lasted hotly-pursued, flirtation with numismatics was all of a piece with the other preoccupations which, in turn, claimed his attention. Each of them was a means to the same end, the end being not so much the edification of his readers as the glorification of Harry Price. In this lifelong enterprise he must be reckoned a success.

XI

The Archaeologist

Harry Price's claim to some local eminence in archaeology in West Sussex started in 1909, the year after his move to Pulborough from New Cross on the occasion of his marriage and the start of his life of independent means. On 29 December in that year a report of a lecture by him on 'Roman Pulborough' was published in the *Sussex Daily News*, in which Price was described as possessing 'an extensive knowledge of antiquities'. In a similar article in the *West Sussex Gazette* on the following day he was stated to be 'a good authority on the subject'. After a period of a little over a year, in which he delivered his lecture, 'Roman Pulborough', to a variety of organisations on at least sixteen occasions, Price's reputation had increased to that of 'Mr. Harry Price, the well-known Sussex archaeologist', in a report 'Echoes of the Past. Lecture on the Roman Occupation of Pulborough', in the *Southern Weekly News* of 25 February, 1911.

So far as I have been able to discover this was Price's last public performance (the phrase is deliberate) in this sphere of activity. It says a good deal, indeed, for his thick-skinned vanity that he continued to deliver the lecture at all, after his claim to archaeological expertise and experience had been so decisively punctured in 1910. It is possible, however, that he was shrewd enough to suspect that the deadly nature of the criticism and the high authority of its provenance would only be fully apparent to persons knowledgeable in a moderately recondite subject. More than thirty years later, when writing his autobiography, *Search for Truth*, Price presumably considered that the passage of three decades was sufficient in any event to enable the old fantasy to be revived without any danger of exposure. Eight years later still, in 1950, Tabori was willing simply to copy from Price's autobiography, with the addition of some mistakes and embellishments of his own.

On page 30 of his book, after describing Price's numismatic activities in 1902–4, Tabori wrote in the compass of a single eight-line paragraph that 'in the same years [Price] excavated a Roman villa in Greenwich Park' and that 'more extensive excavations were carried out under his leadership at Borough, where a Roman villa was unearthed and where he found a Roman ingot'. Tabori was seven years too early in his dating of the latter event, and could not even copy correctly what Price had said about the Roman ingot, which was not found at Borough at all. This apart, however, there is no doubt that it was upon the tales he invented about the excavations at Greenwich and Borough that Price principally based his claim to be a distinguished and learned archaeologist, and which will be examined in this chapter. Price declared on page 49 of *Search for Truth*:

In 1902 I helped to excavate the Roman *villa urbana* (a residence in the country or in the suburbs of a town, not to be confused with the *villa rustico*, or farm-house) in Greenwich Park. The site (known to have existed for many years) lies midway between the Magnetic Pavilion and the Vanbrugh entrance to the Park. Excavating Roman villas is one of the most exciting jobs imaginable.

Price continued (pp. 49–50) by giving an account of the villa and a description of the coins and other objects he claimed to have found there. He asserted (p. 50) that his work at Greenwich was one of the events that made him 'an ardent coin collector'. On page 53 of *Search for Truth* Price wrote:

The Roman villa at Greenwich was not the only one of its kind I assisted to unearth. Quite near to my home is the site of a Romano-British house which I helped to excavate in 1909. It is at Borough, threequarters of a mile from the Stane Street. We turned up the footings of several long walls enclosing a suite of rooms [here followed a long list of the principal finds].

Price said that it was upon this work that his 'popular lecture', *Roman Pulborough* was based.

Dealing first with Greenwich Park, the most significant of the three documents essential to the inquirer (if the least official) is an article contributed by Price himself at the age of twenty-one to *The Askean* (the magazine of the schools associated with the Haberdashers' Company) of December, 1902, three pages in length and entitled 'The Roman Villa at Greenwich'. It is of the greatest interest to discover that nowhere in this essay is there the slightest suggestion by Price that he had any connexion whatsoever with the excavation of the foundations of the Roman villa. Indeed, he admitted that the entire source of his information was A. D. Webster's *Greenwich Park: Its History and Associations*, a 103-page book published by Henry Richardson of Greenwich in 1902. Price said that it dealt 'in a masterly manner, with the complete history of the Park from the earliest times', that it included 'some 40 pages devoted to the recent excavations at the Roman villa, and a complete and descriptive list of all the Roman coins found there', and that it was 'worth every penny of the 3/6 that is charged for it'.

A. D. Webster was the Superintendent of Greenwich Park. The section of his book describing the excavations (pp. 67–100) tells us that these were begun in February, 1902, and were under the guidance of Herbert Jones, F.S.A. In parenthesis, I may add that Herbert Jones read a paper describing his work at Greenwich to a meeting of the Royal Archaeological Institute at 20 Hanover Square, London, on 4 June, 1902. The President, Sir Henry H. Howorth, K.C.I.E., was in the Chair.[1] The photography of the Roman pavement for Webster's book was undertaken by J. P. B. Webster, and the more important of the remains discovered (other than coins) were skilfully drawn by Miss A. Airy. The 'List of Coins found in Greenwich Park during the Excavations' (pp. 76–98) was gratefully acknowledged by Webster to have been 'compiled by Mr. E. H. Tugwell, F.S.M.C., M.P.S., &c., to whom we are greatly indebted for deciphering and classifying them, and also for valuable assistance during the course of the excavations'. It will be seen that Webster was at some pains to acknowledge all the assistance he received. It scarcely seems necessary to say that Harry Price's name is mentioned nowhere in the book,

---

[1] *The Archaeological Journal*, lix, Second Series, ix, 'Proceedings at Meetings of the Institute', pp. 204–10. Price's name was not mentioned.

since we already know that in 1902 he himself made no pretence to have been involved in the work in any way whatsoever. Indeed, so far as I have been able to discover, the first time he published the flat lie that he assisted in the excavations at Greenwich was in *Search for Truth*, when after the passage of forty years he presumably thought it was perfectly safe to do so.

One example will suffice to demonstrate how closely Price copied from Webster. Tugwell's descriptive list of coins in chronological order of the reigns of the Roman emperors was both professional and detailed, dealing with no more than two emperors to the page on average. On page 99, however, is an abbreviated 'Chronological List of the 40 Emperors, etc., who are represented by coins found in the excavations', in which the names and dates of the reigns in Tugwell's twenty-three-page list are compressed into a single page. I fancy that this short list was added by Webster, for two reasons. First, Tugwell's list ends on page 98 with the finality of a double rule. Secondly, when the short list on page 99 is compared with Tugwell's list, four mistakes in the former immediately become apparent, arising either from an inability to copy or a lack of comprehension of what Tugwell wrote. Price copied out the short list, including its introduction virtually word for word, and repeating the four errors in the entries for Marcus Antonius, Faustina the Elder, Postumus and Magnentius. There is, indeed, only one difference between the lists. Price's dates for Maximinus Daza are incorrect by 200 years, presumably due to a mistake in copying or an uncorrected misprint.

Turning now to the allegedly prominent part Price played in the work on the remains of the Romano-British villa at Borough in West Sussex, we recall that Tabori wrote (p. 30) that these excavations were carried out under Price's 'leadership', and that among his discoveries was 'a Roman silver ingot'. In the latter instance it was evidently too much trouble for Tabori correctly to copy even what Price wrote. The latter said on page 52 of *Search for Truth* that the ingot was 'picked up in 1909 on the surface of a ploughed field on top of Park Mount, Pulborough'. Price's account of his 'leadership' of the excavations at Borough, with which the ingot had nothing whatever to do, does not start until the middle of page 53 of *Search for Truth*. Borough is 2½ miles from Pulborough.

Price's lecture, 'Roman Pulborough', consisted of an exhibition of a collection of Roman coins allegedly discovered by him in the district over a period of years (a ridiculous claim, since he had only lived in Sussex for one year by 1909) and an account of his leading involvement in the excavations at Borough. One wonders, in the light of Price's own account (*Search for Truth*, pp. 51 ff.) of his endless perseverance and good fortune in forming his collection, whether he was pleased with one of the early reports of his lecture on 'Roman Pulborough' published in the *West Sussex Gazette* of 30 December, 1909. The writer of the account referred to the 'collection of 130 Roman and Anglo-Saxon coins found at Arundel and Pulborough during a period of 42 years by a ploughman named Micklethwaite, and now in the possession of Mr. Price, who showed them on Tuesday night'. It is noteworthy that no subsequent report of the lecture contained any reference to the embarrassing fact that the collection had been assembled by Mr Micklethwaite.

The exhibition of the coins apart, the remainder of the lecture was typically summarised in a report that appeared in the *Sutton Weekly Record* of 10 February, 1910. It demonstrated the extent to which Price relied on the excavations at Borough for his claim to eminence in archaeology.

At Borough, near Pulboro', the remains of a Roman villa had been unearthed, and it was this work upon which the lecturer had been chiefly engaged. Many years ago excavations were commenced, but little real work was done. With the assistance of the Antiquarian Society [*sic*][1] he and others had been able to expose so much of the ancient foundations as to enable them to provide a plan of a very fine habitation.

While Price was thus spreading his fame as 'the well-known Sussex archaeologist', his claims were fatally punctured from a source that may be perhaps regarded as impeccable. Dr

---

[1] Correctly, the Society of Antiquaries of London, founded *circa* 1572, suppressed on the accession of James I, reformed in 1717 and now the second oldest chartered body (after the Royal Society) in the world. Price was never a member (F.S.A.). I was in my sixties before I was elected a Fellow.

Charles Hercules Read, F.S.A. (1857–1929) had been since 1896 the distinguished Keeper of the Department of British and Mediaeval Antiquities and Ethnography at the British Museum. He was knighted in 1912. In 1910 he was the President of the Society of Antiquaries. On 6 January of that year a particularly flamboyant report of Price's delivery of his lecture on 'Roman Pulborough' was published in the *West Sussex Gazette*. In the issue of the same periodical of 13 January a letter to the Editor was published over Dr Read's signature as President of the Society of Antiquaries, written from the Society's headquarters at Burlington House, Piccadilly, London, W. After referring with commendable restraint to what he described as the 'wrong impression' created by the lecture, Dr Read wrote:

Mr. Charles Praetorius, F.S.A., a local secretary of the Society, reported the discovery of the villa to the Council, and was allowed a grant for excavations on the site. These were undertaken by him, with the permission of Mr. Hugh Davies-Colley, the owner of the land. I understand that the usual report will be presented to the Society by Mr. Praetorius in a few weeks. The Society has no knowledge of Mr. Price in the matter.

As this letter appeared in a newspaper that would be read in Pulborough, where Price lived, he had no choice but to try to defend his position, difficult though this would seem when it is considered that he was so unacquainted with the archaeological scene that he referred to the President of the Society of Antiquaries as 'Mr. Read'. His excuse was that he had sought permission to excavate at Borough, to find that Praetorius and the Society had forestalled him. He concluded his letter by saying:

As far back as last October Mr. Praetorius was fully aware that I intended giving a lecture dealing with the Borough excavations, and I cannot see that my paper had anything to do with the Society of Antiquaries. I fully acknowledged in my lecture (and it also appeared in the public press) the part the Society played in the matter, and I fail to see the point of Mr. Read's letter, which I consider was quite uncalled for.

The Society of Antiquaries took no notice of this letter, nor was any further attention paid to Price. It may be thought that none was necessary. On 10 March, 1910 Charles J. Praetorius, F.S.A., presented his report on the Borough excavations to a meeting of the Society at Burlington House under the chairmanship of the President. He said that the assistance he had received in the work had been limited to 'four labourers accustomed to trenching and familiar with the soil'. Praetorius's paper was published in volume xxiii of the Society's *Proceedings*. It occupied nine pages, and was illustrated by an excellent scale drawing of the foundations, together with five other figures including a view of the hypocaust and photographs of the most important finds. This meeting of the Society was also reported at length in the issue of *The Athenaeum* of 26 March, 1910. It seems hardly necessary to say that in neither of these accounts was there any mention of the name of Harry Price.

The circumstances of Price's pose as an archaeologist differed from his blatant plagiarism as a numismatic journalist in at least one important particular. In the latter activity he was not exposed, while in the former he was, causing him ultimately to retire from all publicised activity in the field of archaeology. Indeed, until the early nineteen-twenties, when he at last found in psychical research the congenial and convenient vehicle for the sensational publicity that satisfied his vanity and exhibitionism, and lasted to the end of his life, he seems to have been mainly interested in collecting scarce books on conjuring and allied subjects. By 1920, as we shall see, he had assembled an important library with the assistance of his wife's money. As we might expect, moreover, he was boldly contributing substantial articles on the subject to appropriate journals, claiming expertise in this new sphere of activity.

XII

The Book-Collector

In *The Magazine of Magic* of November, 1920 was published a six-page essay, 'Some Magical Rarities, Ancient and Modern' by 'Harry Price, F.R.N.S. Member of the Society for Psychical Research, Hon. Librarian, Magicians' Club, London, etc., etc.'. The article was illustrated by three photographic reproductions of old and rare conjuring books, the subject upon which Price's interest as a collector was still principally directed in 1920. It was an informative piece of work in one respect, since Price was describing books he actually possessed, but it was unfortunately marred by some mistakes and more especially by Price's tendency to dilate upon the rarity and value of items in his library irrespective of the facts.

As an example, in his comments upon Henry Dean's *The whole art of legerdemain, or, hocus pocus in perfection,* of which the first edition was published in London by A. Bettesworth in 1722, Price wrote (p. 42), 'The rarest edition of this work is the one published in 1727'. A glance at page 152 of Price's printed *Short-Title Catalogue* (London, 1929) tells us that he did not own a copy of the *editio princeps* of 1722 (an exceedingly rare book of which I know of no copy in private hands)[1] but that he did possess the second edition of 1727, published by A. Bettesworth, D. Pratt, John Willis and Theo. Pettit. The second edition is certainly a rare book, but equally certainly it is not so rare as the first edition of 1722. I know, for example, of at least one free copy of the second edition of 1727, for I possess it myself. Price owned it too, however, and therefore it

---

[1] On pp. 198–9 of my *Old Conjuring Books. A Bibliographical and Historical Study* I mention the two copies of this very rare book in the British Isles known to me. They are those in the British Museum and the Library of the University of Glasgow.

had to be the rarest edition of all, by his standards of accuracy and veracity.

This tendency on Price's part to assert the superiority of the copies of books in his possession is further exemplified in another article, 'My Library', published in *The Magic Wand*[1] of October–November, 1923. In this essay he claimed (p. 133) that his copy of the first edition of Reginald Scot's *The discoverie of witchcraft* (London, 1584), the first book in English to contain an illustrated chapter on practical conjuring tricks as we know them today, was 'the finest in existence, and half an inch taller than the better of the British Museum copies'. Price also asserted that his copy of Scot had come from the Yatton Court Library, where 'it was positively known' that Shakespeare had consulted some of the books, with the added claim 'that Shakespeare was interested in magic, and conjuring as we know it today is certain . . . The subject-matter of this famous work on anti-witchcraft is recognisable in several of Shakespeare's plays'. Shakespeare had therefore, on the basis of these assertions, handled and consulted the finest copy known of Scot's book before Price acquired it.

The remarkable story of Price's published claim to own a second edition of Thomas Denton's *The conjurer unmasked*, uniquely dated 1838 on the title-page, has already been told in my *Old Conjuring Books*. I will include it briefly here, however, for the benefit of those readers who are not bibliographers and may not have seen this work of reference. As is well known to students of old conjuring books, the first, second and third editions of Denton's book, the last two so described on the title-pages, are dated 1785, 1788 and 1790, also on the title-pages.[2] On page 156 of his *Short-Title Catalogue*, however, Price printed the following entry:

Denton (Thomas). The Conjurer Unmasked . . . (Second Edition with large additions and alterations). London, 1838. (See illustration).

---

[1] *The Magic Wand*, founded by my friend the late George Johnson, is, like *The Magazine of Magic*, now unfortunately defunct.

[2] The three editions are described at Nos. 110, 111 and 112 on pp. 39–40 of my *A Bibliography of Books on Conjuring in English from 1580 to 1850* (Minneapolis, 1957). The book was a translation, with some additions, of Henri Decremps' *La magie blanche dévoilée* (Paris, 1784).

Opposite page 140 of the *Short-Title Catalogue* he reproduced as Plate No. 8 a photograph of the title-page and frontispiece of 'The Second Edition' with the date of MDCCCXXXVIII plainly to be seen under the publisher's imprint. The legend under the photograph, moreover,* reads, 'Title-page and Frontispiece of *The Conjurer Unmasked*, by Thomas Denton. London, 1838'. Price also included his unique '1838 Denton' in a selective list of what he regarded as the 500 most rare and valuable items in his collection, *Exhibition of Rare Works from the Research Library* (London, 1934). No. 117 is 'Denton (Thomas), The Conjurer Unmasked . . . London, 1838'.

Astonishing as it may seem, Price's actual copy of the book has the correct date of 1788 ('MDCCLXXXVIII') on its title-page. On the photograph, however, the 'L' has been carefully converted into a 'C' to give the spurious date of 1838 ('MDCCCXXXVIII'). The interested reader can confirm this for himself by examining Plate No. 8 in the *Short-Title Catalogue*, for under a magnifying-glass the alteration of the 'L' into a rather square 'C' is discernible. A conceivable explanation, other than wilful deception, could be that the date came up indistinctly in the photograph, and that Price touched it up (as he invited the late S. H. Glanville to touch up the photographs of the wall-writings at Borley Rectory), altering the date by mistake. It seems fair to say, however, that such carelessness is scarcely expected of a man who believed himself to be the owner of the foremost collection of books in the world dealing with a subject on which he claimed to be a leading expert.

My penultimate example of Price's unreliability as a commentator on the books in his collection (before we turn our attention to his Burmese MS., one of the most astounding mysteries I have ever encountered) is concerned with what he called 'the rarest book known to psychical researchers' in the Introduction to his *Short-Title Catalogue*. The item concerned appeared in the list as:

Adare (Viscount). Experiences in Spiritualism with Mr. D. D. Home. [Privately Printed.] [Two copies]. London [1870]. [See illustration].

In the Introduction to his *Exhibition of Rare Works from the Research Library*, Price wrote:

The rarest book on modern spiritualism is Viscount Adare's *Experiences in Spiritualism with Mr. D. D. Home*, privately printed in 1870. This substantial volume deals with a series of *séances* which Viscount Adare (afterwards Lord Dunraven) had with the famous physical medium Home during the years 1867–9. Fifty copies of this book were printed and circulated among those sitters (including the Master of Lindsay, Mr. and Mrs. S. C. Hall, Sir Robert Gore Booth, etc.) who took part in the experiments. Afterwards, efforts were made to withdraw the work, but a few copies passed into private circulation. The book is not only extremely rare, but is valuable as being the best account extant of Home's alleged phenomena. Two copies are in the Research Library.

In parenthesis, I may say that the fact that the book was in print for private circulation before 1870 is not in doubt, for I have seen two copies inscribed by the third Earl of Dunraven, Adare's father, with a date of 1869 (July and August respectively) to Lady Augusta Vivian, the Earl's daughter, and to J. T. Bayley, from Dunraven Castle, Glamorgan, the family seat. I also believe that the true place of origin of this privately circulated book was Dunraven Castle, and not London, which was merely the place of printing by Thomas Scott, and that the person responsible for its appearance (and subsequent withdrawal) was Edwin Richard Windham Wyndham-Quin, the third Earl of Dunraven, and not his son. I am certain, moreover, that more than fifty copies were printed. This faulty assumption was first published by the late Professor Charles Richet on page 485 of his *Thirty Years of Psychical Research* (London, 1923). Price copied from Richet. Both relied on the fact that the list of 'Names of Persons Present at the Séances' printed on pages xxii–iii of the book numbered exactly fifty. The whole case for a printing of only fifty copies is destroyed by the simple fact that the names of neither Lady Augusta Vivian nor J. T. Bayley are included. It is to be deplored that the originator and copier of the story did not take the trouble to look at the list intelligently, as well as merely counting it, before going into print. It should have been obvious, one would have thought, that extra copies would be needed for relatives and friends. The Earl had three daughters, in any event, and it is reasonable to suppose that they would be treated alike. Did it not occur to the experts, moreover, that Dunraven and Adare would require copies for themselves? Their names are not included in the list of exactly fifty persons. Despite these observations, I have no doubt that the book is a rare item indeed.

In a later book, *Fifty Years of Psychical Research* (London, 1939), Price continued the error on page 276 when he wrote, 'Fifty copies of this book were printed privately and circulated among those friends of Lord Adare who had sat with the medium'. Between 1934 and 1939 he had acquired another copy of *Experiences in Spiritualism*, for on page 277 of *Fifty Years of Psychical Research* he remarked in a footnote, 'I have three copies, with different bindings, in my collection'. Price contributed a lengthy Foreword to Jean Burton's popular biography of D. D. Home, *Heyday of a Wizard* (New York, 1944 and London, 1948), and on page 19 he doubtless caused further confusion to students by writing of *Experiences in Spiritualism*, 'Only thirty copies of the book were printed, and later desperate efforts were made to recall them'. He repeated in the same place that he had three copies in his collection, all with different bindings. I asked Alan Wesencraft, who has the Harry Price Library in his care at the University of London, to inspect the books and give me an independent opinion of Price's statement. He wrote: 'Price's three copies are identical. I can detect no difference to justify the assertion "with different bindings" . . . I have gradually come to the conclusion that in psychical research matters Price was quite incapable of making a simple and accurate statement of fact'.

XIII

The Burmese MS

The tangle of inaccuracy, exaggeration and devious writing described in the preceding chapter apart, there is no doubt about the item, above all others, that Price claimed to be the central jewel of his collection of conjuring books. In the final paragraph of his essay, 'Some Magical Rarities, Ancient and Modern' in November, 1920, already quoted, he wrote:

I will conclude this little monograph with mention of two remarkable and unique items in my library. One of them you have already read about (*Wonderful Book on Playing Cards*. Magazine of Magic, May, 1920). The other is a 'book' of sixty beautifully-inscribed palm-leaves, with three covering leaves finely lacquered in gold and red. It is in Burmese characters, and was executed by a scribe (attached to the court of a local prince) who jotted down and explained the various effects of the native itinerant conjurers who happened to call at the palace. The MS. describes many famous illusions, such as the basket trick, rope-climbing, mango-trick, swallowing the barrel of water, etc., etc. The leaves, both sides of which are worked upon, have gilt edges, and are strung on cords like a Venetian blind. Whether regarded as a work on conjuring or as a literary masterpiece, the 'volume' is unique. There is a note in English to the effect that the MS. has been transcribed[1] by Sir Richard Burton, the famous English traveller, and is dated 1879. Needless to say, I regard this curiosity as the *pièce de résistance* of my collection.

[1] The use of this verb, which *The Concise Oxford Dictionary* defines as simply to 'copy out in writing', seems to me very odd. To transcribe is not to translate. Sir Richard Francis Burton (1821–1890) can scarcely have written out the actual MS. in Burmese from some other source, if we can place any faith in Price's claim in *The Magic Wand* of October–November, 1923 (p. 136) that the MS. was about one hundred years old. In any event, Alan Wesencraft tells me that no such note is to be found on the MS.

In the following issue of *The Magazine of Magic* of December, 1920, the whole of page 62 was devoted to an advertisement by a dealer, Will Goldston, of a forthcoming book, *More Exclusive Magical Secrets*, to be edited and published by him in 1921. Goldston said that he was indebted to Harry Price, 'well-known as the owner of the finest collection of magical works in this country', for allowing him to include in the book the best trick from the Burmese MS., which Goldston called 'The Mysterious Barrel'. When *More Exclusive Magical Secrets* appeared in 1921, the trick (pp. 341–5) was entitled 'Swallowing a Barrel of Water. Freely translated from the Burmese MS. on Native Conjurers' Tricks.'[1] I have never heard of the trick ever being performed and doubt its practicability, since among other difficulties it would involve the performer bearing the weight of 'a large wooden barrel or cask (holding about 40 gallons)' and 'bound around with many iron hoops', on his unprotected chest. I do not believe, moreover, that any of my fellow-members of the Magic Circle would risk the performance of an illusion depending on the assumption that a small hinged trapdoor, lacking any form of fastening other than being just 'stiff enough', would not be forced open at the wrong moment by the weight of 40 gallons of water above it. If my conviction (which I hope to prove) that 'Swallowing a Barrel of Water' was not described in Price's Burmese MS. is right, however, these criticisms of the practicability of the supposed 'illusion' are superfluous. At the conclusion of the entry in *More Exclusive Magical Secrets*, Goldston repeated his gratitude 'to my friend Harry Price' for his contribution of the trick. That Price was responsible for the published description in English (whatever its provenance may have been) is demonstrated by his remark on page 62 of his later article 'My Library' in 1923 (referred to chronologically below) in which he wrote, with a footnote appended:

Elsewhere* I have detailed the 'Swallowing a Barrel of Water' illusion, which is one of the tricks recorded in the Burmese conjuring 'book'.

[1] 'Swallowing a Barrel of Water' is illustrated. There are no illustrations in *The Jātaka*, a book discussed in this chapter.
* *More Exclusive Magical Secrets*, p. 341.

This episode makes it clear that no explanation of the exceedingly curious incident of the Burmese MS., that relies on the possibility that Price was himself deceived in regard to its contents, is possible. Either the MS. was genuine, or the 'freely translated' English extract from it was fraudulent.

Early in 1922 Price placed his library on 'permanent loan'[1] in the Rooms of the Society for Psychical Research at 20 Hanover Square, London, W., and a short unsigned account of the collection, 'Mr. Price's Library', was published in the Society's *Journal* of May, 1922.[2] It included a comment:

In MSS. the collection is well known for the inclusion of a Burmese MS. on the work of the Indian fakirs, which was transcribed by Sir Richard Burton and also for smaller MSS. on magic and astrology.

In Price's essay 'My Library' in 1923, to which reference has already been made, a separate paragraph was devoted to the unique Burmese MS.,[3] repeating in general terms the assertions made in 1920, but stating for the first time that the MS. was 'about one hundred years old'. Immediately after the collection had been removed from the Rooms of the Society for Psychical Research in October, 1927, and transferred to Price's newly formed National Laboratory of Psychical Research at 16 Queensberry Place, South Kensington, S.W.7., the Honorary Director (Price) published an article, 'The National Laboratory Library', in *The British Journal of Psychical Research* of November–December, 1927 (pp. 307–16),[4] using the same photographs of title-pages that had illustrated the essay in *The Magazine of Magic* seven years previously. The now customary paragraph describing the Burmese MS. was included (p. 312) the only difference of interest being that it was now asserted that the MS. had been 'transcribed' by Sir William Burton.

---

[1] The collection was removed from the S.P.R. headquarters in October, 1927 (*Journal*, S.P.R., October, 1927, p. 114).

[2] Pp. 270–1. The article occupied slightly more than one page.

[3] *The Magic Wand*, October–November, 1923, p. 136.

[4] *The British Journal* was published by Price from his 'National Laboratory', which he established in rivalry with the Society for Psychical Research.

In April, 1929, Price published his *Short-Title Catalogue* of his collection as Part II, Volume 1 of the *Proceedings* of his National Laboratory of Psychical Research. The entry for the '*pièce de résistance*' of the library was on page 21:

> Burmese Magic. [A MS. written on 59 palm leaves describing the tricks of Indian fakirs and magicians, transcribed by Sir Richard F. Burton.] [Burma *c*. 1800].

In the Introduction the MS. was described as 'extremely interesting'.

So far as I am aware, the Burmese MS. was not mentioned again in print until it appeared in the *Report of the Library Committee* of the University of London of 11 November, 1936. Price's lease of his office in London, in Roland Gardens, South Kensington, was running out, and he offered his library and equipment 'on permanent loan' to the University of London.[1] That the matter was urgent from his point of view is, I think, demonstrated by the fact that the Report included the information that Price required the collection to be removed from his premises before Christmas, 1936. In these circumstances it is reasonable to suppose that the *Report of the Library Committee*, which recommended to the Senate that the offer be accepted, would necessarily be based, to a large extent at least, on Price's account of his library. It was described as containing 'over 14,000 volumes and pamphlets on psychic phenomena and pseudo-phenomena'. That this was an over-estimate is demonstrated by the later printed report by the Librarian of 1 November, 1938, following the removal of the collection from its temporary storage by the University to the newly completed Senate House in Bloomsbury. In this later factual report prepared by the Library staff, the Price collection was stated to consist of 10,444 items, including bound volumes of periodicals. In the Report of 11 November, 1936, the first item to receive specific mention by name in the description of the library had been the Burmese MS. It was stated that 'a treatise

---

[1] The acceptance of the offer (one condition of which was the bearing of the cost of the insurance of the library by the University) did not deter Price from negotiating with the University of Bonn in 1937 in regard to the transference of the collection to Germany.

in Burmese on Indian magic is particularly interesting'. In the subsequent account of the 'Harry Price Library of Magical Literature' on pages 6–8 of the printed *A Reader's Guide to the University Library*, first issued by the University of London in 1938, however, in which over twenty rare books in the collection were listed individually by name, no mention of the Burmese MS. was made. It was last described in print, therefore, in November, 1936, some four months before the first professional report upon it was prepared by Professor J. A. Stewart.

The late John Alexander Stewart, c.i.e., m.c., m.a., ll.d., who died in 1948, was Professor of Burmese in the School of Oriental and African Studies in the University of London, and the joint author (with C. W. Dunn) of *A Burmese-English Dictionary*. Alan Wesencraft has been unable to discover the precise circumstances in which Professor Stewart prepared a signed report on Price's Burmese MS., dated 24 March, 1937, but this document is on file at the University. A supplementary report was signed by Dr Hla Pe, m.a. (Rangoon), ph.d., Reader in Burmese in the School of Oriental and African Studies in the University of London, on 14 May, 1956, and this is also on the file. These two documents combine to give us a detailed description, leaf by leaf, of the true contents of Price's Burmese MS. Perhaps I should say two things at the outset. First, neither Professor Stewart nor Dr Hla Pe make any mention whatever of the alleged note in English stating that the MS. was 'transcribed' by Sir Richard (or William) Burton, and Mr Wesencraft tells me that he can find no such note in the MS. Secondly, Professor Stewart's report concluded with the following unambiguous statement:

I am quite satisfied that no part of the bundle of MSS. deals with the subject of magic or conjuring.

The MS. consists of 60 palm leaves, of which 7 are blank. Of the remaining 53 leaves, 2 are devoted to a catechism on Buddhism ('*Pănhākattā*') and 2 others to religious treatises ('*Saranādivinicchhaya*'). Of the remaining 49 leaves, Professor Stewart and Dr Hla Pe reported that 32 leaves were devoted to 'Jātaka story 506, *Campeyya*', 10 leaves to 'Jātaka story 509, *Hatthi-pāla*', and 7 leaves to 'Jātaka story 510, *Ayoghara*'. The following comment was made on the whole of the MS.:

> The contents are all *nissaya*, i.e. Pali text, with word for word translations into Burmese; a passage of Pali being followed by the relevant passage of Burmese . . . The two lacquered leaves, used as covering material, contain part of the *kammavācā*, i.e. texts to be recited at consecration or ordination ceremonies.

The paraphrased leaf-by-leaf description of the contents of the MS. falls between the two sentences of the above quotation.

It may be thought that for me, a mere bibliographer and graduate in English, to comment upon the written findings of two distinguished experts in Burmese (a language with which I am totally unfamiliar) would be an impertinence in normal circumstances. Two matters, however, have led me to offer some observations of my own on this extremely curious business. First, there is the quite serious situation that if the MS. contains no conjuring material whatever, as Professor Stewart explicitly declared in his report, then Price stands convicted of deliberate and bare-faced fraud, since he actually published, as the reader is already aware, a supposed translation in English of one of the 'many famous illusions' which he claimed were described in the MS. by 'a scribe (attached to the court of a local prince) who jotted down and explained the various effects of the itinerant conjurers who happened to call at the palace'.[1] Secondly, by great good fortune, I had available to me the one work of impeccable scholarship that enabled me to investigate the matter for myself. More importantly, the interested reader who has access to a good reference library can do so himself.

It will be obvious to the reader that if there is any truth at all in Price's assertion that the MS. consisted of explanations of conjuring tricks (with specific illusions named by him) these could not be contained in the 4 leaves devoted to Buddhist catechisms and other religious material. The only possible place was in what Professor Stewart and Dr Hla Pe described as Jātaka stories 506, 509 and 510. It was therefore a most welcome surprise to me to find on the shelves of the Leeds Library the

---

[1] *The Magazine of Magic*, November, 1920, p. 44.

seven volumes of *The Jātaka, or, Stories of the Buddha's former Births. Translated from the Pali by various hands*, published by the Cambridge University Press from 1895 to 1913, the last volume consisting entirely of a comprehensive index. This large work was produced under the Editorship of Professor E. B. Cowell, sometime Professor of Sanskrit in the University of Cambridge. The translators included W. H. D. Rouse, Fellow of Christ's College, Cambridge, H. T. Francis, Fellow of Gonville and Caius College, Cambridge and R. A. Neil, Fellow of Pembroke College, Cambridge.

The Jātaka stories Nos. 506, 509 and 510 are all in Volume IV, commencing respectively on pages 281, 293 and 304. Each consists of a story told by Buddha, and under the number and title of each is an introductory comment on the text that follows:

No. 506. Campeyya-Jātaka. This story the Master told while dwelling in Jetavana, about the fast-day vows. The Master said, 'It is well done, lay Brethren, that you have taken upon you the fast-day vows. Wise men of old likewise even renounced the glory of being a Serpent King [Campeyya], and lived under these vows'. Then at their request he told a story of the past.

No. 509. Hatthi-Pāla Jātaka. This story the Master told, while dwelling at Jetavana, about the Renunciation. Then with these words, 'It is not the first time, Brethren, that the Tathagāta made the Renunciation, but it was so before', the Master told them a story of the past.

No. 510. Ayoghara-Jātaka. This story the Master told about the Great Renunciation. Here again he said, 'This is not the first time, Brethren, that the Tathāgata has made the Great Renunciation, for he did the same before'. And he told them a story of the past.

These epitomes give some idea of the content and flavour of the stories told by Buddha. None of them contain any explanations or descriptions of conjuring tricks whatever. The scribe attached to the court of a local prince, who according to Price was the author of the MS. and who jotted down and explained the various tricks performed by the itinerant conjurers who called at the palace, is also conspicuous by his absence.

I examined the index volume to see if there was any reference anywhere to 'the basket trick, rope-climbing, mango trick, swallowing the barrel of water, etc., etc.', the 'illusions' (allegedly among many others) specifically mentioned by Price in his description of the MS. in *The Magazine of Magic* in 1920. No 'basket trick' is mentioned in the entire work. A footnote on page 93 of Volume 1 explains 'the three divisions, or "three baskets", of the Buddhist scriptures', but this has no reference to conjuring. No 'rope-climbing' is mentioned anywhere in the index volume, the only references to rope being a 'rope of sand' (vi, p. 168) which was a counter-quip of the sage Mahosadha, used against a playful quip of the King, and 'rope-rubbing' (iv, p. 284) which was simply a term used in snake-charming. As regards the trick of 'swallowing the barrel of water', there is no mention of a barrel or a cask in the index of the entire work. The long entry for water in the index is worth quoting, not only for its complete lack of any reference whatever to conjuring, but for the cross-section it gives of the atmosphere of the Jātaka stories:

Water, of consecration, coronation, *see* Ceremonial sprinkling; delicate, so that all things sink, vi, 55; of donation, gift, respect, *see* Gift; filtered, i, 76, 77; not defiled by elephants, ii, 15; poured on betrothed, iii, 180.

Only the mango trick remained as a possibility, and it was with great interest, therefore, that I found an entry for it in the index (page 28):

Mango-trick of conjurers, iv, 204; performed miraculously by Buddha, iv, 168; by Ananda, iv, 145.[1]

---

[1] The miracles of Buddha and Ananda have no connexion with conjuring, as is demonstrated by the description of the first of these (iv, p. 168). 'Even as the crowd stared it grew into a mango tree of a hundred cubits, with a trunk fifty cubits and branches of fifty cubits in height; at the same time flowers bloomed, fruit ripened; the tree stood filling the sky, covered with bees, loaden with golden fruit; when the wind blew on it, sweet fruits fell; then the Brethren came up and ate of the fruit, and retired.' This had no connexion with the Burmese MS., being in story No. 483, Sarabha-Miga-Jātaka, which dealt with supernatural power and 'the descent from the world of gods', as the epitome at the beginning makes clear.

I also found on page 10 of the index an entry, 'Conjurers, *see* Jugglers', and page 21 the entry, 'Jugglers, iv, 308;[1] i, 135;

> 'Lions and tigers, panthers, seize their prey,
> And all devour it, struggle as it may;
> From fear of their devouring death is free:
> So I'm resolved—a holy life for me.
>
> Upon the stage a juggler with his sleight,
> Performing can deceive the people's sight,
> To cozen death, no trick so quick can be;
> So I'm resolved—a holy life for me.
>
> Serpents enraged will with venomed bite
> Attack at once and kill a man outright;
> To death no fear of poison-bite can be:
> So I'm resolved—a holy life for me.'

mango-trick, *see* Mango [iv, 204]; trick of cutting a man piece-meal, etc., iv, 204'. The important reference is to page 204 of volume iv, and to the mango trick and the trick of cutting a man piece-meal. This page is part of 'No. 489. Suruci-Jātaka', which means that it forms no part of the Burmese MS. However, it was still of interest to see that the passage concerned bore no relation to practical conjuring, and offered no explanation of tricks:

Then came two clever jugglers, Bhandu-kanna and Pandu-kanna, Crop-ear and Yellow-ear, and say they, 'We will make the prince laugh'. Bhandu-kanna made a great mango tree, which he called Sanspareil, grow up before the palace door; then he threw up a ball of string, and made it catch on a branch of the tree, and then he climbed into the Mango Sanspareil. Now the Mango Sanspareil they say is Vessavana's mango. And the slaves of Vessavana took him, as usual, chopt him up limb-meal and threw down the bits. The other jugglers joined the pieces together, and poured water upon them. The man donned upper and under garments of flowers, and rose up and began dancing again. Even the sight of this did not make the prince laugh.

---

[1] This reference is to one verse in a 32-verse poem recited by the King's son, who insisted on renouncing the throne and upon embracing the religious life. Each 4-line verse ends with the line, 'So I'm resolved—a holy life for me.' I quote the (only) verse mentioning conjuring, with those that precede and follow it, so that the reader has a cross-section of the meaning of the poem as a whole:

At the foot of the page is a footnote linked to 'Vessavana's mango', which says 'The juggling trick here described is spoken of by mediaeval travellers. See Yule's *Marco Polo*, vol. i, p. 308.'

Although on the authority of Professor Stewart and Dr Hla Pe we know that this passage, occurring as it does in Jātaka story 489, forms no part of Price's Burmese MS., it will not have escaped the reader that in it there are some points of coincidence with Price's original description of his most valued item. First, it is an account of the entertainment of a prince. Secondly, the prince's palace is mentioned. Thirdly, albeit in a wildly exaggerated way, the *general effect* of the mango tree trick is described. Fourthly, although there is no entry for rope-climbing in the index of *The Jātaka*, in the quoted passage Bhandu-kanna does climb up a string into the Mango Sans-pareil.

All that can be said about these similarities is first that Professor Cowell's book was available in 1920. Secondly, a careless and unscrupulous person, determined to claim that the MS. was a unique conjuring item and having been told in general terms that it contained Jātaka stories, might have referred to the index volume of *The Jātaka*. If he had looked for an entry dealing with conjuring he would have found 'Conjurers, *see* Jugglers', and would so have been led directly to page 204 of volume iv, and the passage I have quoted. It is an odd business, one of the most curious points about it being that despite the importance Price claimed for the *'pièce de résistance'* of his collection, he never disclosed in print how it came into his possession.

XIV

The Book Plates

Book-collectors almost invariably indulge their pride in the ownership of their treasures by the use of a book-plate, often defined as 'a label pasted inside the cover of a book, bearing the owner's name, crest, coat-of-arms or other personal device'. Harry Price was no exception to this rule, and at various times no less than four different plates have been associated with his collection, two of which are of very great interest indeed. It will be convenient first to discuss in the reverse of chronological order the three book-plates bearing Harry Price's name. When that has been done, I will offer my solution of the separate and singular mystery of the plate bearing the name of 'Robert Ditcher-Price', that is present in some of Price's books.

Alan Wesencraft tells me that when Price's collection was transferred to the University a high percentage of the items had no book-plates inserted at all. A number did bear one or other of Harry Price's two early personal plates, and some others were distinguished by the extraordinary 'Robert Ditcher-Price' book-plate, a mystery that has fallen to my lot to attempt to solve. Mr Wesencraft informs me that the Library staff 'never remove, efface or erase any book-plate belonging to a book's previous owner: in fact, we normally take great care to preserve them'. This admirable precept, followed by most librarians and collectors, ensures that the record of a book's provenance remains permanently available.

It is admittedly odd that Price put comparatively few of his earlier plates into his books, bearing in mind that he must have incurred the expense of having them designed and printed, presumably in fairly large quantities. It is possible, however, that the considerable task of inserting the plates into a collection of books and pamphlets variously declared as containing 20,000 items in Price's last entry in *Who's Who* in 1948, and as 'some thirteen thousand volumes' in Tabori's biography published two years later,[1] was one that Price, a prolific and busy writer and journalist, never found the time or energy to undertake.

In the case of Price's collection, the task of inserting into the books, as the University of London Library did, a new book-plate depicting the arms of the University over the words 'University of London. Harry Price Library',[2] was made easier by one of the owner's idiosyncrasies. Mr Wesencraft tells me that in most cases (but not all) Price's original plates had been pasted on to the front free end-papers of his books, rather than in the usual position inside the front cover, and that the latter position was therefore generally available for the addition of the University of London plate. This habit of Price's is unusual in my experience, for unless one is particularly skilful in the use of adhesives, there is a tendency to produce crinkling on the verso of the free end-paper. A book-plate pasted inside the front cover, furthermore, is a more permanent proof of ownership. The historian, however, can only record the facts as he has tried to ascertain them, curious though some of them may seem to be.

The result of these procedures is that today the majority of the books in the Harry Price Library simply bear the University of London/Price plate inside the front cover. In other examples, one or other of Price's earlier personal plates, or the 'Robert Ditcher-Price' plate, is also present on the opposite free end-paper. In those cases where Price had perversely pasted one of his earlier plates inside the front cover, these have been left *in situ* by the Library staff.

Price's first printed *Short-Title Catalogue* of his library was published in April, 1929 as Part II of Volume I of the *Proceedings* of his self-styled National Laboratory of Psychical Research. Plate 16, opposite page 204, is a photographic reproduction of Jaspar Isac's engraving 'Abomination des Sorciers'. On page 234 of the text this item is listed and described:

Isac (Jaspar), [Engraved by], Abomination des Sorciers. [Engraving of the Witches' Sabbath, reproduced for Mr. Harry Price's magical book-plate.] Paris [*c.* 1613]. [*See illustration.*]

[1] The records of the University of London Library show that both these totals were inflated.

[2] See Plate 5.

It follows that the book-plate in use by Price in 1929, before his collection was moved to the University of London in 1936, was the one described above, with 'EX LIBRIS' and 'HARRY PRICE' above and below the reproduction of the Isac engraving.[1] We know, in fact, that this plate existed as early as 1923, for it was used as one of the illustrations in Price's article, 'My Library', published in *The Magic Wand*, No. 119, vol. xii, of October/November, 1923. It succeeded the spurious crested plate, next to be described, the existence of which as early as 1913 is proved by evidence available within twenty miles of my own home.

My initial knowledge of what I believe to have been Price's earliest book-plate came from a xerox kindly sent to me by Alan Wesencraft. It is still displayed in a few items in Price's collection, and in at least one other place. My first encounter with the actual book-plate, as opposed to seeing a photograph of it, was in the Leeds Library during the winter of 1975. After the period of Price's attempt to establish a reputation for himself as a numismatic journalist (presumably not without financial reward) in the first decade of the present century, to be followed by his exploits in archaeology, he evidently sold his copy of George C. Williamson's *Trade Tokens issued in the Seventeenth Century in England, Wales and Ireland. A New and Revised Edition of William Boyne's Work* (2 vols., London, 1889 and 1891) to Bernard Quaritch, Ltd., the London booksellers, some time previous to 27 June, 1913. On that date, as the Leeds Library's accession records show, this standard work on trade tokens had been bought by the Library from Quaritch for £2.11s.2d, as we have seen. The long arm of coincidence was certainly in operation when, 62 years later, the President of the Library, the present writer, opened the first volume and was confronted with a book-plate bearing the name of 'Harry Price' on an elaborate scroll, below a crest which he had certainly no right whatever to display.[2] Indeed, when I sent a photograph of the plate to Mr C. W. Scott-Giles, o.b.e., f.s.a., of Cambridge, the Fitzalan Pursuivant Extraordinary and a former Editor of the standard work on British heraldry, his comment on it in his letter to me of 30 November, 1975 was

---

[1] See Plate 6.   [2] See Plate 7.

unambiguous. 'What a complete fraud Harry Price was! . . . What satisfaction can a man get from using heraldic honours to which he knows he is not entitled?'

A very old family named Price (anciently 'ap Rhys'), originating in Denbighshire, bore as its crest, 'a lion rampant or, holding a rose gules, stalked and leaved vert'.[1] An early description of this crest, which Harry Price adopted for his book-plate, is to be found under 'Price (Denbighshire)' in the alphabetical but unpaginated section 'The General Armory' in John and Bernard Burke's *A General Armory of England, Scotland and Ireland* (London, 1842). If we assume that in the process of copying the crest Harry Price looked up the relevant lineage of this distinguished family in works of heraldic reference, a sentence on page 14 of *Search for Truth* assumes some significance:

> One headmaster went so far as to tell me that my proper name was 'Henry Ap Rhys' (Henry the son of Rhys), which is probably true, though I am glad the name has been whittled down through the centuries. This particular head was a Welshman.

The same reference books would certainly have told him that his own descent from the Prices of Dudley, Worcestershire in the eighteenth-century (claimed by him on page 15 of *Confessions of a Ghost-Hunter* to be 'an old Shropshire family') had no connexion whatever with the Prices whose crest he used, and who were created baronets in 1804. The distinguished descendant who was so honoured was Sir Charles Price (1748–1818), who became Lord Mayor of London in 1803, and whose seat was Spring Grove, Richmond, Surrey. The crest he adapted from that of his Denbighshire ancestors was of 'a lion rampant argent, in the dexter paw a rose slipped proper'. The fifth baronet, who succeeded his brother Sir Frederic Price in 1873, assumed by royal licence in 1874 the additional name of Rugge, and became Sir Arthur James Rugge-Price, which has remained the family name to this day.[2]

---

[1] In the works of reference quoted in this chapter, some of the words used in the descriptions of the crests and arms are abbreviated. For the sake of clarity, I have given them in full.

[2] Sir Bernard Burke, *A Genealogical and Heraldic Dictionary of the Peerage and Baronetage* (London, 1891), pp. 1132–4.

An additional point of interest is that the motto used by Sir Charles Price was 'Vive ut vivas' (Live that you may live). Harry Price's faked book-plate, however, bears the more hedonistic motto 'Dum vivimus, vivamus' (Let us live while we live), the maxim of the Epicureans, which is not included in Fairbairn's 'Mottoes',[1] but is commonly featured in lists of words and phrases from Latin, French and other languages in household dictionaries such as those published by W. & R. Chambers, Ltd.

My first encounter with the mystery of the book-plate of 'Robert Ditcher-Price' was in one of Price's many editions of a seventeenth-century book containing conjuring tricks, John White's *A rich cabinet with variety of inventions, unlock'd and open'd for the recreation of ingenious spirits*. The customary procedure in regard to book-plates, already described in the preceding pages, had been followed by the University. The 'University of London. Harry Price Library' plate had been inserted inside the front cover of the book by the Library staff. Opposite to it on the free end-paper, however, had been preserved another plate, already *in situ* when the collection had been transferred to the University Library. This plate occupied a similar position, therefore, to that of the majority of the two early plates bearing Harry Price's name and inserted by him, but was entirely different from either of them in every particular. It bore a crest, arms and motto, with the words 'Ex Libris' and 'Robert Ditcher-Price, Norton Manor, Radnor', respectively above and below.[2]

The impression given by the book-plate was clear enough, and superficially convincing. It was that this copy of the seventeenth-century White's *A rich cabinet*, together with a number of other books in the collection, had come into Harry Price's possession from the old family manor house of the Ditcher-Prices at Norton in Radnor in Wales. Price's father's name was Ditcher Price. On the other hand, the inquiry already conducted into that gentleman's life and circumstances, and his unremarkable background in Shropshire and London, did

---

[1] *Fairbairn's Book of Crests of the Families of Great Britain* (Fourth Edition, 2 vols., London & Edinburgh), i, Part II, 'Mottoes'.

[2] See Plate 8.

not suggest a family history involving ancient manor houses in Wales or anywhere else. It seemed clear that an investigation of the 'Robert Ditcher-Price' book-plate was necessary.

In the autumn of 1975 I was invited to deliver a lecture in Churchill College, Cambridge, and it was my very good fortune during my stay of two nights in college to be able to spend an afternoon as the guest of Mr C. W. Scott-Giles, who lives on the outskirts of Cambridge. I took with me a photo-copy of the mysterious book-plate of Robert Ditcher-Price, and it was therefore subjected to scrutiny in the very appropriate milieu of a room in Cambridge, the walls of which are lined with heraldic and genealogical works of reference.

The crest, 'a female's head affrontée couped below the shoulders proper, habited azure, on her head a wreath of roses alternatively argent and gules', was identified as that of the ancient family of Parr of Parr and Liverpool, Lancashire.[1] The arms below the crest, 'Argent two bars azure a bordure engrailed sable a crescent for difference' were also positively identified as those of the same family, which had younger branches in Kendal, Westmoreland and Lythwood, Shropshire.[2] The latter was a very young branch indeed, since Thomas Parr (who was alive in 1842) only took up residence in Shropshire after his retirement as one of the most eminent merchants in Liverpool. He was the fourth son of John Parr of Liverpool and West Derby, descended from the Parrs of Kendal, who in turn derived from the marriage of Sir William Parr of Parr, Lancashire, with Elizabeth de Roos, the grand-daughter and heiress of Sir Thomas de Roos, Baron of Kendal. The arms, crest and motto of the younger branches of the family were the same as those of Parr of Parr, 'except that some authorities vest the crest ermine instead of azure; and others place a crown on her head instead of a wreath; some give both, the crown above the wreath'.[3]

The motto on the book-plate of 'Robert Ditcher Price' is 'Amour avec loyauté', which is precisely that of the Parr family as recorded by Fairbairn, except that the latter authority

[1] Fairbairn, *op. cit.*, i, p. 431.
[2] *Papworth's Ordinary of British Armorials* (London, 1874), p. 30.
[3] John and Bernard Burke, *A General Armory*, *op. cit.* (unpaginated).

gives 'loyauté' [*sic*.] as the spelling of the last word.[1] This, then, was the third and final confirmation that the plate was a fake, using, as it did, the arms, crest and motto of the Parr family, who never lived at Norton Manor.

There has been a Price family of ancient lineage at Norton Manor, Radnor, since the seventeenth century at latest. In 1874, Richard Green, heir to his uncle Richard Price, (1773–1861), M.P. for Radnorshire, of Norton Manor, Radnor, took the surname of Green-Price and was created a baronet. The arms and crest of this distinguished family bear no resemblence whatever, as might be expected, to those used on the faked book-plate of 'Robert Ditcher-Price', being respectively, 'Sable, a chevron invected argent between three escutcheons of the last, each charged with a spear-head of the first embrued proper', and 'In front of a dragon's head erased vert, holding in the mouth a dexter hand, couped at the wrist gules, three escallops argent'. The family motto is 'Vive hodie' (Live today).[2]

To tie the matter up completely, I wrote to the present baronet, enclosing a photo-copy of the spurious book-plate. Sir Robert Green-Price was in Tokyo, but his mother, Lady (Jean) Green-Price, was kind enough to write to me on 4 January, 1976. One paragraph of her letter was in quite definite terms:

I have never heard of Robert Ditcher-Price, and am quite certain that he never resided at Norton Manor. I telephoned two of the older members of the family to ask if they knew anything, and they have never, on any occasion, heard the name 'Ditcher' mentioned, nor does it appear in the family tree in my possession. Nor have I ever seen the armorial book-plate.

To attempt to follow Harry Price's devious motives and actions is not easy. However, the evidence of the presence of the plate in some of his books is incontrovertible, as is the fact that his father's name was Ditcher Price, albeit without the embellishment of the hyphen. No trace of a Robert Ditcher-Price has been found among the Prices of Shropshire or

[1] Fairbairn, *op. cit.*, i, Part II, 'Mottoes', p. 4.
[2] *Debrett's Peerage, Baronetage, Knightage, and Companionage* (London, 1953), p. 690.

Worcestershire. An investigation has proved that the plate is completely spurious, since the arms, crest and motto are those of an entirely different family, and nothing is known of anyone named Ditcher-Price ever having lived at Norton Manor.

Who was the forger? The short answer is that a man who will fake one book-plate will fake another, and that it is significant that both Price's spurious crested plate, appropriated from the Denbighshire family of the same name, and the Robert Ditcher-Price plate, are to be found in books owned by Price. I have already suggested the motive, common to both, which was to support the fantasy that Harry Price was a member of an ancient, distinguished and armigerous family.

A number of books and pamphlets in Price's collection boast a book-plate quite different from any of those described in the foregoing paragraphs. In each case the plate is pasted inside the front cover, and is that of the Society for Psychical Research. Alan Wesencraft has sent me xeroxes of the title-pages and facing book-plates of four examples of such items. I list them below with some details:

(1)   Judge J. W. Edmonds, *An Appeal to the Public on Spiritualism* (Spiritual Tracts No. 1) New York, 1858. A pamphlet of 15 pages, bearing the plate of the Society for Psychical Research, 14 Dean's Yard, Westminster, S.W., the Society's first address following its foundation in 1882. On the title-page is the signature of its original owner, F. W. H. Myers, a founder of the Society, and the book-plate states that it was presented by him to the S.P.R. Library.

(2)   A. T. Myers, *The Life-History of a Case of Double or Multiple Personality*. A pamphlet of 10 pages, stated at the top of the first page to be 'Reprinted from *The Journal of Mental Science*, Jan. 1886'. Dr Myers was the brother of F. W. H. Myers. This item bears the Dean's Yard book-plate of the S.P.R., and has an embossed oval stamp on the wrapper, 'Society for Psychical Research. Founded 1882'. It is stated on the book-plate that this pamphlet was presented to the S.P.R. Library by Mrs Gurney, the wife (and later widow) of Edmund Gurney, the Society's first Honorary Secretary.

(3)   August Forel, *Der Hypnotismus: seine Bedeutung und seine Handha-bung* (Stuttgart, 1889). A book of 88 pages, bearing the book-plate of the S.P.R., 19 Buckingham Street, Adelphi, W.C.

(4) [Louis Hensel] *Anhang zur Philosophie des Geistes* (Steglitz, 1885). A book of 79 pages, bearing the book-plate of the S.P.R., 14 Dean's Yard.

All these four items were present in the S.P.R. Library at a date which may reasonably be estimated as late 1926 or early 1927. A printed catalogue of the collection was compiled at that time by the Hon. Librarian, Theodore Besterman, and was published in December 1927 as Part 104 of the Society's *Proceedings*. It was a substantial volume of 367 pages, giving authors, titles, places of publication, detailed pagination and notes, and clearly took many months to prepare, print, proof-read and publish. The items with which we are concerned were recorded respectively on pages 124, 253, 140 and 32.

How, we may ask, did these and other publications which formed part of the S.P.R. Library, none of which show any cancellation stamp, find their way into Price's collection at some date subsequent to the early months of 1927? One thing seems probable to the point of certainty, on the basis of the example of the first item, *An Appeal to the Public on Spiritualism*. This rare pamphlet had belonged to a founder and President of the Society, F. W. H. Myers, and had been presented by him to the Library. It may be thought that in no circumstances would the S.P.R. Council of those days have agreed to dispose of it to Price, either by sale or exchange.

Price's collection, we recall, was deposited on 'permanent loan' in the S.P.R. rooms from 1922 to 1927. In the latter year he was asked to remove his books for reasons of space by a decision of the Council reported on page 114 of the *Journal* of the S.P.R. of October, 1927. At first sight it seems not entirely unreasonable to conjecture that when moving his own books Price might accidentally have taken some of those belonging to the Society. This charitable hypothesis ceases to carry any conviction, however, when we consider two facts. First, Dr Dingwall, who in 1927 was a paid official of the S.P.R., has told me that when the Price collection was housed in the Society's rooms it was kept separate from the S.P.R. library in its own book-cases. Secondly, a more important obstacle to any theory of accidental removal arises from a circumstance for which there is documentary evidence.

After Price had transferred his collection from the S.P.R. rooms to his National Laboratory of Psychical Research at 16, Queensberry Place, South Kensington in the latter part of 1927, he prepared a printed catalogue of his library. It was a substantial volume of 422 pages, and was published in April, 1929 as his *Short-Title Catalogue*, being Part II of volume 1 of the *Proceedings* of the National Laboratory of Psychical Research. It may be presumed that Price prepared the catalogue for the printer in 1928. He gave no details of pagination, but he recorded authors, titles in full, places of publication and dates. It may be thought that he must have at least opened each book at the title-page in order to ascertain these particulars. The four examples of items removed from the S.P.R. library now under consideration are included in the *Short-Title Catalogue* on pages 171, 287, 184 and 213. We may think that when recording these books and pamphlets Price cannot have failed to notice the S.P.R. book-plates inside the front covers, facing the title-pages. It will be recalled, moreover, that *The Life-History of a Case of Double or Multiple Personality* has the embossed stamp of the Society on the front cover. If these items had been brought away from the S.P.R. rooms by accident, why were they not returned with apologies to the Society?

The catalogue cards prepared by Price for these four books and pamphlets do not give any indication whatever of their provenance, information that he usually included if books had come to him from other collections (as opposed to booksellers) thus making them association copies. A number of quite valuable items in Price's library, for example, bear the plate of Montague Summers. Under the heading 'Remarks' on the catalogue cards for each of these books, Price inserted 'From the Montague Summers Collection'. Conversely, the catalogue card for *An Appeal to the Public on Spiritualism*, for example, gives no indication that it had originally belonged to F. W. H. Myers, one of the pioneers of psychical research, and that it had been presented by him to the library of the S.P.R. during that organisation's earliest years at 14 Dean's Yard.

The Life-History of a Case of Double or Multiple Personality comes into the same category, being an association item presented to the S.P.R. in its early years by Mrs Gurney. We may think that it almost certainly had been owned originally by her husband Edmund Gurney, who committed suicide in 1888. Gurney had been a founder of the S.P.R. and its first Hon. Secretary, and a close friend of Dr A. T. Myers, the author of the pamphlet. No mention of the interesting provenance of the item is present on Price's catalogue card. Instead, under 'Remarks', Price copied precisely, even to the abbreviated 'Jan., 1886', the line of printing at the head of the first page already quoted in my earlier description of the booklet, a circumstance which we may think demonstrates beyond any doubt that Price opened it for cataloguing purposes, to be faced by the S.P.R. book-plate.

There are four other words inserted under 'Remarks', following the others and uniformly typed, but heavily crossed out by two horizontal strokes in ink. These words are, however, still readable if closely examined. Alan Wesencraft tells me that he has no knowledge of any alteration of this kind having been made by the Library staff at London University. The additional comment on the card under 'Remarks' thus incompletely obliterated is 'The only copy printed', which seems to me nothing short of astonishing in the surrounding circumstances.

I do not think that a solution of the mystery surrounding the actions half a century ago of so extraordinary a person as Harry Price is possible in final terms. However, since the placing of the words 'The only copy printed' follows the first phrase under 'Remarks' beginning 'Reprinted from . . .', and neatly completes the second line of uniform typescript, it is reasonable to suppose that Price was responsible for this remarkable comment. It was his catalogue card, so that the probability is very great. If this be assumed, then it seems that at some point in time Price was claiming that this pamphlet, bearing both the book-plate and the embossed stamp of ownership of the Society for Psychical Research, was the only copy in existence. Looking at the documentary evidence laid out on one's work-table in a quiet room in a Yorkshire country town fifty years after the event, the implications of the statement seem so obvious that one can only marvel, not only that Price recorded such a comment at all, but that he made such a clumsy job of his later attempt to obliterate it.

We may think that if Price coveted these scarce and desirable items contained in the S.P.R. library and decided to add them dishonestly to his own collection, then his failure to remove the book-plates and his inclusion of the titles in the catalogue of his library would result in a grave risk of detection. It may be urged that a man in his right senses would not take such a chance, and that the circumstances recorded in the foregoing pages must have some other explanation. It seems to me that there are three answers to this argument. First, it is a matter of simple fact that the items concerned were the property of the S.P.R. and are now in the Harry Price Library. Secondly, on the point of the risk of detection it is pertinent to remember that both collections were very large, containing thousands of books listed in catalogues of hundreds of pages, making both losses on the one hand and the identification of individual titles on the other easy to overlook, a state of affairs rather obviously demonstrated by the fact that this curious business has only now come to light after an interval of fifty years. Thirdly, again on the question of the risk involved, it does not seem to me that what Price appears to have done in this instance differs from the many other examples recorded in this book of his reckless audacity and apparent belief that he could get away with anything, a characteristic abundantly displayed in so many of his activities.

A final comment on Price's lack of ability and patience as a bibliographer is perhaps not out of place. Dr Myers' *The Life-History of a Case of Double or Multiple Personality*, as we know, was 'Reprinted from *The Journal of Mental Science*, Jan. 1886'. Price's entry for this pamphlet in his *Short-Title Catalogue* (p. 287) was 'Myers, (A. T.), The Life-History of a Case of Double or Multiple Personality. No place, 1886'. It was evidently too much trouble to ascertain that *The Journal of Mental Science* (Published by authority of the Medico-Psychological Association) had been edited by D. H. Tuke and George H. Savage and was published in London.

XV

The Schneider Brothers

Since this is not a book about psychical research *per se*, it is not my purpose in this chapter to offer any judgment upon the alleged physical mediumship of the notorious Schneider brothers, Willi and Rudi, of Braunau-am-Inn, Austria, both of whom were supposed to produce paranormal movements of objects, visible materialisations, invisible touches and other phenomena. Price was closely involved with both mediums over a considerable period, and long and detailed accounts of both Willi and Rudi are included in his *Confessions of a Ghost-Hunter*, *Leaves from a Psychist's Case-Book*, *Fifty Years of Psychical Research* and *Search for Truth*, and in many magazine articles. He wrote two full-length books about the younger of the two brothers, *Rudi Schneider. A Scientific Examination of his Mediumship* (London, 1930) and *An Account of some Further Experiments with Rudi Schneider* (London, 1933),[1] followed by a short pamphlet of 31 pages, *Rudi Schneider: The Vienna Experiments of Professors Meyer and Przibram*, published later in 1933.[2] Much has been written by other investigators, moreover, about the mediumship of both Willi and Rudi, resulting in a formidable literature describing events that were frequently and often sensationally featured in the press of the 1920s and 1930s. The present chapter is concerned mainly to discover, by an examination of the various texts and some unpublished documents, whether Price's published accounts of these matters can be relied upon at all.

The habitual liar can often be detected by his inability to present the simple truth in small things, and it is therefore of interest to trace Price's story of how he was introduced in 1922 to Willi, the elder and first established of the two mediums,

---

[1] *Bulletin IV* of Price's National Laboratory of Psychical Research.
[2] *Bulletin V* of Price's National Laboratory of Psychical Research.

from his earliest account of this occurrence published in 1923 to his final version of it in *Search for Truth* nineteen years later. Price had joined the Society for Psychical Research in 1920, and had become acquainted with Dr Dingwall, who in February, 1922 was appointed part-time Research Officer to the Society. Despite their widely differing family and educational backgrounds, Price and Dingwall had common interests in conjuring, book-collecting and the alleged physical phenomena of the séance-room, and collaborated in the editing and publishing of *Revelations of a Spirit Medium. Facsimile Edition, with Notes, Bibliography, Glossary and Index* (London and New York, 1922).[1] It will be recalled that in the previously unpublished note of his relations with Price, Dingwall wrote of this period:

Although Mr. Price claimed to have been actively engaged in psychical research for twenty years he did not then seem to me to know very much about the scientific side of the subject, although his knowledge of fraudulent methods led him to propose co-operating with me in editing and reprinting a famous American book, *Revelations of a Spirit Medium*. It was during this time that I spent several hours almost every day with Harry Price. He was a man of immense energy, with an exceptionally keen and ingenious mind, and I soon came to the conclusion that were he to have opportunities of observing genuine physical phenomena (if such exist) he might develop into a psychical researcher of great ability. Accordingly, at the end of May 1922 I invited Mr. Price to accompany me to the series of sittings with the medium Willi Schneider which Dr. Schrenck-Notzing had asked me, as Research Officer to the Society for Psychical Research, to attend in Munich.

The truth of Dingwall's account of the circumstances is demonstrated by both published and unpublished evidence. The invitation extended by Schrenck-Notzing to Dingwall to go to Munich in his capacity as Research Officer to the S.P.R. was arranged by the Hon. Everard Feilding (1867–1936) the second son of the eighth Earl of Denbigh, and a member of the Council of the S.P.R. and its joint Honorary Secretary. In a letter to Dingwall dated 17 May, 1922 Feilding wrote:

---

[1] The original edition of this anonymous work, which is of the greatest rarity, was published in St. Paul, Minnesota in 1891.

The following is from a translation of another very illegible letter from Schrenck received today about your visit. 'I have received your letter and I agree with you entirely. If Mr. Dingwall likes to come to see Willi's phenomena, I am very ready to show him . . .'. He does not say anything about Price, although in my letter I asked whether he might accompany you. I am writing to him today and will revert to that point, but meanwhile, as everybody seems to be now in agreement that you should go, I hope you will make ready.

The visit to the Bavarian capital was made, and in the S.P.R. *Journal* of June, 1922 (p. 293) it was announced that a paper, 'Physical Phenomena recently observed with the Medium Willi Sch.[neider] at Munich', would be read by E. J. Dingwall, the Research Officer, at a Private Meeting of the Society on Thursday, 13 July, 1922, at 5 p.m. The meeting was reported in the S.P.R. *Journal* of October, 1922. Under the chairmanship of Sir Oliver Lodge, Dr Dingwall read his paper, which was illustrated with lantern slides. The lantern was operated by Mr Harry Price.

In the following year Price contributed an article 'Convincing Phenomena at Munich', to the quarterly journal *Psyche*.[1] In his opening sentence he wrote:

It was with mixed feelings that I accepted the invitation of Mr. E. J. Dingwall, the Research Officer of the Society for Psychical Research, to accompany him to Munich in order to witness the phenomena alleged to occur through Willy Sch., a boy medium and *protégé* of Dr. A. Baron von Schrenck-Notzing, who had kindly arranged some sittings for us.

To the ordinary person, accustomed to the simple truth, it would seem that if Price felt it necessary to record in print the *fons et origo* of his visit to Munich, there was nothing else he could say other than that it was at the suggestion of the Research Officer of the S.P.R. As Dingwall wrote to Price on 26 March, 1923, 'We all have to learn, and had it not been for me you would never have had any chance of coming to Munich to see Willi. Things are very difficult, and I was glad to find somebody who had a certain amount of spare time and know-

---

[1] Vol. iii, No. 4, (New Series), April, 1923, pp. 317–27.

ledge of magical devices.' In his reply of 2 April, 1923, Price said, 'It was certainly due to you that I went to Munich'. It is precisely because the facts are so simple and are so completely documented, and because they were admitted by Price in 1923 both in published writings and in private correspondence, that the Munich incident is so perfect an example of Price's blatant and unnecessary distortion of the truth.

In his obituary of Schrench-Notzing printed in his *British Journal of Psychical Research*, March/April, 1929, Price wrote:

> I was peculiarly indebted to Baron Schrenck on account of the fact that I owed to him the opportunity of witnessing phenomena which at last convinced me that all was not fraud and illusion. This was in the early summer of 1922 when the Baron arranged that I should be present at some experiments with Willi Schneider. The Baron's München séance room became the grave of my doubts as to the *possibility* of abnormal manifestations, and both Dingwall (who was with me) and I returned to London satisfied that we had seen *real* phenomena at last. I met the Baron several times after that and was on the point of visiting him concerning the Kraus MS. when I was shocked to hear of his sudden end.

It may be thought surprising that in the whole of the four pages of the obituary there is no reference to Dr Dingwall other than the casual 'Dingwall (who was with me)' in the quoted paragraph above. It was the beginning of the purposeful reduction of Dingwall to a secondary rôle in Price's accounts of the visit to Munich, before his final total extinction, as we shall see.

Four years later, in the opening chapter of Price's *Leaves from a Psychist's Case-Book*, Dingwall's supposed lesser part in the affair was confirmed. Price said that his interest in Willi Schneider had been aroused by 'a number of inquiries which I had made in various parts of the continent' and that 'I obtained an introduction to Baron von Schrenck-Notzing, who invited me to participate in his experiments with Willi'. Price continued:

> I was invited for the specific purpose of *detecting trickery if I could find it*. Of course I accepted, and the end of May 1922 found me in the beautiful Bavarian capital. I was accompanied by Dr. E. J.

Dingwall, also an amateur conjurer, and a well known investigator. The Baron met us on Munich station and cordially greeted us, at the same time telling us what arrangements had been made for our visit.[1]

From this point onwards (p. 19, second paragraph) Price copied from his article from *Psyche* published ten years previously in 1923 in his description of the sittings, and pages 318 to 326 of the latter were used almost *verbatim* in *Leaves from a Psychist's Case-Book*, except that one highly significant sentence on page 325 of *Psyche* was omitted. This alteration will be considered in another context not lacking in interest. It is not directly concerned with the elimination of Dingwall, which finally occurred in 1942, on pages 138–9 of *Search for Truth*:

During the early part of 1922 I heard a good deal about the alleged marvellous phenomena that a young Austrian boy was producing for Baron Schrenck-Notzing at Munich. I learnt that savants from all over Europe were being impressed with the marvels they had seen—*and* with the conditions under which they had seen them—in Schrenck's séance-room. Imagine my delight, then, when Schrenck invited me to witness these things for myself. In effect Schrenck said: 'You are a great sceptic; you know all about mediumistic trickery; come to Munich and if Willi is tricking us, tell us how he does it'. So I went. I had my first séance on May 29, 1922.

The name of Dr Dingwall does not appear in the account, nor in the index of *Search for Truth*.

It may be helpful to recall here that Dr Albert Freiherr von Schrenck-Notzing (1862–1929) was the best known and most flamboyant impresario and publicist of sensational psychical research in the German history of that subject. He was an impecunious medical man before his very advantageous marriage. In his obituary written by Price in 1929, already quoted, it was said:

An event now occurred which was to make all the difference in the world to psychical research in Germany—he married. Very

[1] It will be noticed that in this intermediate account the Society for Psychical Research disappeared from the scene.

poor himself, he had the good fortune to meet one of the richest girls in Germany, a daughter of the famous Siegle family of Stuttgart—probably the largest chemical manufacturers in Germany and now partly incorporated in the great Frankfurt chemical combine. The sudden acquisition of great wealth enabled Schrenck-Notzing to realise one of the day-dreams which—he once admitted to me—always inspired his early work in München: a life's devotion to psychic research.

The parallel between the lives and circumstances of the two men is of some interest. I once asked Dingwall, who knew them both well, whether he agreed with me that Price might have returned from Munich to England in 1922 with the ambition to become in this country what Schrenck-Notzing had made himself in Germany. Dingwall replied that in his opinion I was almost certainly right.

It seems possible that Price may have been impressed by the social standing and publicity value of the persons, including the Prince and Princess of Parma, who gathered at Schrenck-Notzing's house in the Max-Josefstrasse in Munich to witness the marvels of the séance-room in 1922. Spiritualist mediums were all the rage in the nineteen-twenties when as many heads as tables were being turned, particularly among those persons with the necessary leisure and money to attend the séances and pay the fees. In 1929–30, when Price put on similar performances in London with Rudi Schneider, those attending the séances included Susan, Countess of Malmesbury, Sir Edward and Lady Naylor-Leyland and Captain the Hon. A. Cochran Baillie. Perhaps more importantly from the point of view of publicity value, however, a number of the sitters were well-known persons in the world of entertainment, including Frank Lawton of 'Young Woodley' fame, Miss Marjorie Mars, Laurence Olivier and Stanley and Mrs Holloway.[1]

Dr Dingwall was a member of the Occult Committee of the Magic Circle of London, a group founded by the late J. Nevil Maskelyne to investigate the claims of spiritualism. He wrote to Price:

I do think that it would be gracious of you to invite a couple [of

[1] *Rudi Schneider. A Scientific Examination of his Mediumship*, pp. 224–5.

members of the Committee] to attend a sitting or so, as they are really anxious to see something of the kind you say takes place with Rudi. But you are, of course, quite justified in excluding them and inviting actors and actresses who shriek and are a bit scared! It is inexplicable to me if you believe in the 'phenomena', but natural if you are giving a show, and also very amusing.

Price refused to invite any members of the Committee. Dingwall was doubtless referring to an incident on pages 150–1 of *Rudi Schneider. A Scientific Examination of his Mediumship*, on which an interview with Frank Lawton reported in *The Star* of 31 December, 1929 was reproduced:

'I have never been so scared in all my life, but it was jolly impressive', Mr. Lawton stammered, as he tried to put his experiences into words . . . 'Marjorie Mars shrieked when these phenomena began to happen, and I was a bit scared myself, so we gripped hands a bit harder'.

In his reply to Dingwall's letter, Price asserted:

Your suggestion that I invite actors and actresses who shriek has no foundation. I have never invited an actor or an actress to a séance in my life. Occasionally a Member has asked me if I would allow actor friends to be present, and I have consented. That is all.

In the report of the interview with Frank Lawton in *The Star* it was stated:

Until yesterday Mr. Lawton had never been to a spiritualist or psychic séance, and when he was invited to see Rudi Schneider exhibit his psychic powers to the actors and actresses playing in *The Last Enemy*, a spirit play at the Fortune Theatre, Young Woodley thought he was going to hear all about his past and future.[1]

Despite their lack of experience, Lawton and Miss Mars were appointed controller and assistant controller of the medium.[2] It is only fair to record that Lawton was impressed by his experience:

'I dunno what to think, you know', he concluded. 'What I mean to say is, well, there must be something in it, don't you think?'[3]

---

[1] *Rudi Schneider*, p. 150.   [2] *Ibid*., pp. 150 and 225.
[3] *Ibid*., p. 151.

As we have seen, in his glowing obituary of Schrenck-Notzing in 1929, Price referred again to his climacterical experience in Munich in 1922. He was, moreover, almost ecstatic in his enthusiasm over the mediumship of both the Schneider brothers in 1930, when he published his book, *Rudi Schneider. A Scientific Examination of his Mediumship*. Page [v] of this substantial volume was occupied by the following:

To the Memory of Dr. Albert Freiheer von Schrenck-Notzing, whose courage, initiative and scientific experimentation with many mediums, but especially with Willi and Rudi Schneider, have made this work possible, this vindication of his methods is affectionately dedicated.

In the final chapter of the book Price wrote (p. 213):

The manifestations have occurred under every condition of change or control, and both the mediumship and this report are unassailable and final, and nothing can shake them. On behalf of the Council of the National Laboratory of Psychical Research, I have handed Rudi Schneider a letter—really a certificate—stating that *absolutely genuine* phenomena have been produced through his mediumship, under triple control conditions which have never previously been imposed on any psychic known to the writer. Not the slightest suspicious action was witnessed by any controller or any sitter. Rudi did everything we told him, at any time, and never queried any experiment. If the Laboratory issued a 'gold medal' or 'diploma' for genuine mediumship under our own scientific conditions we should have no hesitation in awarding it to Rudi.

It may be thought that nobody could say more. Price was, moreover, highly critical on the first page of the first chapter of the book of what he called 'the attack by W. J. Vinton and the negative séances recorded by Dr W. F. Prince during his visit to Europe in 1927 for the Third International Congress of Psychical Research'.[1] Price continued:

[1] 'Experiments with Physical Mediums in Europe', *Bulletin VIII*, Boston S.P.R., 1928. Dr Prince became the President of the London S.P.R. in 1930.

I am not going to waste the reader's time and patience in analysing the reports of these negative séances. I have often wondered why Vinton descended on Braunau (the boys' home) like a bolt from the blue. Why this tyro should have chosen the Schneiders to experiment with I can only surmise. But apparently the journey to Austria was worth while, since he filled forty-five pages[1] of his journal telling us what ought to have happened, but didn't.

Price's scornful reference to 'the attack by W. J. Vinton' was in regard to one of the most detailed of all the accounts of the mediumship of both the Schneider brothers published in a magazine. It was printed in the journal *Psyche*, of London and New York, in April, 1927. The article, 'The Famous Schneider Mediumship. A Critical Study of Alleged Supernormal Events', by Warren Jay Vinton, was 43 pages in length. Mr Vinton, an S.P.R. member, was invited by Dr Dingwall, in the latter's capacity as Research Officer to the Society for Psychical Research, to be present at four sittings in London in March and April, 1926, with Willi Schneider. In July of the same year, Vinton was present at a sitting with Dingwall in the home of the Schneiders at Braunau-am-Inn in Austria at which Rudi was the medium. Vinton stayed on in Braunau for three weeks in order to study the Schneider family and the alleged phenomena. He was present at ten consecutive sittings, four with Willi and six with Rudi. During the fourth séance, with Rudi as the medium, Vinton discovered the presence in the 'cabinet' of 'a figure crouching close behind the medium's chair'. The father of Willi and Rudi insisted that this must have been 'a great mass of "ectoplasm" withdrawn from Rudi and huddled in the darkest corner of the cabinet' (p. 26). Vinton observed dryly in his account, 'I remarked that a body of the size and solidity I had encountered must have abstracted a good half of Rudi' (p. 26).

It is fair to observe that the possibility of confederacy was in Vinton's mind during the sittings. He remarked on pages 24–5 of his article:

There were thus at least four possibilities for entering and leaving the cabinet; there was only the Schneiders' word for it that no

[1] Vinton's article occupied pp. 3–45 of *Psyche*, April, 1927.

confederate ever did enter it. On the other hand, I already had many reasons for believing there was a confederate. Mr. E. J. Dingwall had strongly suspected the use of a confederate as early as 1925, and the London séances of 1926 had greatly strengthened this belief. Mr. Dingwall had publicly stated his suspicion of confederacy, and this had been duly reported to Baron Schrenck-Notzing.[1] So when the Baron heard that Mr. Dingwall was coming to Braunau in the summer of 1926, he wrote to Father Schneider. Mr. Dingwall's statement, he said, cast discredit on 'our science', and he therefore forbade Father Schneider to grant any further sittings to Mr. Dingwall unless he first signed a retraction.

Vinton's paper is moderately worded, and contains one of the most illuminating accounts of the peculiar psychology of the séance-room I have seen. At the end of his long narrative of his experience, which included a meeting with Schrenck-Notzing, he came to the conclusion that the performances of both Willi and Rudi were entirely dependent on trickery and collusion. We may think that it was logical of Vinton to consider the mediumship of the brothers together, on the reasonable assumption that either genuine mediumship (if such exists) ran in the Schneider family, or that Rudi had simply learned his elder brother's tricks. Vinton's experience caused him to prefer the second alternative, and he concluded his article in *Psyche* with the following words:

They work hard for all they gain. They sit up late of nights, they exhibit great ingenuity and daring, they have a genius for making the best of simple means, and are quick to use any loophole left open to them. The result is a performance exciting enough to raise your goose-flesh, and I for one do not grudge what I paid to see it. And after all, their deception is no greater than that practised in many more respectable and exalted places. Yet in the interest of those who wish to know things as they are, I have thought it worth while to record my conviction that the processes of Nature within the Schneider family are just what they are in all other parts of the world.

As we have seen, in 1930 Price was highly critical of Vinton's

---

[1] The theory of confederacy was suggested by Dingwall at a Conversazione at the S.P.R. on 9 December, 1925 (*Journal*, S.P.R., July, 1927, p. 108).

article. In 1933, however, when he displayed a startling change of front in regard to the Schneider brothers in his *Leaves from a Psychist's Case-Book*, it may be thought that two sentences in that book referred to the Vinton account without disapproval. When Price wrote his own article 'Convincing Phenomena at Munich' in *Psyche* in 1923 he had stated his belief in the genuineness of the phenomena produced by Willi Schneider without qualification. This is made clear beyond doubt by a paragraph on page 325 which he revised significantly in *Leaves from a Psychist's Case-Book*. When he prepared that book for publication in 1933, he copied out the details of the 1922 Munich sittings from his *Psyche* article, which had occupied nine of its eleven pages (pp. 318–26) to form pages 19–28 of the first chapter of *Leaves from a Psychist's Case-Book*. The copying was virtually *verbatim* apart from the alteration of the paragraph I have mentioned, which I quote below for comparison:

Psyche, p. 325.

The above notes were taken either at the sittings or immediately after them. Mr. Dingwall also took notes, independently of myself, which upon comparison were found to agree in nearly every particular with my own. Both of us are convinced that we witnessed absolutely genuine phenomena.

Leaves from a Psychist's Case-Book, p. 27.

The above notes were taken either at the sittings or immediately after [them]. Mr. Dingwall also took notes, independently of myself, which upon comparison were found to agree in nearly every particular with my own. [Both of us are convinced that we witnessed absolutely genuine phenomena].

It will be seen that the effect of the omission of the vital sentence from the text of *Leaves from a Psychist's Case-Book* was to withdraw Price's unqualified declaration in *Psyche* that he believed the phenomena to be genuine. On pages 53–4 of *Leaves from a Psychist's Case-Book*, moreover, Price went further in this disclaimer. He said that despite his *verbatim* notes of the sittings, taken from his case-book, there were 'other factors to be taken into consideration'. He wrote that although he had been impressed with the first sittings with Willi in 1922 in the home of Schrenck-Notzing, 'the conditions were not so scientifically perfect as we, in our enthusiasm, imagined them to be'. He added that it was significant that 'no physicist of note ever duplicated [Schrenck-Notzing's] results with Willi', and that if confederacy be assumed, at least some of the effects he had seen at Munich could have been produced by normal means. He added, in support of his drastically amended view, the observation (p. 54) 'that the Schneider family has been consistently accused of confederacy and the production of spurious phenomena. There is some evidence that this is the case.' The reference to 'the Schneider family' clearly included both Willi and Rudi. I fancy that what Price called the evidence for 'confederacy and the production of spurious phenomena' can reasonably be identified, in part at least, with the Vinton article. It was, without question, by far the most substantial and important criticism of the Schneider mediumship dealing with the hypothesis of fraud to have appeared during the years immediately preceding the publication of *Leaves from a Psychist's Case-Book*. As I remarked at the beginning of this chapter, it forms no part of my purpose to suggest whether Vinton was right. My aim is simply to present the evidence to enable the reader to judge whether Price wrote about these matters honestly, or, as Mrs Anita Gregory has asserted, 'with complete lack of scruple'.[1]

Price published two other works in 1933 in addition to *Leaves from a Psychist's Case-Book*, and it may be thought that this was the reason for the adroit manipulation of the text of the latter book, the details of which have been discussed. The earlier of the two additional books was *An Account of some Further Experiments with Rudi Schneider*, and was *Bulletin IV* of Price's National Laboratory of Psychical Research. It was mentioned at the beginning of this chapter. In it Price claimed that the medium had been caught in flagrant fraud by means of photography at a sitting at the Laboratory on 28 April, 1932. An epitome of *Bulletin IV* was included as a chapter, 'How the Camera Caught Rudi Schneider', on pages 68–88 of *Leaves from a Psychist's Case-Book*, and Price wrote on page 75 of that book that the camera 'has provided us with incontrovertible proof' of trickery on the part of the medium.

---

[1] In a paper *The Physical Mediumship of Rudi Schneider*, read to the Parapsychological Association in Freiburg in 1968.

It was stated on the front cover of *Bulletin IV* that the book was 'Published by the Council at the Rooms of the National Laboratory of Psychical Research', and Price's Preface, dated January, 1933, began:

The Council of the National Laboratory of Psychical Research has pleasure in submitting to its Members an account of a further series of experiments with Rudi Schneider, the young Austrian physical medium.

Commenting on this sentence Lord Charles Hope, a member of the Council, wrote:

It would appear, however, from a joint manifesto signed by most of the active members of Mr. Price's Council, which was published in *Light* on 7 April, 1933, and from a letter written the previous week by H. G. Bois, the acting President [of the National Laboratory of Psychical Research] that these members were ignorant of the charge of fraud made against Rudi, and therefore the responsibility for the whole report must rest solely upon Mr. Price . . . No hint was given to those who had financed the series of sittings then closing of any suspicious incident having recently occurred, and later in the summer [of 1932] when Mr. Price again sought financial support from some of us for a proposed further series of sittings to be held in the autumn of 1932, he omitted to mention the photographs in question. Later, those of us who subscribed towards the cost of the publication of his report were not informed that in it any accusation of fraud was to be made against Rudi. Most of the members of Mr. Price's Council learnt for the first time of the charges to be brought in the report from a sensational newspaper article appearing ten months after the sitting.[1]

Nearly twenty years ago Dingwall and I published the evidence of Mrs K. M. Goldney, a Vice-President of the Society for Psychical Research and in 1932 a Member of the Council of the National Laboratory of Psychical Research in regard to the probable motives that actuated Price to behave as he did in 1932 and 1933. Since then Mrs Anita Gregory has confirmed Mrs Goldney's account of the matter, and in addition has published what amounts to an accusation of forgery on Price's part

[1] 'Report on a Series of Sittings with Rudi Schneider', *Proceedings*, S.P.R., xli, 1932–3, pp. 284–7.

in connexion with the all-important photograph. I reproduce the paragraphs from the account published by Dingwall and myself in 1958:

Several Council members contributed to the cost of the second Schneider inquiry, among them Lord Charles Hope, whose large donation justified his feeling that he might have some control of the experiments. Any real co-operation, however, was never possible with Harry Price; and it seems that Lord Charles Hope was not able to carry out his own ideas for investigation. He therefore asked Rudi Schneider whether, when Price had finished with him, he would go to Lord Charles Hope for further investigation. Price became aware of this arrangement through a remark of the medium, and was extremely angry about it, and Lord Charles Hope attended only one more sitting.

The twenty-fifth sitting of the series on 28 April, 1932, furnished the material for Price's later alleged exposure of Rudi. A photograph automatically taken during this séance at which Price was acting as controller, showed Rudi with one arm free and stretched behind him. Price discovered this when developing the plate himself on the following day and according to him, he taxed Rudi with trickery immediately and received an unsatisfactory reply. Surprisingly, Price said nothing at all about his discovery (which according to him would have accounted for some of Rudi's phenomena) to the Laboratory Council, and proceeded to the twenty-sixth sitting on 3 May, 1932, when the photographic apparatus was not used.

Mrs. Goldney stated that shortly after the last sitting she called on Price at the Laboratory. Price said that he had some important news but before he disclosed it, Mrs. Goldney must give her word to reveal it to nobody without his permission. Mrs. Goldney did so. Price then produced the photograph of Rudi with his hand free and stretched behind him. Mrs. Goldney said that he must tell the other members of the Council. Price refused to do so. He said that he intended to say nothing until Lord Charles Hope had completed his sittings with Rudi in the latter part of 1932 and had published his report. Then, Price said, he would publish his 'exposure' of Rudi and make Lord Charles look foolish.

The bombshell burst when Price's critical report was published on 6 March, 1933, together with the appearance in the *Sunday Dispatch* of 5 March of a review and a long article on the exposure of Rudi Schneider.[1]

[1] E. J. Dingwall & T. H. Hall, *Four Modern Ghosts* (London, 1958), pp. 56-7.

In her paper on Rudi Schneider read to the Parapsychological Association in 1968,[1] Mrs Anita Gregory both confirmed Mrs Goldney's account and presented some evidence in regard to the photograph that was the centre-piece of the whole incident. She said that the photograph, purporting to show Rudi's arm freed from control while 'phenomena' were occurring, was of very poor quality, but that while Price was alive and was not prepared to give access to his negatives, it was not possible to investigate the matter. After Price's death, however, Mrs Gregory discovered the plate in Price's collection in the University of London Library. Examination showed that the plate 'was almost certainly a fake—a composite picture; one of the exposures was clearly taken at the séance in question, but the other was taken on another occasion; the medium's legs point in another direction from that of the back, an anatomical absurdity. There is also clear evidence of retouching on the supporting plates, claimed to be stereograms taken on the same occasion.'

Mrs Gregory declared that Price's motives for what he did emerged quite unambiguously from the evidence. Since Price considered himself to be the discoverer and stage-manager of Rudi Schneider in England, 'he decided to denounce Rudi in order to ruin the reputation as a careful researcher of Lord Charles Hope who had, as Price saw it, taken Rudi away from him . . . Also, Price was clearly feeling vindictive towards the medium who, he felt, had shown himself unfaithful and ungrateful.'

I record these observations by Mrs Gregory without offering any opinion as to whether she is right or wrong. I will say, however, as a matter of simple fact, that Price's published comments on the matter of the fees paid to Rudi Schneider demonstrate his change of attitude between 1930 and 1933. In the former year, in his enthusiastic book *Rudi Schneider* (p. 215) Price wrote of the sittings of 1929–30, on which that book was based:

A most extraordinary notion has got abroad that if you are a medium you must work for nothing! As a matter of fact, we paid

---

[1] An abridged version of the paper has been published in the *Proceedings* of the Parapsychological Association, No. 5, 1968, pp. 19–21.

5 Book-Plate, University London, Harry Price Library (see p. 125)

6 Book-Plate, Harry Price "Abomination des Sorciers" (see p. 126)

7 Book-Plate, Harry Price with spurious crest and motto (see p. 126)

DUM VIVIMUS, VIVAMUS

Harry Price

8 Book-Plate, Robert Ditcher-Price, with spurious crest, arms, motto and address (see p. 128)

EX LIBRIS.

Amour avec Loyaulte

ROBERT DITCHER-PRICE.

NORTON MANOR, RADNOR.

Rudi only what he would have earned at his trade, from which we took him. We *ought* to have paid him more, but so many expenses were incurred through the investigation that we did not remunerate him as much as we would have liked. Though of course members of the Laboratory paid for their sittings, there was a considerable deficit to be made up, and on behalf of our Council I would like to thank Lord Charles Hope for his very material assistance in this direction.

Three years later, on the first page of his Preface to *Bulletin IV* Price wrote:

In 1929–30, the Laboratory paid him £3 per week and his hotel expenses and fares—a sum in excess of what he would have earned in Austria as a motor mechanic, to which trade he was apprenticed . . . The financial problem in the case of highly-paid mediums is a very difficult one.

Small matters can be revealing.

On the factual basis of the Borley Rectory papers, moreover, there was another reason why Price was doubtless furiously angry with Lord Charles Hope in April, 1932, of which Mrs Gregory may be unaware. It was on 1 April that Lord Charles wrote to Price:

I would be obliged if you could find it possible not to mention my name in connection with your 'Borley Rectory' lecture on Wednesday, or if you do, please say that I was not impressed and thought the phenomena were produced by normal means.

This was an echo of one of the only two visits paid to Borley by Lord Charles, when in notes compiled on 6 July, 1929 he had written:

I left Borley with the definite suspicion that Mr. Price might be responsible for some at least of the phenomena which had occurred while I was present.

The implication of the letter Lord Charles wrote to Price would, we may think, be very clear. It was received at the beginning of the very month of April, 1932 in which Price, according to

Mrs Gregory, decided to 'ruin the reputation as a careful researcher of Lord Charles Hope'.

The final event in this curious story was the publication of *Bulletin V* of the National Laboratory of Psychical Research in the summer of 1933, under the title of *Rudi Schneider. The Vienna Experiments of Professors Meyer and Przibram*, with a Foreword by Price. In it he wrote that 'Professor Dr. Stephan Meyer and Professor Dr. Karl Przibram, of the Institut für Radiumforschung der Akademie der Wissenschaften, Vienna, had experimented with Rudi Schneider in 1923-4 and detected him evading control. They discovered—as we did—that the young Austrian was able to free a hand and thus produce the telekinetic "phenomena" himself'. *Bulletin V* also repeated the charge of fraud by Rudi Schneider at the London sittings in 1932 at the National Laboratory of Psychical Research, and how he was caught by the camera with his arm free, producing 'phenomena'. On pages 17 and 19 of *Bulletin V* Price specifically accused Rudi of lying as well as producing fraudulent 'phenomena'.

Bulletin V was the subject of a review in the *Journal* of the S.P.R. of July, 1933, in which Lord Charles Hope remarked:

It seems that Mr. Price is seeking to justify the charges brought by him against this medium in *Bulletin IV* by raking up some very doubtful evidence of fraud, said to have been obtained nine years ago under dissimilar conditions and in regard to a different kind of phenomena. If Mr. Price attaches such importance to the suspicions of Professors Meyer and Przibram, why did he not include their testimony in his book *Rudi Schneider* published in 1930?

Whether we are believers or sceptics, we can scarcely quarrel with the logic of the last sentence. I will let Lord Charles Hope have the last word, which is contained in his criticism of *Bulletin IV* in which it will be recalled that Price, writing in 1933, declared that he had caught Rudi Schneider in fraud on 28 April, 1932. Lord Charles wrote:

Not that Mr. Price was silent as to the result of those sittings. In several newspaper articles written by him between the close of those sittings [and therefore after the alleged exposure on 28 April, 1932] and the publication of his report he wrote in eulogistic terms of Rudi and his phenomena. In the *Empire News* for 8 May, 1932 he says, 'For three years he has been under laboratory tests in England and France and has emerged unscathed from his very strenuous ordeals', and again in *Light* of 20 May, 1932 he writes, 'This is the third time he [Rudi] has been in England, and on each occasion he has added to his laurels' . . . What does emerge damaged from Mr. Price's report is his own reputation as controller, conductor of investigations and critic. Mr. Price asks us to consider how much of Rudi's phenomena, produced in different series of sittings, ·can, after this 'exposure', still be considered genuine. I am quite prepared to face that problem, but what exercises me, and perhaps other readers of the report, still more, is what weight is now to be attached to any report, whether positive or negative in its conclusions, or any phenomena, produced under Mr. Price's direction or control or recorded by him?[1]

[1] *Proceedings*, S.P.R., xli, 1932–3, pp. 290–1.

XVI

Joanna Southcott's Box and the Bloksberg Tryst

In the Introduction to this book I offered the opinion that when Price embraced psychical research at the age of nearly forty, he had at last found the vocation that was to satisfy his thirst for publicity for the rest of his life. In the last sentence of Dr Dingwall's previously unpublished study of Price, quoted in the Introduction, he remarked that it was 'the desire for publicity which had been the mainspring of [Price's] activities'. In his later years, when Price had made himself the most prolific and successful psychic journalist of his generation, he had no need to seek publicity. In the early days of the National Laboratory of Psychical Research, however, which we recall Price founded in the mid-twenties, this situation had not yet been achieved. It is therefore of interest briefly to consider two episodes in Price's career during this earlier period which seem to have been contrived simply to attract wide public attention to Price and his Laboratory.

The first was the affair of his opening of what purported to be the Joanna Southcott box in 1927 in the presence of the Bishop of Grantham. One reason for a brief examination of this very odd business is the fact that reference is actually made to the event (although Price is not mentioned by name) in the 14-line entry for 'SOUTHCOTT, JOANNA (1750–1814), a religious fanatic', on page 739 of *The Oxford Companion to English Literature*, Oxford University Press, 1960 edition) edited by Sir Paul Harvey. After a short account of Joanna's life it is stated:

She died of brain disease, leaving a sealed box with directions that it should be opened at a time of national crisis in the presence of the assembled bishops. It was opened in 1927, one bishop being present, and was found to contain nothing of interest.

In a shorter 8-line entry for Joanna on page 847 of the second volume of the *Oxford Illustrated Dictionary* (1962) as republished in 1964 by the Oxford University Press and the Reader's Digest Association, the last phrases read:

Left a box which was to be opened in a time of national crisis; it was opened in 1927, but contained nothing of interest.

Some near coincidences of wording may cause us to think that these extracts in regard to the opening of the box may have been based on the substantial entry for Joanna Southcott in 1929 in the fourteenth edition of the *Encyclopaedia Britannica*,[1] with a correction of the error of the year 1928:

She left a locked box with instructions for it to be opened by all the bishops together assembled at a time of national crisis. The box was finally opened in 1928 in the presence of one of the bishops, but it was found to contain nothing of interest at all.

No mention whatever is made of the box in the entry for Joanna Southcott in the eleventh edition of the *Encyclopaedia Britannica* (1910–11), and this omission is continued in the twelfth and thirteenth editions, which were simply three-volume supplements to the eleventh edition. We must concede, therefore, that Price was responsible for the *début* in 1929 of Joanna Southcott's box in the fourteenth edition of the best known of our works of reference. An earlier mention of a box had appeared in 1920 on page 756 of volume xi of the *Encyclopaedia of Religion and Ethics*, edited by James Hastings. The description of the box and its contents was quite different, however, from the specimen that came into Price's hands in such mysterious circumstances in 1927, as will be seen. The article, 'The Southcottians', was contributed by W. T. Whitley, who stated that an immense mass of Joanna Southcott's MSS., totalling 9,000 pages partly written in a peculiar shorthand, was 'sealed in a large case corded up till the next crisis of world-history'. Over half a century later, among the advertisements published in the *Daily Mail* of 2 August, 1977 was included a prominently displayed statement by the Panacea

[1] Vol. xxi, pp. 87–8.

Society of Bedford, 'CRIME & BANDITRY, DISTRESS OF NATIONS & PERPLEXITY WILL CONTINUE TO INCREASE UNTIL THE BISHOPS OPEN JOANNA SOUTHCOTT'S BOX OF SEALED WRITINGS'.

The most interesting reference of all to the matter is a letter written on 2 November, 1922 at the direction of the Archbishop of Canterbury by his Private Secretary to the Rev. G. C. Robinson, on the subject of 'Joanna Southcott and her mysterious box'. The letter is reproduced on pages 1200–1 of *Randall Davidson. Archbishop of Canterbury* (Oxford University Press, Second Edition, 1938) by G. K. A. Bell, Bishop of Chichester. The Archbishop had been importuned 'for many years past' by misguided persons to convene a council of Bishops before whom the box should be opened, in accordance with Joanna's dying instructions, representing, it was suggested, the four-and-twenty elders of the Apocalyptic vision. In addition to the Bishops, it appeared that Joanna's requirements included the presence of '2000 maidens in white', representing angels, which the Archbishop dryly described as 'a not very easy arrangement'.

The Archbishop had 'always been strongly against such a course, feeling, as he does, that the whole idea of opening the box in such circumstances is fantastic'. He added that sensible persons, as opposed to the followers of Joanna, 'cannot fail on reflection to see in what an absurd position the Bishops would be placed if, having consented to the conditions demanded, the box were opened in their presence and found to contain nothing more than an additional collection of the strange writings of that strange woman[1]—or, conceivably, nothing at all!'. The whole concept struck the Archbishop as 'partly profane and partly ridiculous' according to his biographer's text immediately following the reproduction of the letter. As Bishop Bell remarked in the next sentence, however, 'The opening of the box was at last achieved on July 11, 1927. The scene was the Church House, Westminster, under the auspices of the National Laboratory of Psychical Research'. The first two objects extracted from the box 'were a woman's night-cap

---

[1] It would seem that the Archbishop was following the concept of the contents of the box suggested by W. T. Whitley in 1920.

and a book called *The Surprises of Love: or an Adventure in Greenwich Park*. Bishop Bell added mildly that 'the remaining treasures were a little less strange, but of hardly greater importance to the destinies of the world'. He added in a foot-note on page 1201 that in 1935 episcopal aid was solicited for the opening of another box, also claimed to be 'a true box'.

According to the story told by Price in Chapter XVI of his *Leaves from a Psychist's Case-Book*, 'a bulky metal-bound walnut coffer' was delivered without previous warning at the office of the National Laboratory on 28 April, 1927, accompanied by a letter written on the note-paper of the Carlton Hotel, London. Price concealed the name of the signatory under the initials 'F. M---- F------', but said that he immediately telephoned the hotel and was told that 'a gentleman of the name of F------ had been staying at the hotel and had the previous day departed for New York'. I am informed that no such letter is to be found among Price's correspondence files in the University of London Library, although these start much earlier than 1927. However, the full text of this document is reproduced in Price's book. So far as I am aware, its contents have not previously been the subject of published comment, which is surprising.

Mr 'F------' told Price that two servants employed by his family and himself were the children of a lady named Rebecca Pengarth who, 'as a young girl', had been the sole companion of Joanna Southcott during the years 1798 to 1814. On her death-bed (she died on 27 December, 1814) Joanna entrusted the box to Rebecca with a dying injunction 'that it was to be opened only in the time of dire national need and in the presence of a number of bishops. The contents of the box would reveal to an astonished nation means of saving the country and would benefit the common weal'. Rebecca swore a solemn oath that in no circumstances would she allow the box to be opened except under the required conditions. Fifteen years after the death of Joanna (i.e. in 1829) Rebecca 'married rather late in life a Welshman named Morgan by whom she had four children, the last surviving being John, who died in 1925 aged eighty-one'. John was one of the servants of Mr F------, and retired on pension, having in-herited the box from his mother. On his deathbed he insisted

that Mr F------ should take the box 'and do what was right
with it'. Almost his last words were that the box must be
opened in the presence of bishops. 'Don't forget the bishops',
he said. As Mr F------ was leaving England forever in 1927
he felt that the National Laboratory was the proper place for
Joanna Southcott's box. According to his letter to Price,
Mr F------ wanted no personal publicity and no correspondence, and therefore gave no address in America. He
considered, however, that there might be 'something of
extraordinary value in the box', and therefore asked Price to
publish 'in the South American papers' a description of the
contents of the box when it was opened. Mr F------ was of the
definite opinion that the Bishops should be present at this
event.

Price said that the pedigree of the box bore the stamp of
authenticity. He decided to open it in the prescribed conditions,
and audaciously wrote to eighty bishops inviting them to be
present at the ceremony which he proposed to hold at the
Hoare Memorial Hall, Church House, Westminster on 11 July,
1927, an event which Price announced in *The Times*. During
the weeks between the receipt of the box and the public
opening, Price invited a number of mediums to test their
powers by divining what the box contained, amid very con-
siderably publicity.

Price remarked on page 300 of *Leaves from a Psychist's Case-
Book* that 'the bishops let us down very badly', and only the
elderly Bishop of Grantham[1] was present. More importantly
from Price's point of view, we may think, the opening ceremony
'aroused extraordinary interest among the public and the large
hall was crowded', a long account appearing in *The Times* of
13 July, 1927. The box was found to contain a rusty and
innocuous horse-pistol, a night-cap, a number of pamphlets, a
puzzle, a set of money weights, a purse of coins and trade
tokens and other miscellaneous *bric-à-brac*. There was nothing
in it capable of saving Great Britain from calamity, and
nothing that could not have been obtained in 1927 by an
experienced collector without prodigious effort or expense.

[1] Dr J. E. Hine is pictured in the plate opposite p. 320 of *Leaves from a
Psychist's Case-Book*.

If it be thought that the entire incident was invented by Price to attract publicity to himself and his newly founded National Laboratory, including the faking of both the box and the letter from Mr F. M---- F------ (if indeed this document ever existed at all) then many suspicious circumstances surrounding the whole story would be explained. Why, for example, was it necessary for Price to conceal the name of Mr F. M---- F------, who set sail for New York so conveniently the day before the supposed delivery of the box at the National Laboratory? The tale that the box contained something of such importance that it could only be revealed in the presence of an assembly of bishops, and would astonish the nation and save the country from peril was nonsense, on the simple basis of the prosaic contents of the box. The only person who benefited from the publicity aroused by such a fantastic story was Price. To these considerations we may add the fact that the supposed history of Rebecca Pengarth, the sole companion of the religious fanatic from 1798 to her death in 1814, is not confirmed by the quite detailed account of Joanna Southcott's life by the Rev. Alexander Gordon in *The Dictionary of National Biography*.[1] Rebecca Pengarth's name is not mentioned, and instead it is stated of Joanna, 'On 11 October 1813 she shut herself up from society, seeing only Jane Townley and Anne Underwood, who lived with her', to her death on 27 December, 1814.[2] How, then, we may ask, could the box have been given to an unknown person named Rebecca Pengarth by Joanna on her death-bed?

The dates contained in Mr F------'s letter present formidable difficulties when they are examined. Rebecca 'as a young girl between the years 1798 and 1814 was the sole companion of Joanna'. She married Mr Morgan 'rather late in life' in 1829. This phraseology is vague, but there is one firm date afforded to us. Her son John, it was alleged in the letter, died in 1925 at the age of 81, which gives us his year of birth as 1844. If we assume that 50 is about the limit of a woman's age for child-

---

[1] Vol. liii, pp. 277–9.

[2] In the account by W. T. Whitley in the *Encyclopaedia of Religion and Ethics*, already quoted, it is stated that Jane Townley was Joanna's 'most intimate friend'.

bearing, then Rebecca would be born no earlier than 1794 and would be 35 when she married Morgan in 1829, which in the early nineteenth century could be regarded as 'rather late in life'. This is totally contradicted, however, by Mr F------'s statement that Rebecca 'as a young girl' started her supposed period as the sole companion of Joanna Southcott in 1798, when she would be no more than about four years old. If we try to make sense of the latter part of the tale, on the other hand, by assuming that Rebecca must have been in her early 'teens when she became Joanna's companion in 1798, then a year of birth of about 1784 is forced upon us. This in turn becomes impossible, however, when we recall the firm date of the birth of her son John, 60 years later. Leaving out of account, therefore, the fact that Joanna's real sole companions during the years leading up to her death were Jane Townley and Ann Underwood, who lived with her, the internal evidence of the supposed letter from Mr F------ demonstrates that it was a clumsy fake.

*   *   *   *   *

On page 226 of his biography of Price, Tabori said that the case that brought his subject 'the greatest international publicity' was that of the Bloksberg Tryst, and that three large scrapbooks in Price's collection 'are filled with over a thousand cuttings, all referring to the Brocken experiment'. This is a slight exaggeration, in that while Price's press-cutting albums Nos. 12 and 13 are wholly devoted to the Bloksberg affair, No. 14 is only partly so, and by my count the cuttings number nearer eight hundred than a thousand, but I do not dispute Tabori's general assertion. The highly publicised and photographed nocturnal activities of Price and Dr C. E. M. Joad in June, 1932 on the summit of the Brocken (anciently Bloksberg), the highest of the Harz Mountains in Germany, were the subject of sensational articles, many illustrated and under headlines, in newspapers published in Great Britain, Germany, Austria, Switzerland, Holland, Belgium, Denmark, Sweden, France, Italy, America, Canada, Australia, New Zealand, South Africa, Cuba, India and Ceylon. We may think that this second attempt by Price to attract wide public attention to himself and his National Laboratory succeeded beyond even his expectations.

Price's scientific pretentions and academic ambitions must have been encouraged by headlines such as those carried by the *Daily Herald* of 8 June, 1932, 'Scientists to Test Magic. Girl and Goat in Magic Ring' and by a cutting (source unknown) on the first page of his twelfth album headed 'Goat Spurns Maiden's Plea to become her Young Man', in which he was twice described as 'Professor Harry Price'. We may wonder whether it was this kind of publicity that emboldened him five years later to conclude his article on Borley Rectory in *The Listener* of 10 November, 1937 with the extraordinary sentence, 'As a scientist, I can guarantee you a ghost'.

Contrived publicity-seeking apart, the Brocken affair displayed some suspicious resemblances to Price's involvement with Joanna Southcott's box. We notice first the mysterious circumstances in which the essential document supposedly came into his possession on 9 November, 1931. 'A person whose name is unknown' deposited a 'most interesting old manuscript entitled *The Bloksberg Tryst*' at the National Laboratory.[1] Secondly, in both examples the oddly surreptitious delivery of the package at the National Laboratory was quickly followed by the planning of the highly-publicised dénouement. In December, 1931 Price delivered a lantern lecture at the National Laboratory on the Bloksberg Tryst during which, according to Tabori, he announced within one month of his acquisition of the manuscript that the experiment would be conducted by him on the Brocken.[2] 'He proposed to stage the experiment on January 23, 1932 . . . In January there was thick fog on the Brocken, and the moon was invisible, so the date was fixed for March. Then it was postponed to the night of April 30 . . . After various postponements, June 18, 1932 was fixed as the definite date. With Dr Joad, Harry Price went off to Germany'.[1]

Some additional light was thrown on the circumstances surrounding the arrival of the Bloksberg Tryst at the National Laboratory of Psychical Research in a two-part article, 'The

[1] Tabori, p. 227.   [2] *Ibid.*, p. 227.   [3] *Ibid.*, pp. 227–9.

Brocken Tryst', by Dion Fortune,[1] a well-known student of magical texts, who attended Price's lecture:

It appears that a manuscript of antique appearance was left at the college [*sic*] by an unknown person while everybody was out at lunch, the donor promising to call again, but so far not having done so. The manuscript, when examined, proved to be a magical rite for changing a virgin he-goat (rare beast!) into a beautiful youth . . . My verdict upon the Bloksberg Tryst is, 'A tale told by an idiot'. If Mr. Price really wanted to make an experiment in ceremonial magic, he was wasting his time with such a piece of goods; but if, on the other hand, he simply wanted publicity regardless of accuracy, I do not think he could improve on the method employed, though I doubt if it will add to the credit of the National Laboratory of Psychical Research.

It will be recalled that when Price boasted that his copy of the rare and valuable first edition of Reginald Scot's *The discoverie of witchcraft* was 'the finest in existence and half an inch taller than the better of the British Museum copies', he was proud to reveal its provenance. It came from the Yatton Court Library where, according to Price, 'it was positively known' that Shakespeare had consulted the books. By contrast, the mystery surrounding the sources of his Burmese MS., the Bloksberg Tryst manuscript and Joanna Southcott's box causes the critic unease in regard to the authenticity of all three items.

The Brocken manuscript is listed on page 16 of Price's *Supplement* to the *Short-Title Catalogue* of his library:

Bloksberg Tryst, The. [Old manuscript giving formula for magical experiment on the Brocken.] [With transcription.] No place, *n.d.*

Neither the Burmese MS. nor the Bloksberg Tryst are included in Price's *Exhibition of Rare Works*, in which are listed his selection of the 500 rarest and most desirable items in his collection.

---

[1] *The Occult Review*, lvi, No. 1, July, 1932, pp. 21–5 and No. 2, August, 1932, pp. 102–7. In the Editorial of the first of these issues, Price's antics were summed up as 'merely a stunt to secure publicity'.

On pages 334–5 of his *Confessions of a Ghost-Hunter* Price wrote:

In the autumn of 1931 I acquired a manuscript which is an early eighteenth-century transcript of a page of the so-called 'High German Black Book'—a hand-written volume of magical formulae which is preserved in one of the German museums. The 'Black Book' dates from about the fifteenth century, and contains much ritual for the practice of transcendental magic; and amongst the experiments is one called the Bloksberg Tryst . . . The MS. is written in an early nineteenth-century hand in faded brown ink, almost illegible in places. In the centre of the MS. is the magic circle painted in two colours (red and blue) with the usual symbols. On the reverse of the MS. is an engraving (undated) of the town of Bacharach, on the Rhine, by the German artist, R. Püttner.

Alan Wesencraft of the University of London has kindly supplied me with a xerox of the Bloksberg Tryst in the Harry Price Library. It is in English and consists of a single folio sheet of exceedingly cramped handwriting, very difficult to read in places, with the 'magic circle' in two colours in the centre of the sheet. If the engraving of Bacharach was present on the reverse of the sheet it is not now visible, for Mr Wesencraft tells me that the MS. is pasted or glued on to a piece of thin board. Mr Wesencraft has also sent me a xerox of the 'transcription' referred to in Price's catalogue entry, which is simply a typescript copy of the MS., also on a folio sheet, but lacking the illustration.

On page 335 of *Confessions of a Ghost-Hunter* Price wrote:

In 1932 was celebrated throughout Germany the centenary of the immortal poet Goethe. The Harz Goethe Centenary Committee (the *Harzer Verkehrsverband*), hearing that I possessed a copy of the ritual of the Bloksberg Tryst, invited me to reproduce the experiment as part of the *Goethejahr* celebrations. I consented.

Several curious points about this story will not have escaped the reader. First, it seems a remarkable coincidence that Price acquired the Bloksberg Tryst from an anonymous source in November, 1931, only seven months before the celebration of the centenary of Goethe (1749–1832) in June, 1932, in which

Price was to become publicly involved as a result. Secondly, it seems surprising that the *Harzer Verkehrsverband*, with the Bloksberg Tryst available to them in the *High German Black Book* in their own country and in their own language, should have sought to rely upon Price's possession of an English translation of unknown provenance. If Price's story of the spontaneous approach to him has any truth in it, one wonders how the Germans knew of its availability in the light of his brief ownership of the MS. Unfortunately, investigation of these curious events is not easy, as Alan Wesencraft tells me that Price's correspondence files at the University of London contain 'absolutely nothing' in regard to the Bloksberg Tryst whatever.

The fact that correspondence must originally have existed between Price and acquaintances in Germany is demonstrated by a two-page pamphlet, obviously composed by him, of which I found a loose proof in one of the press-cutting albums most kindly loaned to me by the University of London Library. It is printed on the headed notepaper of the National Laboratory of Psychical Research, and was circulated to the members with an intention that is made perfectly clear by its contents. I quote the last four paragraphs, which read like a travel brochure with Price acting as the agent in England. In view of his reference to the Laboratory's 'German Correspondents' we are entitled to wonder whether there may have been some mutually advantageous collaboration between Price and the *Harzer Verkehrsverband* to make the Brocken experiment a tourist attraction. The references to the fall in prices and low railway fares in Germany, the special trains to the summit of the mountain and the convenience and excellence of the Brocken Hotel are all of interest in this regard.

Elaborate preparations are being made for the experiment and a most enjoyable evening will be the result. Addresses on Goethe, *Faust*, magic, witchcraft, etc., will be given in English and German; Harz Mountain peasant dancers in appropriate costumes will perform the age-old witches' dances on the *Hexentanzplatz*, and it is intended that the evening shall be interesting, enlightening, historical, magical, and amusing.

This is to notify Members of the National Laboratory that they are cordially invited to be present at the experiment on June 17th.

The Harz Mountains are very easy of access and it is possible, by leaving London (Liverpool Street) at 8.30 p.m., via Harwich and the Hook of Holland, to be on the Brocken by the following evening. It should be mentioned in parenthesis that, owing to the fall in prices and the much lower railway fares, living in Germany is only *10 per cent* higher than it was before the depreciation of the pound sterling. There will be special trains to the summit of the Brocken, where there is an excellent hotel.

A number of the Laboratory's German Correspondents and other scientists will attend the Brocken experiment, and the daughter of one of them will be the 'maiden pure in heart' mentioned in the MS. It is thought that Members of the Laboratory will be glad to meet their German representatives.

For information regarding local arrangements, Members are advised to communicate with the Direktor, Harzer Verkehrsverband, Markstrasse, 30, Wernigerode, Germany. This organization will also gladly reserve accommodation for Members at the Brocken Hotel on request.

In an article, 'White Magic on the Brocken', published in *The Listener* of 6 July, 1932 Price described how, 'accompanied by Dr C. E. M. Joad, whose interest in magic and psychic matters is well known', he arrived on the Brocken on Friday evening, 17 June, 1932 'and found everything in readiness except the moon'. It was perfectly obvious that his German friends had collaborated by making all the necessary arrangements in advance, from Price's own words:

A 'magic circle' accurately designed in mosaic had been laid down 'neer the Granit Altar', and a white kid, specially chosen at birth, was trotted out for our inspection. The 'maiden pure in heart', in the person of Miss Urta Bohn,[1] daughter of Dr. Erich Bohn, of Breslau, was awaiting us, and her spotless white dress did not seem out of place at a magical experiment.

Price said that 42 photographers and 73 pressmen were in attendance, accompanied by a 'cinematograph set-up'. Typical of the hundreds of press-cuttings of the event is that taken from the *Hull Daily Mail* of 18 June, 1932, under the heading:

[1] Miss Bohn was perhaps better known as Gloria Gordon, the film actress, although Price did not say so.

'GOAT OUTWITS MAGIC. NO CHANGE OF FORM DESPITE GREAT SHOW OF WITCHERY. EERIE MIDNIGHT SCENE.

The article read in part:

Many believers in black magic received a rude shock last night on the summit of the Brocken, in the Harz Mountains, when all their hopes of witnessing a great transformation scene ended in miserable failure. A snow-white goat, duly anointed with great ceremony, was covered in a mystic sheet in a magic circle. A formula was canted which, according to believers, should have turned the goat into a 'youth of surpassing beauty'—but the goat remained adamant, and is still a goat.

It was a weird midnight scene, this attempt carried out by prominent British scientists to realise by black magic the old legend of Beauty and the Beast, and the established formula was carried out with meticulous adherence. All that was needed was a maiden 'pure in heart', a witches' potion of bat's blood, scrapings from a church bell, soot and bee's honey, a bottle of red wine, a bed sheet, and a magic circle . . . But maybe the ingredients of the ointment were not mixed in the right proportion. Too much bat's blood, for example, and not enough scrapings from a church bell. Or perhaps, since it was Walpurgis Night, when witches and warlocks and werewolves foregather, there should not have been quite so many trippers at the unhallowed spot. Anyway, the whole experiment was a failure, and the goat, instead of turning into a handsome young man as everyone would have liked, obstinately, after the manner of his kind, remained a goat.

The magic circle was duly painted in white on the summit of the Brocken, a triangle was drawn inside with its apex towards Kassel and its base facing the witches' dancing place, the cabbalistic signs were there, the weather was fine, the goat and the virgin all in order, the proper Latin incantations were used, and all the fantastic ritual carried out down to the smallest detail, but nothing happened. The beautiful girl, clad in a snow-white robe, visible only by the eerie rays of the moon, stepped into the triangle wherein stood Billy the Goat. The pine fire, which up to then had been crackling beside the magic circle, was put out, the incense-burner extinguished, and the remainder of the formula carried out by moonlight. More incantations, and the girl poured a flask of 'fair red wine' over the goat, all the time intoning an imprecation against profane spirits.

Then, when the moon was 'obscured by a blackness', and a point of light shone from the tower of Kassel nearby, the maiden threw a white sheet over the goat, completely covering it. All waited for the expected apparition to appear, but when the cloth was snatched away lo! there stood the goat. Don't blame the goat. He certainly did his best. In the interests of science he submitted to being turned round three times anti-clockwise inside the magic circle; he did not even object to being anointed with the extraordinary ointment which looked and smelt like boot polish, nor did he shy at having a bottle of wine poured over him and being covered by the white cloth . . . Mr. Harry Price, Honorary Director of the National Laboratory of Psychical Research, accompanied by Professor C. E. M. Joad, of London University, undertook the experiment, but did not expect any real results. The promoters propose to try again tonight in spite of their set-back, but no doubt the result will be just the same.

The *New York Herald Tribune* of the same date added the information that the incantations were uttered by Harry Price in 'a weird monotone'. The *Daily Sketch* reported Price as saying that 'The top of the Brocken has been described as the most haunted spot in Europe. It has been declared that if black magic could succeed anywhere, it would reveal itself on this spot where Goethe set a famous scene in *Faust*'. Both the *Hull Daily Mail* and the *Leicester Mail* reported that 'thousands of people' gathered on the Brocken to watch the proceedings.

The spiritualists were not enthusiastic. *The Christian Spiritualist* of 6 July, 1932, devoted only a single paragraph to the performance:

Several readers have sent us newspaper cuttings of the Harry Price Brocken adventure. We are not a bit interested. Price seeks advertisement, even as he thrives upon it. One newspaper thought he put himself to a good deal of expense and trouble to prove his disbelief in witchcraft. Nothing of the kind; he did all that to get limelight; and the papers were silly enough to waste space on giving it to him. We can employ both our time and space to better effect, and with better subject matter.

Hannen Swaffer, normally well-disposed towards both Price and psychical belief, wrote in the *Daily Herald* of 20 June, 1932:

I am seriously concerned at the stupidity of so-called 'scientists', joined by a writer on philosophy, going to the Harz Mountains to make a goat stand in a ring at midnight to see if when a Latin incantation was recited the animal would turn into a young man. My friend Harry Price, who organised it, is Director of the so-called 'National Laboratory of Psychical Research', and should know better. Still, photographs were taken, and several people got their names into the papers.

Lady Conan Doyle, the widow of the greatest spiritualist in the history of the movement, was reported in the *Sunday Graphic* of 19 June, 1932 as saying that the whole episode was 'pure rubbish', adding 'I never heard of such nonsense. The world is sufficiently topsy-turvy as it is without people indulging in this sort of thing'. The view of the Wesleyan divine, Dr Dinsdale T. Young, was reported in the same place:

At a time when the world has to think of so many serious things it is almost criminal that people should waste time and money in dabbling in a relic of a barbarous age. It is equally deplorable that they should go to the Bible for phrases to be used as incantations in performing their ridiculous rites. People concerned in these futile experiments would be better employed helping their fellow men.

I shall doubtless be accused of being a chauvinistic Yorkshire-man by quoting one of England's greatest journalists, the late Sir Linton Andrews, LL.D., the distinguished Editor of the *Yorkshire Post* for many years and the author, under the pseudonym 'W.L.A.' of the famous column 'IT SEEMS TO ME'. Sir Linton wrote:

Scientists, indeed! I felt a trifle scornful when I saw that scientists were to make a motor-car search of the Harz Mountains for a witch to anoint a virgin he-goat with ointment from the scraping of church bells, bats' blood, soot and honey, and to utter an incantation that might turn the animal into a youth of surprising beauty. Scientists, indeed! said I to myself. There is more theatrical showmanship than science in all this. I read on. There was to be a 'maiden pure' in these strange doings on top of the Brocken. Indeed? Could it be that she was a 'maiden pure' of the silver screen? Sure enough, there was an actress in the story. We met her first as the daughter of a German professor, but a little later we were told that she has adopted Miss Gordon as a stage name. Yes, a stage name: I was getting warm. Further, the whole scene was to be flood-lit and filmed. Just so.

The Brocken experiment was specifically quoted in the obituary of Price published in the *Journal* of the Society for Psychical Research of May, 1948. It was cited as an example of the kind of highly publicised activity on his part that was 'incompatible with work conducted under the auspices of an old-established Society'. One cannot help wondering, moreover, whether the enormous press coverage attracted by the ridiculous Bloksberg Tryst affair in 1932 may not have been an important ingredient in the decision of the University of London two years later to decline Price's offer to endow (with his wife's money) a Department of Psychical Research. If this is true, then the final sentence of Dr Dingwall's note on Price, quoted in the Introduction to this book, is worth mentioning again:

Perhaps he himself realised, before his death, that the desire for publicity which had been the mainspring of his activities may have rendered impossible the achievement of that academic recognition that had been one of his dearest ambitions.

The participation of the late C. E. M. Joad in the Brocken farce is of particular interest, for he was the Head of the Department of Philosophy and Psychology at Birkbeck College, and a well-known broadcaster and writer on philosophical subjects. He was a close friend of Price's, and became the Chairman of the so-called University of London Council for Psychical Investigation (an organisation that had no official connexion with the University) when it was formed to replace the old National Laboratory. Dr Joad ardently supported Price's offer to the University, and it was through him personally that the proposal was put forward to the Senate.[1]

When more information was sought, Joad prepared the necessary report, which included some account of the history and work of the National Laboratory.[2]

Joad and Price were frequently photographed together.[3]

[1] *Search for Truth*, p. 98. [2] *Ibid.*, pp. 98–9. [3] See Plate 9.

The frontispiece of *Leaves from a Psychist's Case-Book* bears the legend:

Harry Price (left) and C. E. M. Joad investigating in Germany, photographed by the famous Goose Girl fountain, Göttingen.

This picture was originally used in many of the Brocken newspaper articles and the original, preserved in Price's album No. 14, bears the inscription:

Harry Price (left) and Dr. C. E. M. Joad photographed at Göttingen, June 15th 1932, on their way to the Brocken for the experiment in Magic. Famous goose girl fountain in the background.

In *Confessions of a Ghost-Hunter* is a photograph of Price and Joad (with goat) 'in the Magic Circle on the Brocken. Next to Joad is Fräulein Urta Bohn, who took the part of the "maiden pure in heart" in the *Goethejahr* experiment'. Joad had twenty-one entries in the index of *Search for Truth*, and the book is embellished with a press photograph of Price and Joad side by side in a supposedly haunted bed in a private museum at Chiswick. In the same volume is a different and much less flamboyant Brocken photograph showing Price and Joad 'examining the preparations for the reproduction of a magical scene in connexion with the Goethe Centenary celebrations on the Brocken', with ostentatious care. We may suppose that by this time (we recall that Price's autobiography was published in 1942) the Brocken 'experiment' was being prudently played down. Indeed, on page 172 Price remarked that he would not describe it, 'as it has been done so often'.

While Price clearly regarded his friendship with Joad as greatly to his advantage, affording him familiarity with the academic circles he courted so assiduously, this happy state of affairs suffered at least a temporary eclipse early in 1939. A long article by Joad, 'Adventures in Psychical Research', was published in the June, 1938 issue of *Harper's Magazine*. Joad opened his account with the following:

Let me begin by stating my credentials. I have had at different times a certain amount of firsthand experience of what I will non-committally call abnormal phenomena. This experience has been due largely to the facilities afforded in London by the National Laboratory of Psychical Research.

Joad claimed that 'by the courtesy of the Director of the Laboratory, Mr. Harry Price' he had enjoyed the advantage of sitting with a number of well-known mediums, and said that he had 'witnessed at different times a considerable number of varied phenomena'. Three of these mediums were Mrs Duncan, Rudi Schneider and Eleonore Zügun.

In January, 1939 Price was warned privately (and evidently in some detail) by a prominent member of the Society for Psychical Research that Joad's article in *Harper's Magazine* was to be subjected to a severely critical review in the Society's *Proceedings*. The grounds of the criticism were to be that certain supposed incidents described by Joad as personal experiences, were complete invention, and that this could be proved by reference to documents already in print, published by Price himself. Price was exceedingly concerned about the dis-advantage to himself that would result from such a criticism of the Chairman of the University of London Council for Psychical Investigation, if it were well-founded, as it seemed to be. He wrote to a well-informed friend:

I am only concerned with the effect of such an attack. Our Council has been in cold storage for some time and I have, more than once, contemplated closing the whole thing down. This action I most certainly shall have to take when the S.P.R. article is published. I shall not be able to help myself. I shall have to see Joad and discuss the position. It is an unfortunate tangle to get into, but of course it is his own fault. But the Council could not exist for twenty-four hours after such an article which it is proposed to publish.

The reply Price received was not reassuring. It was pointed out that many independent scientific men were of the opinion that the statements published by psychical researchers were of little value, and that it was suspected that many of the stories told were wholly or partly fictitious. It was added that if the charges anticipated in the review were substantiated, the effect on scientific and academic opinion could be very serious indeed.

The notice of Joad's 'Adventures in Psychical Research' was published in the *Proceedings* of the S.P.R., xlv, Part 158, March, 1939. It was written by W. H. Salter, a Member of the Council of the Society. The criticism was that the occurrences described by Joad were claimed by him to have taken place under his personal observation, and that in some instances these assertions were totally contradicted by Price's published writings. Joad described vividly, for example, his supposed experiences at the five séances with the 'materialising' medium Mrs Helen Victoria Duncan held at the National Laboratory in 1931. In the same year Price's *Regurgitation and the Duncan Mediumship*, a 120-page book with many photographs, was published by the National Laboratory as its first Bulletin. Each of the separate accounts of the five sittings included a precise list of the persons present, and on page 105 was a composite 'List of Sitters who examined the Duncan Manifestations'. Joad's name was mentioned in none of these lists, nor did his name appear in the index.

The case of Eleonore Zügun, an exponent of supposed telekinesis with accompanying stigmata, was worse. Joad described in detail an extraordinary experience on his homeward train journey after meeting Eleonore in London. While reading a newly acquired book in the train he discovered that some of the pages were unopened.[1] On taking out his pen-knife he discovered to his complete surprise that it was encircled with a metal letter 'C', wedged so tightly that it was only ultimately removed with the help of a mallet and chisel. Price's account of the National Laboratory séances with the medium Eleonore in 1926 was published in January, 1927 as 'A Report on the Telekinetic and other Phenomena witnessed through Eleonore Zügun' and was Part 1 of volume i of the *Proceedings* of the National Laboratory of Psychical Research. As in the example of the affair of Mrs Duncan, Joad's name was not mentioned in Price's account, nor did it appear in the index. Appendix C. of the report (pp. 55–8), written by

---

[1] Both Joad and Tillyard's accounts described the pages as 'uncut', which is bibliographically imprecise.

Dr R. J. Tillyard, F.R.S. is entitled 'The Occurrences of Friday, October 22nd 1926'. The late Dr Tillyard described how after a day in London which included lunching with Professor Julian Huxley at King's College, visiting the Natural History Museum, attending a meeting at the Imperial College of Science and having a brief meeting with Eleonore at the National Laboratory, he caught an evening train to Rochester. Professor Huxley had presented him at lunch with a signed copy of his *Essays of a Biologist*, which he started to read in the train after looking through the evening paper. He discovered that some of the pages were unopened. When he brought out his pen-knife he discovered to his complete surprise that firmly attached to the knife-case was a metal 'C'. Figure 4 on page 58 of Price's report is a drawing of the knife-case with the mysterious metal 'C' *in situ*. Mr Salter remarked with restraint, 'It is certainly strange that Dr. Joad and Professor Tillyard should both have experiences so strikingly similar on the same occasion. Difficulties and discrepancies such as these are the despair of the psychical researcher'.

Price's University of London Council for Psychical Investigation remained in 'cold storage', as he himself described it, and was not revived during the three years of his life that remained to him when the war was over.

XVII

The 'Psychic Child', 'Dear Old Nigger' and Katie Boreham

Friends whose opinion I value and who have read this book in typescript have expressed astonishment at the recklessness with which Price palpably distorted the truth by telling varying stories in different published texts. Did he not realise, they argue, that a critical reader of all his books and articles might compare one with another, and point out the discrepancies? The simple answer is that the texts are there, for anyone to examine. One of the most remarkable examples of this, in my opinion, is what I will call the case of 'the psychic child' and 'dear old Nigger'.

One version of the story was told by Price on pages 82–4 of his *Confessions of a Ghost-Hunter*, introduced in the following words:

In my capacity of Foreign Research Officer to the American Society for Psychical Research I scoured Europe in investigating the facts, frauds and fallacies of psychical research. From Oslo to Athens and from Lisbon to Bucharest I found many psychic adventures—but some of the major mysteries were found on British soil; one, in my own bedroom. For want of a better title, this particular mystery is down in my case-book as 'the psychic child'.

Price said that because there was no electricity in his 'quiet Sussex village' of Pulborough at the time,[1] he kept a powerful electric torch by his bedside. In the small hours he was awakened from a sound sleep as suddenly 'as if someone had thrown me out of bed'. He heard 'the soft patter of naked feet

---

[1] Price never gave any indication of the date of the supposed experience.

round my room as if a little child were running round the bed'. Price described his bedroom in some detail, with the information that it 'was nearly forty feet from the ground', and that as he lay in bed in the darkness listening to the pattering feet, which 'exactly resembled those of a child of three', he discounted the possibility that any small animal could have climbed into his bedroom.

I knew that my dog was fast asleep in his bed by the kitchen fire, and I possessed no other animal. But the sound of the pattering feet was not that which could be caused by any animal with which I was acquainted.

After listening to the little footsteps for ten minutes or so, Price chose a moment when the sounds were close to his bed, and switched on his torch. The pattering stopped instantaneously, and there was nothing to be seen. He searched the room, moving every article of furniture, and found nothing. 'I explored the house without result. No one was about and my retriever was sound asleep in his basket in the kitchen, the door of which was closed'. Price concluded this remarkable story with these words:

In my career as an investigator there have been few mysteries for which I could not find some sort of solution—but I must admit that the 'baby feet' in my bedroom puzzle me to this day. If it is possible for spirits to return to this earth, and demonstrate exactly as humans, then my 'psychic child' is capable of this explanation.

During the thirties, an undated 94-page paper-backed book entitled *The Soul of a Dog. Illustrated by True Stories* was published by the Churchman Publishing Co. Ltd., at a price of 2/-. The author, using the pseudonym of 'F. M. Archer' on the title-page, was Arthur Wellesley Pain. The two advertisement pages at the front and rear were wholly devoted to the work of the R.S.P.C.A. Like most ephemera of its kind, published between the two world wars, *The Soul of a Dog* is now a very scarce item, and since I bought my own copy I have never seen the title included in a bookseller's catalogue. Although both the front cover and the title-page bear the words 'Foreword by Harry Price', there is no entry for this item in the checklist of Price's

published writings included in Tabori's biography. The theme
of the book is contained in its title, and argues that there is no
reason to suppose that dogs, being noble, intelligent and
affectionate creatures, devoted to man, should not have souls
and an after-life. The idea is attractive to persons like myself
who have gained much happiness from the companionship of
dogs.

Most of Price's Foreword to *The Soul of a Dog* duplicated his
account of the inexplicable noise of pattering feet in his bedroom at Pulborough exactly, except that in this version of the
tale no mention was made of a 'psychic child' with 'baby feet':

> The pattering continued, first on one side of the room and then
> on the other. Once or twice I could distinctly hear it under the bed
> on which I was lying. After due consideration I decided to switch
> on a powerful electric torch which I always have at hand. I listened
> until the pattering appeared to be nearest me and flashed on the
> light. Silence—the sounds ceased simultaneously. I jumped out of
> bed and searched every nook and cranny of the bedroom and the
> dressing-room leading out of it, but not a vestige of life could I find.
> (*The Soul of a Dog*, p. 19)

Another of the differences between the two stories was that
in the account in *The Soul of a Dog*, Price did not go downstairs
to make sure that 'my retriever was sound asleep in his basket
in the kitchen, the door of which was closed' (*Confessions of a
Ghost-Hunter*, p. 84). There was a very good reason why, in
this version of the tale, such an investigation would have been
superfluous, as we discover from some earlier passages on
pages 17–18 of *The Soul of a Dog*:

> Under my study window, a few yards from where I am penning
> this Foreword, is the grave of the dearest, noblest, and most 'human'
> black retriever that ever raised a paw to be shaken or a muzzle to
> be caressed. More intelligent than the majority of villagers with
> whom I am surrounded, more lovable than most of the people with
> whom I claim acquaintanceship, more dependable than many of
> the people who daily cross my path, 'Nigger' was our loving friend
> and companion for more than thirteen years . . . Is it so very
> extraordinary that something much stronger than affection should
> bind a loving dog to a loving master? Isn't it reasonable to suppose

that there should be formed some *nexus* which should bridge the grave, assuming that the souls of dogs survive the grave? I emphasise this query because soon after the death of our dear old dog I had a very curious experience. Though I am not at all a light sleeper, about two o'clock one morning I was awakened as suddenly as if a pistol had been fired over my head. As I wondered what had disturbed me, I heard a pattering of feet round the room. . . .

The rest follows. The 'psychic child' totally disappeared from the story and was replaced by 'dear old Nigger'. Price concluded his Foreword to *The Soul of a Dog* with the sentence:

I wish I could have proved that it was 'Nigger' who was trying to make himself known to me, as I am as certain as I am breathing that the dear old boy would have returned to me, if possible, even from that place 'whose portal we call Death'.

The reader will have noticed another minor difference between the two stories. In one, Price was wakened from sleep as suddenly 'as if someone had thrown me out of bed', and in the other as suddenly 'as if a pistol had been fired over my head'. Another small variation is that in *Confessions of a Ghost-Hunter* (p. 83) Price's bedroom was 'nearly forty feet from the ground', whereas in *The Soul of a Dog* (p. 19) it was only 'thirty feet from the ground'. But these are over-shadowed by the essential difference between these two blatantly reckless pieces of psychic journalism, i.e. that in one 'dear old Nigger' was fast asleep in the kitchen, and that in the other he was in his grave in the garden.

Price seldom wasted material of this kind by confining it to a single book or article.[1] If the reader, unable to find a copy of *The Soul of a Dog*, wishes to read a moving paragraph from it, he need only turn to page 303 of *Search for Truth*, which is headed 'Dear Old Nigger'. There are two introductory sentences:

Do animals survive? I understand that the Archbishop of Canterbury's commission, in their private report, considered it

---

[1] As will be seen in a later chapter, in a third version of the story the footsteps in Price's bedroom became those of a mischievious poltergeist.

reasonable to suppose that if humans survive, so do animals. A few feet from where I am penning these remarks are the earthly remains. . . .

Sixteen lines follow from *The Soul of a Dog*. There are small differences, exemplified in this account by the retriever's grave being only a few feet from Price's study window, as opposed to a few yards. But in the main it is a nearly *verbatim* copy of Price's earlier description of the *nexus* between his dog and himself.

The exposure by simple comparison of these two examples of unscrupulous writing has been made possible merely by reference to Price's published work. By contrast, however, some of his misrepresentations and distortion of evidence can only be examined by comparing them with unpublished material. The story of Kate Boreham, which is of great interest, falls into this second category.

In May 1937 Harry Price rented the empty Rectory at Borley for one year for the sum of £30. He advertised for and obtained the honorary services of some forty observers, who in small groups stayed for days and nights in the lonely, dilapidated house[1] and supplied Price with reports of their experiences. The late Sidney H. Glanville, a man of absolute integrity, was one of the most conscientious of these observers. He was a consulting engineer and a brilliant artist, and died in December, 1953. With his son, Roger H. Glanville, and their friends Mark Kerr-Pearse and Alan J. Cuthbert, Mr Glanville spent a good deal of time at Borley during the summer and autumn of 1937 and the winter of 1937–8. He prepared the excellent plans and most of the photographs of the rectory used by Price to illustrate *The Most Haunted House in England*. His experience of 'phenomena' during his vigils in the vast empty house is perhaps appropriately expressed in a letter he wrote to the late Lionel Algernon Foyster on 8 October, 1937[2] after reading the latter's typescript *Fifteen Months in a Haunted House*[3]:

---

[1] See Plate 10.   [2] *Locked Book*, p. 79.
[3] An account of supposed 'phenomena' at Borley now conceded by Mr Foyster's widow to be largely fictitious.

I must say that it is the most astonishing document I have ever read. Compared with my own experience of a few mild taps, it is simply astounding.

In 1953 Sidney Glanville, whom I came to know well during the investigation on which the report published in 1956 was based, presented me with the *Locked Book* (*The Haunting of Borley Rectory. A Private and Confidential Report*). This unpublished and unique document was prepared by him in 1937–8. It became known as the *Locked Book* because Harry Price, during the period that he borrowed it to assist him in the writing of *The Most Haunted House in England*, had it bound and fitted with a Bramah lock. Price oddly presented it to the University of London Library, from where Sidney Glanville withdrew it in 1948. His inscription of the book to me reads:

To Trevor with my kindest regards, and appreciation of his help and encouragement at a time when the making of a re-statement of the history of Borley Rectory seemed to be beyond my capacity.
Sidney.   27 July 1953

Sidney Glanville told me that he never finished reading Price's *The End of Borley Rectory*, and that he had no belief whatever in the results of the table-tilting and planchette séances that he and his family and friends held in the Rectory and elsewhere, mainly to pass the time during fruitless vigils. These are included in the *Locked Book*, and edited versions of some of them are printed in Price's books. Sidney Glanville was fully aware of the influence of suggestion in this kind of experiment. A letter from him quite unconnected with Borley is before me as I write:

A few months ago I was receiving letters from a man living in a desolate part of Wales, a man whom I have never seen and probably never shall. He wrote disjointedly and badly about some alleged paranormal noises that were worrying him and his housekeeper; knocks, footsteps, sounds of furniture being moved etc. Purely as an experiment my son and I used the planchette. It promptly wrote about garden paths, gates, names, deaths and dates. The name most frequently written was 'Evan'. The letters were from Wales and Evan is a common Welsh name. I knew the garden had paths and gates. I presume that our subconscious was at work.

Sidney Glanville and I were able to discuss the case of Kate Boreham and Price's misrepresentation of it with complete mutual frankness. It is fully recorded in the *Locked Book*. On 6 October, 1937, seventeen days before the first table-tilting experiment at Borley Rectory, Sidney Glanville travelled to Sevington in Kent to meet for the first time the late Rev. G. Eric Smith, formerly Rector of Borley. He was regaled with a good deal of what Price himself described in *The End of Borley Rectory* as 'legends of suicide, murder and sudden death connected with Borley—and much scandal'. While this kind of gossip is not uncommon in country villages, it is perhaps not usual for it to be repeated with conviction by a clerk in holy orders.[1] However, the sensational stories told to Glanville about deceased members of the Bull family at Borley by Smith are recorded on pages 74–8 of the *Locked Book*. The one ultimately involving Kate Boreham is on page 75:

It is alleged, and Mr. Smith believes it to be true, that a cook in the service of Mr. Bull[2] died in his arms in the kitchen. She had given birth to a child, but the infant was never seen. The matter was 'hushed up', it is said.

On the night of 23 October, 1937, seventeen days after Smith had told this tale, the first table-tipping experiment took place at Borley Rectory. 'Carlos' was said by some to be a nickname of the Revd. Henry D. E. Bull. The record is on page 135 of the *Locked Book*:

Is it Carlos?	Yes.
Then you are Henry Bull?	Yes.
Did something unfortunate happen in the kitchen?	Yes.
Did a servant girl die in your presence there?	Yes.

[1] It is, however, fair to point out that during a visit paid to Borley on 28 July, 1929 by Lord Charles Hope, accompanied by the Hon. Richard Bethell, the former recorded in his notes that 'it was in connexion with old Bull, I gathered, that the tales of village girls were concerned'.

[2] The Revd. Henry Dawson Ellis Bull, who was Rector of Borley from 1862 to his death in 1892, when he was succeeded by his son, the Revd. Harry Foyster Bull, who died in 1927.

Did she die a natural death?	No.
Was there a baby?	Yes.

On the following day Sidney Glanville looked at the Borley Parish Register and found an entry:

Kate Boreham of Sudbury died Easter Day, 1888 aged 31.

That same evening, 24 October, 1937, a further table-tipping séance was held in the rectory. The appropriate extract from the record is on page 139 of the *Locked Book*:

Is it Kate?	No.
Is it Katie?	Yes.
Were you a maid here?	Yes.
Have you a message?	Yes.
Will you please spell it out?	Light, Mass, erslre.

The final relevant experiment was with a planchette at Sidney Glanville's home at 25 Lewin Road, Streatham, S.W.16 on 31 October, 1937. The important sections are recorded on pages 156 and 158 of the *Locked Book*:

Did you know Katie?	Yes.
Please spell her surname.	Boreham.
What year did she die?	18890. [*sic*].
Please try again.	1888.
Can you tell us the month?	April.
Where did Katie Boreham die?	Kitchen.
From what?	Child.
Was the child's father there?	Yes.

*   *   *   *   *

Is that Henry Dawson Ellis Bull?	Yes.
Do you wish to leave Borley?	Yes.
Are your own past actions the cause of your being unable to leave?	Yes.
What was that action?	Death.
Whose?	Katie.

On page 144 of *The End of Borley Rectory* Price wrote of the séance of 31 October 1937:

> At this same séance the name 'Katie Boreham' emerges. We have heard of Katie before [i.e. in the séance of 24 October] but the script reveals her surname, and that she died in 1889, afterwards corrected to 1888, in April. Immediate steps were taken to consult the register of Borley Church and under 'Deaths' is the following entry: 'Kate Boreham of Sudbury died Easter Day, 1888, aged 31'. Kate Boreham of Sudbury may have no connexion with the 'Katie' Boreham' who is alleged to have communicated at both Borley and Streatham; but if not, it is a most extraordinary coincidence. Even the year of her death is given, and 'April' and 'Easter Day' are sufficiently close to be remarkable.

It is clear that in this passage Price was telling his readers that *after* the full name and particulars of Kate Boreham had been revealed during the séances, the church registers were *then* consulted and provided startling confirmation of the previous earthly existence of a young woman of the same name, living within two miles of Borley, who had died on approximately the same date. It was a flat lie, and Price knew that it was when he wrote the paragraph in *The End of Borley Rectory*, published in 1946. He was fully aware of the precise circumstances as early as 1938, before his first book on Borley was published. He did not, however, risk including this deception in *The Most Haunted House in England*, which it may be thought supports my view that the degree of recklessness in Price's published falsehoods was progressive.

In 1938, when Price read the séance scripts in the *Locked Book*, he wrote to Sidney Glanville to inquire about Katie Boreham, although the plain sequence of events was before him in the record. The reply he received from Glanville dated 13 October, 1938, was unambiguous:

> I looked up the planchette writing and find that we had the story of the maidservant who, it is alleged, died in the kitchen of the rectory. [I.e. from the story told by the Revd. G. Eric Smith at Sevington on 6 October, 1937.] Then we looked up the burial registers in the church and found the name of Kate Boreham of Sudbury. Immediately after that [i.e. the evening of the same day,

9   Harry Price and the late C.E.M. Joad at a meeting of the Ghost Club at the Savoy Hotel (see p. 169). Reproduced by permission of the University of London Library

10 Borley Rectory, Essex, 1937 (see p. 178)

(a)

(b)

(c)

(d)

11 The Borley Medals (see p. 209). (a) Obverse of brass St Ignatius Medal i.e. the "Medallion with Latin words on it and the head of a monk". (b) Reverse of (a), i.e. the "brass Romish medallion". (c) Obverse of gilt "French Roman Catholic Confirmation medal" claimed by Price in *MHH* to have been found with (d) at Borley Rectory on 5 July 1929. (d) Obverse of "French Revolution medal or badge" (actually a pass issued to members of the National Assembly) of similar dubious provenance

24 October, 1937] the table persistently tapped out 'Katie' and the planchette repeatedly wrote 'Katie Boreham'. So I am afraid it was not a confirmation.

Price replied on 14 October:

I note what you say about Katie Boreham—What a pity!

Eight years later, he purposefully falsified the sequence of events in *The End of Borley Rectory*.

If Price had been the sceptical, cautious and thorough investigator that he claimed to be, instead of the unscrupulous psychic journalist that he was, he might have taken the trouble to obtain a certified copy of the death entry of Kate Boreham from the General Register Office. This is before me as I write. Kate Boreham was the wife of Walter Boreham of Sudbury and according to the entry followed no other occupation, and was therefore not a maid or a cook. She died not in April but on 27 March, 1888. She died not in the kitchen of Borley Rectory, but in her home in Priory Walk, Sudbury. The informant was 'Walter Boreham, Widower of the deceased. Present at the death. Priory Walk, Sudbury'. Mrs Kate Boreham died not in child-birth but from 'Acute Cerebritis. 48 hours', the cause of death being certified by Dr W. Inglis Mason.

Two comments seem applicable to this disgraceful piece of deception. First, as a result of Price's deliberate distortion of the true sequence of events, the tale in its doctored form apparently offered some evidence for survival and the possibility of communication with the dead. Secondly, it is of interest to compare the transparent honesty of Sidney Glanville with Price's lack of this quality.

XVIII

The Poltergeists

The largest single sample of Price's psychic journalism between two covers was *Poltergeist over England*, published in 1945. This 423-page book was the penultimate product of what one imagines was his by no means unpleasant war spent in Pulborough, the period during which he had at last become a successful writer. It is reasonable to suppose that the total estate of £17,000 Price left at his death (less the considerable amount represented by the substantial value of his library and other chattels) largely consisted of the money he made from his last four books published from 1940 to 1946. These were *The Most Haunted House in England, Search for Truth, Poltergeist over England* and *The End of Borley Rectory*.[1] Among the papers presented to me by Dr Dingwall in 1975 was a copy of a letter written by Price to a friend on 12 January, 1944, in which he said:

I am working flat out on my *Poltergeist over England* which is nearly complete. Then I have another Borley book to do, and Mrs. Beatrice Hastings bequeathed to me her 'Diary', which I am hoping to edit and publish under the title of *Diary of a Split Personality*. An amazing case. She died on the day her MS. was posted to me! *Country Life* tell me that they could sell 100,000 copies of my Poltergeist book—had they the paper. They are printing a 5000

---

[1] These four books were respectively published by Longmans, Green & Co., Collins, Country Life and George Harrap & Co. Lest it be assumed that Price began to drive hard bargains when his books became popular, I may say that his literary record demonstrates that he constantly changed his publishers, the earlier firms concerned being Kegan Paul, John M. Watkins, Hurst & Blackett, Methuen & Co., Putnam & Co., Victor Gollancz and St. Hugh's Press. Six of his books, moreover, were published over the imprint of his National Laboratory of Psychical Research.

first edition, which is probably sold out now. It will not appear until the autumn.[1]

In his Foreword to *Poltergeist over England* Price declared that 'for some years I have been acquiring books, tracts and other records of these mischievous "entities" with a view to preparing a comprehensive work on the whole subject'. Price underlined this assertion under the title of Appendix B of the book, 'Bibliography. Poltergeists in Print', consisting of 119 titles. He wrote:

Most of these works have been acquired specially for use in the preparation of this monograph; all have been studied, and many are cited in the text.

The first phrase of this sentence (which was untrue, as I hope to show) is worth examination. It may be thought that it was designed to give the reader the impression that *Poltergeist over England* was the result of original historical and literary research, based on the deliberate and patient assembly of the relevant source works for the specific purpose of preparing the definitive book on the subject. It was calculated, we may think, to persuade the general reader that the book was not a 'pot-boiler', impressive only by reason of its great size, hastily put together by 'working flat out' in order to get it published while the market was propitious. The allaying of such a suspicion was desirable from Price's point of view, we may think, since he must have been fully aware that the whole subject of poltergeists had already been extensively covered by the published work of writers who had preceded him like Alexander Aksakoff, Sir William Barrett, Hereward Carrington, Mrs Catherine Crowe, Hon. Everard Feilding, Cammille Flammarion, Nandor Fodor, Dr Richard Hodgson, Dr James

[1] In the same letter Price said that he had been asked whether he would consent to his name being included in the next Honours List. If this was true, his comment that it seemed that his work was at last to receive the recognition it deserved does not suggest that the invitation was refused. Price lived for another four years, however, evidently without any summons to Buckingham Palace.

Hyslop, Andrew Lang, Frank Podmore, Dr Walter F. Prince, Sacheverell Sitwell and Father Herbert Thurston.

That *Poltergeist over England* was not regarded as the authoritative work by two well-known writers on the subject was demonstrated within five years of Price's death. In 1953 Hereward Carrington and Nandor Fodor published *The Story of the Poltergeist down the Centuries*.[1] Pages 23–78 were occupied by 'The March of the Poltergeist', a list of what the authors considered to be the 375 most important and typical cases arranged chronologically from A.D. 355 to 1949. Each entry was accompanied by the literary source upon which the authors relied. *Poltergeist over England* was cited as the reference in only ten cases. By contrast, a book by the distinguished French astronomer Camille Flammarion (1842–1925) entitled *Haunted Houses* was cited fourteen times. *Haunted Houses*, moreover, was published as early as 1924, and the last case in Carrington and Fodor's list taken from it (p. 65) was dated 1921, whereas the tenth and last example in the list (p. 77) extracted from *Poltergeist over England* was dated 1943. Out of cases available by reason of date, therefore, Flammarion was notionally quoted as the authority more often than Price by a large margin. Flammarion's book, moreover, discussed many curious subjects in which he believed in addition to poltergeists, including apparitions of the dead and hauntings in general, veridical and premonitory dreams, hysteria, spiritualism, thought transference and somnambulism. The title *Haunted Houses* was a considerable oversimplification of its contents, and the fourteen poltergeist cases cited with page-numbers by Carrington and Fodor are concentrated in only five of the thirteen chapters of the book.[2]

Price's story that he collected most of the list of 119 titles specifically for the purpose of writing *Poltergeist over England* is not supported by the evidence. Half of them were already recorded in his two printed catalogues of his collection in 1929 and 1935. No later list was issued, as additions to the library were insignificant after 1936, when the books were transferred

---

[1] It was a considerable enlargement and revision of the same two authors' *Historic Poltergeists* (London & New York, 1935).

[2] Chapters III, VI, VIII, IX and X.

to the University of London Library on permanent loan. The curious history of Price's collection is recorded in a later chapter, but suffice it to say here that Price was grievously disappointed that the University would not form a Department for Psychical Research in 1934 and give him a doctorate *honoris causa* in exchange for his library and an endowment. The subsequent 'permanent loan' of the books to the University was in my view entirely motivated by his desire for free accommodation and insurance for his collection after the closing down of his National Laboratory of Psychical Research, where the books had been housed since 1927, the year of their removal from 'permanent loan' to the Society for Psychical Research.

There is a letter on file from Price to Miss M. S. Quinn, the Sub-Librarian of the University of London Library, dated 12 November, 1940, five years before the publication of *Poltergeist over England*, which we may think reflects his true attitude, as opposed to the tale in his book. He enclosed 'one item for the H.P. Library'. It was not named, but as Price remarked that 'It is just completed, and it may as well go into the library', it seems probable that it was a copy of the newly published *The Most Haunted House in England*. Price added lugubriously, 'I am afraid I have not much heart to collect these days', which I suspect may have been (for once) a statement of fact.

In addition to the fifty or sixty titles that Price had owned for many years, used by him in the writing of *Poltergeist over England*, a substantial additional number can reasonably be identified by date and title as those 'old and rare books' obtained for him on loan by the Librarian and staff of the Reform Club, which were 'not in my collection or in their own magnificent library', a favour which he acknowledged in his Foreword. Twenty-seven titles were simply articles in periodicals such as the *Journals* and *Proceedings* of the British and American Societies for Psychical Research, to which Price subscribed. Two articles by Andrew Lang from the *Encyclopedia Britannica* were included, and four of Price's own works. These calculations have not been made easier by Price's irritating habit (discussed with examples in the later chapter devoted to the history of his library) of cataloguing articles in journals as if they were books, in order artificially to swell the true total of his collection by several thousand titles.[1]

In order to fill the many pages of *Poltergeist over England* Price relied heavily on the extensive published work on poltergeists by those writers who had preceded him, some of whom I have listed on an earlier page. He was able significantly to enlarge his book, moreover, by including lengthy accounts of cases of alleged haunting, which did not even come within his own terms of reference. He wrote on page 1:

Whereas the ordinary ghost of our story-books is a quiet, in-offensive, timid, noiseless, and rather benevolent spirit, with—usually—friendly feelings towards the occupants of any place where it has its abode, the Poltergeist is just the reverse. According to the many reports of its activities, in all lands and all ages, the Poltergeist is mischievous, destructive, noisy, cruel, erratic, thievish, demon-strative, purposeless, cunning, unhelpful, malicious, audacious, teasing, ill-disposed, spiteful, ruthless, resourceful and vampiric. A ghost *haunts*; a Poltergeist *infests*.

With Price's definition before us, making a firm distinction between ghosts and poltergeists, it is amusing to notice that the first chapter of his *Confessions of a Ghost-Hunter*, devoted to his supposed adventures as a schoolboy in the 'manor house' at 'Parton Magna' in Shropshire, is entitled 'The Ghost that Stumbled'. In *Poltergeist over England* precisely the same story (*verbatim* except for the omission of one paragraph) becomes Chapter XVIII, 'The Poltergeist that Stumbled'. More amusing still is the solemn appearance in the latter book of Price's alleged experience in his bedroom at Pulborough of the pattering feet, which it will be recalled he attributed to his 'psychic child' in *Confessions of a Ghost-Hunter*, and to the spirit of his retriever, 'dear old Nigger', in his Foreword to *The Soul of the Dog*. In *Poltergeist over England* (p. 26) Price had the shameless audacity to claim that this incident was 'my only

---

[1] In his last entry in *Who's Who* Price claimed that he owned 20,000 volumes. A more accurate estimate would be nearer half this number, as will be seen.

real personal experience of a Poltergeist', adding hastily[1] 'I mean the only poltergeist that has ever invaded my own home'. The tale was exactly the same as that quoted in an earlier chapter of the present work, with its familiar opening:

> One January night I was instantly awakened by hearing pattering footsteps in my bedroom. I could hear the soft patter of naked feet round my room as if a little child were running round the bed. Sometimes the pattering came from *under* the bed, proving that the 'intruder' was of very small stature . . . When I judged the 'footsteps' were nearest to me, I switched on a powerful electric lantern that I kept by the side of the bed (there was no electric light in my village). The noise ceased instantly.

In this third version of the tale, blatantly inserted into *Poltergeist over England* to swell its pages, both the 'psychic child' and 'dear old Nigger' disappear from the story and their place is taken by a 'destructive, noisy, cruel, erratic, thievish' Poltergeist, to use only five adjectives from Price's definition. If we wonder how Price thought he could get away with this patent and clumsy published deception, which by itself, it may be thought, is sufficient totally to destroy his credibility as a writer, the fact of the matter is that he evidently has done until now. I know of no previous criticism of his three different versions of the same supposed incident.

Price's definition of a poltergeist did not deter him from devoting the whole of Chapter XI of *Poltergeist over England* to the case of Ballechin House and its alleged haunting, which had been the subject of a book, *The Alleged Haunting of B------ House*, by Ada Goodrich Freer and John, Marquess of Bute, first published in 1899, with a second edition in 1900. The single illustration of the chapter on Ballechin in *Poltergeist over England* (p. 225) shows the 'slight black figure . . . dressed as a nun' of Ishbel, the alleged apparition and communicator by means of an ouija board, who was the central figure of the

---

[1] Possibly inserted after writing 'The Poltergeist that Stumbled', the later chapter in the same book mentioned above, in which he claimed to have encountered a poltergeist at 'Parton Magna' when still a schoolboy. One imagines that a good memory is necessary for this kind of writing, especially if 'working flat out'.

story of 'the most haunted house in Scotland'.[1] On page 2 of our book on Borley Rectory my collaborators and I pointed out that the only reported objective 'phenomenon' at Ballechin seemed to be the supposed pulling of the bedclothes, depending entirely on the uncorroborated tale of the former butler, Harold Sanders, in a newspaper.[2]

Another remarkable achievement, even for Price, was to bring his favourite medium Stella C. into the scope of *Poltergeist over England*, where her name appears ten times in the index. On pages 25, 30, 169, 322 and 382 Stella is described as 'a Poltergeist medium', simply because she produced alleged physical phenomena at her séances. The reader will search in vain for any such previous description of Stella either in Price's book about her, *Stella C. An Account of some Original Experiments in Psychical Research* (London, 1925), or in the whole chapter

---

[1] This phrase is printed on pp. 76–7 of the first edition of *The Alleged Haunting of B—— House* and on p. 70 of the second edition. There can be little doubt that Price used Ballechin as a blue print for his *The Most Haunted House in England*. Following the procedure adopted at Ballechin, he took a tenancy of Borley Rectory and invited observers to stay there to watch and listen for the alleged phenomena, aided by printed suggestions as to what they might expect to see and hear. I also think it probable that Ballechin was the inspiration for the title of Price's first book on Borley, as against the unlikely tale he told on p. 15 of *The End of Borley Rectory*. 'Before I begin my narrative I must first answer a question that is often put to me: Who first called the Rectory "the most haunted house"? I do not know. On my first visit to the house, on June 12, 1929, as I swung my car into the market square at Sudbury, I found I had come to the end of my instructions for finding the Rectory and was at a loss how to proceed. I inquired from a bystander how I could get to Borley Rectory. "Oh", he said, "you mean the most haunted house in England". And that is how and where I first heard the phrase.' Price owned *The Alleged Haunting of B—— House* as early as 1929, for it is listed on p. 199 of his first catalogue.

[2] A critical study of the Ballechin case is contained in two chapters devoted to it in *Strange Things* (London, 1968) by Dr John Lorne Campbell and the present writer, based on many unpublished documents and the discovery of the real names of the persons involved in the affair, concealed by Miss Freer. The latter lady was a very strange person indeed. When she died in 1931 her husband, Dr Hans H. Spoer, believed her to be 56 years old. She was 73. Her birth and death entries are reproduced in *Strange Things*. Virtually the whole story of the haunting of Ballechin House, apart from noises caused by earth tremors (for which the situation of Ballechin was notorious) depends upon Miss Freer.

devoted to her in his *Fifty Years of Psychical Research*. It seems hardly necessary to say that she is not included in the list of 375 poltergeist cases prepared by Carrington and Fodor, to which reference has already been made. If it be urged that since Stella C. was used to swell the pages of *Poltergeist over England*, Price might as well have gone the whole hog by claiming that all other physical mediums were really the agents of poltergeists, despite the fact that such inclusion would completely contradict his own definition of his subject, the simple answer is that this is what he did. Willi and Rudi Schneider both have long entries in the index, and on pages 169 and 382 are lumped together with Stella C. as 'Poltergeist mediums', on the grounds that all three 'rang bells experimentally on many occasions. Bells in sealed wooden boxes were rung under conditions that precluded fraud'. On page 322 even mediums such as D. D. Home, Stainton Moses, William Eglinton, Franek Kluski and Jean Guzik are drawn into the same net, apparently on the grounds that they 'produced lights on many occasions', coupled with the curious qualification, 'Some of the phenomena were probably fraudulent'.

Another odd example of Price's admittance that some of the cases he was quoting were fraudulent occurs on page 249. There he wrote, 'But the greatest feat, of the Poltergeist order, connected with any medium, was that of Mrs Samuel Guppy who, in 1871, was instantly precipitated from her home in Highbury to a house in Lamb's Conduit Street, some three miles away. Of course the whole thing was a swindle; but this modern "transit of Venus" (who was wearing only her underclothes and weighed seventeen stone) was never proved to be a swindle'. The fact that Mrs Guppy was a fraud and had nothing whatever to do with poltergeists, however, did not prevent page 250 of *Poltergeist over England* being a full page illustration of the moonlit flight in London, with Mrs Guppy comfortably floating over the house tops.

Stella C., in her new role as a 'Poltergeist medium', provides us with an excellent example of Price's manipulation of facts. In the index of *Poltergeist over England* is a substantial entry, 'Puberty and Poltergeists', a traditional and favourite theme copied by Price from the writers who had preceded him and exemplified by his assertion on p. 371:

We are certain that there is some connection between Poltergeists and puberty and that the mysteries of sex enter largely into their doings.

Clearly, from Price's point of view, Stella had to be fitted into this pattern if she was to justify her ten entries in the index of *Poltergeist over England* and the many pages devoted to her in the text. Accordingly, on page 278 Price remarked, 'The psychic powers of Miss Stella C. did not manifest themselves until she had first menstruated', and on page 375 he used Stella as one of 'several examples of the link between phenomena and pubescency'. Nowhere in *Poltergeist over England* is the reader given any indication of Stella's age except on page 248, where she is simply described as 'young'.

The innocent reader of *Poltergeist over England* in isolation might think that Price's information in regard to Stella's puberty was first-hand, which it was not. We know, indeed, from page 83 of *Search for Truth* that Price claimed that he first met Stella in 1923 by a chance encounter in a railway-carriage. On page 119 of *Fifty Years of Psychical Research* he gave us a description of her at this time:

She was twenty-one years old, perfectly normal, healthy, good-looking, and a typical specimen of the modern, well-educated English girl. By profession she was a nurse.

In the same year of 1923, in a letter to the Managing Director of Messrs. Scott and Turner, Ltd., of Newcastle-on-Tyne, the proprietors of Andrews Liver Salt, Price described Stella as 'a young girl of good family'.

Even if Stella had only been twenty-one in 1923, Price's own account makes it plain that he could have no personal knowledge of any manifestations of her supposed psychic powers when she first menstruated. Dorothy Stella Cranshaw (the name on both her birth entry and that of her marriage to Leslie Irving Deacon on 4 August, 1928) was in fact born on 1 October, 1900 at 3 Woodman Cottages, North Woolwich. She was therefore 23 years old in October, 1923. Her father was James Henry Cranshaw, a charcoal burner, described as a deceased Civil Servant on Stella's marriage entry.

Price's understatement of Stella's age in 1923 was either a pointless deception on his part, or the careless reporting of incorrect information provided by his protégé. In considering the second alternative, it has to be borne in mind that Price and Stella were evidently close friends, and that he must have known a great deal about her life and circumstances. James Turner reproduces in his book some of Stella's affectionate 'Dear Harry' letters to Price, using the expressions 'Well, dear' and 'Lots of love', and even that of 15 October, 1923 when Stella terminated the sittings because of her engagement to Leslie Deacon:

'You see, I am now engaged to be married and had the sittings been entirely business it would have been different, but under the circumstances it is not fair to either of you if I see you again.

This letter was written on the day following the last and thirteenth sitting on 14 October, 1923. It is of great interest that on page 101 of the first edition of *Stella C.*, published in 1925, Price gave a totally different account of Stella's letter written to him after the thirteenth sitting, and her reason for terminating the séances:

The number thirteen proved 'unlucky' as far as we were concerned, for after this séance Stella informed me by letter that she had decided not to continue the sittings. Her employment fully occupied her time, and she said the sittings made her feel tired, which is more than probable.

Paradoxically, the reader can check these two entirely different stories for himself within the pages of a single book devoted to unqualified praise of Price. They are printed on pages 36 and 119 of the 1973 edition of *Stella C.*, edited by James Turner.

I know of no evidence whatever to suggest that Stella C.'s alleged psychic gifts depended on the activities of mischievous, noisy and destructive poltergeists, a circumstance which I think will be made abundantly clear when Peter A. Bond's forthcoming study of the whole complex case is published. I have no intention of anticipating the contents of this book, which is based securely on the scrutiny of original documents and historical research. With the kind permission of Peter

Bond, however, and because a brief comment on the matter is appropriate to a study of Price's literary idiosyncracies, I will draw attention to the very odd business of Stella's surname and its treatment by both Price and herself. I refer to the peculiarity which Dorothy Stella Cranshaw shared with Lucy Violet Kay, Price's first secretary, of having the letter 'e' grafted on to her name during her association with him. Lucy Kay is variously referred to in the literature both with and without the final 'e', and sometimes as 'Lucie Kaye'. She appeared in this form in *The Most Haunted House in England* and elsewhere, and it was in this name that she contributed a short memoir of Price to Tabori's biography.

In the case of Dorothy Stella Cranshaw, Price was very reluctant to disclose her name at all in 1923. On 2 April of that year, for example, in a letter to Dr E. J. Dingwall, he refused to do so:

Re Stella C. I am not 'hiding her identity'. That is her Christian name and the first letter of her surname. She will publicly reveal her full name only if and when she decides to take up mediumship.

Although Stella became a medium in 1923 and was paid for her services, her surname was still concealed when Price published his book, *Stella C.*, in 1925. In formal correspondence with Price, however, she was addressed as 'Miss Cranshawe', and Price ultimately recorded her name with the embellishment of the additional 'e' on page 143 of the *Short-Title Catalogue* of his library, published in 1929:

'Cranshawe (Stella), [*Pseud*: "Stella C."], [Medium]'.

So far as Peter Bond and I have been able to ascertain, the only person previously to comment in print on the curious Cranshaw/Cranshawe puzzle is James Turner, in a footnote on page 18 of his edited 1973 edition of *Stella C.* which is unfortunately mistaken. Mr. Turner tells us that Stella herself always left out the final 'e', whereas in fact she included it, for example, in her signature to a letter written to Miss Ethel Beenham, Price's second secretary, on 25 April, 1928. On the other hand, her formal letter to Price terminating the sittings on 15 October, 1923 is clearly signed 'Stella Cranshaw'. In his equally formal reply Price perversely addressed her as 'Dear Miss Cranshawe', an amusing fact which is not revealed to Mr. Turner's readers because of the incorrect omission of the final 'e' in the printed reproduction of Price's letter on page 37 of the 1973 edition of *Stella C.*

There can be little doubt that Price was the instigator of this curious embellishment of the surnames of both his favourite medium and his first secretary. Unimportant in itself, it is significantly in accord with all the other evidence that has come to light in this study of Harry Price's writings and activities. I refer to his fundamental inability to leave the simple truth of any matter unadorned.

The late W. H. Salter, a former President of the Society for Psychical Research and its Hon. Secretary for many years, was one of the most active advocates of a full investigation of the Borley Rectory affair and the publication of the report in which I ultimately became involved. In his original notes on the project, written before the inquiry had started and therefore wholly or mainly based on his reading of the two books on Borley, Salter remarked that 'Price gets away with his story by ingeniously suggesting connexions between occurrences belonging to different periods, happening under different conditions and due to different causes (hallucination, faulty memory, fraud, etc.)'. This criticism is equally applicable to the whole text of *Poltergeist over England*, in which Price consistently supports one shaky case by quoting another equally weak, on the basis of the illogical theory that if one leaking bucket will not hold water, two might. An interesting example of his use of this device, with which this chapter can appropriately be concluded, occurs on page 316:

A phenomenon sometimes associated with rectories is that of the paranormal displacement of coffins in nearby vaults. In the crypt of Borley Church, about 1880, some of the coffins were found to have been paranormally moved from their prescribed positions. At Staunton, in Suffolk, something similar happened. A number of leaden coffins were displaced three times, about the year 1760.

On page 50 of *The Most Haunted House in England*, published five years previously, Price gave the provenance of the Borley story:

Other interesting incidents connected with the Borley mystery were related to us by Miss Ethel Bull. Some of the old coffins in the crypt of Borley Church have been found moved from their prescribed positions. This has occurred on several occasions and no explanation has been found for the displacements.

Price added that the phenomenon of displaced coffins had also occurred at Staunton in Suffolk, 'a few miles from Borley, in 1810'. It will be noticed that no date was given by Miss Bull for the alleged movement of the Borley coffins, and that Price's date of 1810 for the Staunton disturbances differed by fifty years from his mention of the case in *Poltergeist over England*. 'Staunton', which was described as the old alternative spelling of Stanton as early as 1904, as will be seen, is about nine miles north-east of Bury St. Edmunds and therefore 25 miles from Sudbury, the nearest town to Borley. Price's attempt to link the two cases topographically by describing Staunton as 'a few miles' from Borley was therefore guesswork. Staunton does not occur as a place-name on twentieth-century maps of Suffolk, and it will be clear from what follows in the present chapter that Price made no effort whatever to look into the Staunton case. It would seem, moreover, that Price attached little importance to the story of the coffins told to him by Miss Ethel Bull on 13 June, 1929, when he wrote *The Most Haunted House in England*, for it is not mentioned at all in his Appendix F. of that book, 'Chronological Record of Principal Events, 1362–1939'. The first date given for an alleged paranormal event at Borley (p. 245) is 1886, the year when Miss E. Byford, a young nursemaid, left the service of the Bull family at Borley on account of what Price called 'ghostly footsteps' (an expression never used by Miss Byford), the whole tale being contradicted by her when she was interviewed by the *Saffron Walden Independent Press and Chronicle*, as reported in the issue of that newspaper of 9 November, 1951.

Price must have known that the tale told to him by Miss Ethel Bull was pure hearsay, for it is clear from the text of *The End of Borley Rectory* that in 1943 she did not even know the whereabouts of the entry to the crypt of Borley Church. I would say here that Miss Ethel May Bull, who died at her home at Chilton Lodge, Great Cornard, near Sudbury on 29 April, 1961, was most certainly in full possession of her faculties as late as 4 April, 1953. On this date Dr Dingwall, my first wife and our son and daughter and myself were most kindly entertained to tea by Miss Bull and her brother, the late Alfred Richard Graham Bull, who died on 17 March, 1956. It was an enjoyable and interesting occasion, which threw a flood of light on some incidents in Price's books.

In the spring of 1943 Price, who had been under pressure from Canon W. J. Phythian-Adams for two years to dig in the cellars at Borley, agreed to do so. He wrote on pages 231–2 of *The End of Borley Rectory*:

As I was going to Borley, I thought I would kill two birds with one stone and make an attempt to find the entrance to the crypt of Borley Church. I wished to ascertain whether there were any records of documents deposited with the Waldegrave coffins in the crypt—those coffins which, as the reader will remember, were supposed to have been moved paranormally . . . We continued our search for an entrance to the crypt, without result. Then the masons inspected likely spots near the church, in the churchyard, where they concluded the opening to the crypt must be. Unfortunately, time did not permit us to start digging up the churchyard, as we were anxious to get down to the more important task of digging up the cellars.

Miss Ethel Bull was very much alive in 1943 and lived only three miles from Borley. If there was any substance in the tale of the disturbances in the crypt 'about 1880', when Miss Bull was about twelve years old and her father, the Revd. Henry Dawson Ellis Bull (d. 1892) was alive, why was she not asked the simple question that might have avoided the abortive search?[1]

[1] Paul Tabori and Peter Underwood do not throw any additional light on the matter on p. 137 of *The Ghosts of Borley*. 'One of the long-standing mysteries of Borley involves conflicting statements about a crypt in Borley church. In *The Most Haunted House in England* (p. 50) Price stated that Miss Ethel Bull spoke of coffins in the crypt having been moved on several occasions. Yet she told Mr Peter Underwood that she knew nothing of a

I turn finally to the Staunton case, quoted by Price in juxtaposition with the Borley crypt affair as supporting evidence.
When that evidence is subjected to critical inquiry, we find
that it is limited to a single letter, five sentences in length,
addressed to the Editor of *The London Magazine* and published
in that journal in 1760 (volume 29, p. 371).[1] The letter was
unsigned and no indication of its provenance was given, which
may reduce our opinion of the evidential value of this document, upon which the entire case relies. The unknown writer
said, 'At Staunton, in Suffolk, is a vault belonging to the
family of the French's', adding that several coffins, which were
leaden with wooden cases, were found to be displaced when
the vault was opened, following a death in the family. This
initial event was described with irritating vagueness by the
anonymous correspondent as having occurred 'some years ago'.
The two later discoveries of displacement were stated to have
occurred 'about seven years ago' (presumably about 1753) and
'two years after' (presumably about 1755). The unknown writer
concluded his letter with a curious sentence rarely quoted by
commentators, 'It was occasioned by water, as is imagined,
though no signs of it appeared at the different periods of time
that the vault was opened'.

Despite the anonymity and imprecision of this communication, it was re-printed in the same year of 1760 in *The Annual
Register* (First Group, p. 121),[2] presumably because it was the
first story of the displacement of coffins in a vault. Over half a
century later the account was again re-printed in *The European
Magazine* of September, 1815, under the heading 'The Curious

---

crypt at Borley and had not made the statement attributed to her. To add
to the confusion, on 3 July, 1972 Mr. G. Croom-Hollingsworth told us
that he held evidence about Miss Ethel Bull knowing all about the crypt
and that she had been down the vault!' On pp. 182–3 and 217–18 of the
same book it is reported that Croom-Hollingsworth saw the 'Nun' at
Borley in 1970 clearly at a distance of 'about fifteen feet'. The time was
1.50 a.m., but Croom-Hollingsworth could see that the apparition's 'skin
looked hard and dry' and that 'she had a mole or a spot on her left cheek'.
The observer experienced a feeling of coldness that 'seemed to penetrate
every bone in my body'.

[1] *The London Magazine*, first edited by John Scott, ran from 1732 to 1785.
[2] *The Annual Register* was founded in 1758 by Robert Dodsley.

Vault at Staunton, Suffolk'. This republishing of the letter
without any indication that the original document was 55 years
old misled Andrew Lang and other psychical researchers into
assuming that the case occurred in 1815. Lang discussed it in a
paper read to the Folk-Lore Society in 1907, and afterwards
published in the Society's *Journal*. The confusion over the date
was corrected by the late Father Herbert Thurston, S. J. in his
paper 'Do Poltergeists invade the Tomb?' published in *The
Month* in March, 1938, and afterwards as Chapter XIV of his
book *Ghosts and Poltergeists* (London, 1953).

What may not be generally known perhaps, is that in his
undated MS. account of the Barbados coffin case,[1] with which
he became involved in April, 1820, the Hon. Nathan Lucas
wrote:

> Being informed that a similar occurrence had been said to have
> happened in England, I had the account looked for, and the
> following copy was given to me. I did not see the work from which
> it was extracted, but I have no reason to doubt the accuracy of it.

What followed was clearly a copy of *The European Magazine*
printing of the story of five years previously, because the title
'The Curious Vault, Etc.' was used, but with two alterations
made by the Hon. Nathan Lucas, which strongly suggest that
unlike the contented copiers who had preceded him, he had
made some inquiries of his own. The title was altered to 'The
Curious Vault at Stanton [as opposed to Staunton][2] in Suffolk',
with an inserted query underneath by Lucas, 'Which of the
Stantons?' The reader will, I suggest, find a search for any
mention of these very interesting amendments in modern
works on psychical research unrewarding, despite their
importance.

The Hon. Nathan Lucas was quite right in his topographical
supposition, and it is to be regretted that the fact that he was
not resident in England evidently prevented his pursuing the
inquiry, presumably begun by him from works of reference.

[1] Now in the Public Library of Bridgetown, Barbados.
[2] W. A. Copinger, in his *County of Suffolk. Its History as disclosed by Existing
Records*, vol. 5, 1904, gives Staunton as a very rare alternative spelling of
Stanton.

The place-name Staunton does not exist in Suffolk today, but Stanton All Saints and Stanton St. John were originally adjoining small parishes about nine miles north-east of Bury St. Edmunds. They have been amalgamated for over a century, being simply marked as 'Stanton' on the map, and single incumbents have been appointed since the early sixteenth century. The present Rector is the Revd. Eric K. Andrews, who was preceded by the Revd. Canon C. J. H. Mills. The County Archivist states that there is no record of any other place in Suffolk called Stanton or Staunton, or similar name. The Hon. Nathan Lucas's query, 'Which of the Stantons?', early in the last century was therefore exceedingly relevant, and there can be no doubt about the location of the case reported anonymously in 1760 in five sentences in *The London Magazine* in July of that year, which constitute the whole of the evidence for what is alleged to have occurred in 'a vault belonging to the family of the French's' in Stanton in Suffolk.

The County Archivist has searched the indexes of the records in his care and can find no trace of any persons named French ever having lived at Stanton. The Parish Registers of both All Saints and St. John have been searched from 1750 to 1760 by the Revd. Canon Mills with a similar negative result. The Rev. Eric K. Matthews has informed Archdeacon Charles O. Ellison (who kindly undertook the ecclesiastical correspondence on my behalf) that the name French has no significance in Stanton that he can discover, either past or present, and that neither he nor his sexton of many years service have any knowledge of the existence of a vault. The whole case, therefore, falls to pieces when examined; perhaps not unexpectedly when we recall that its flimsy provenance was a single anonymous letter written over two hundred years ago.

Price, as we have seen, was sufficiently lacking in knowledge of the case to refer to it in 1945 on page 316 of *Poltergeist over England* as having occurred at 'Staunton, in Suffolk', which a glance at a map would have corrected. In his footnote on the same page, however, he referred to the accounts of the case in both *The London Magazine* and *The European Magazine*, which suggests that he had access to enough of the relevant documents to prompt a literary and historical examination of the affair, had he any inclination to do so. Serious and impartial investi-

.gation, however, forms no part of the activity of the successful psychic journalist, 'working flat out' to finish a book like *Poltergeist over England*. Price knew, moreover, that 'so many people prefer the "bunk" to the "debunk" ', as he himself had written in his Foreword to J. R. Sturge-Whiting's *The Mystery of Versailles*, published in 1938. Cases like those of 'Rosalie' (which even his friend C. E. M. Joad could not accept)[1] and Borley, to quote two outstanding examples, and books like *Poltergeist over England*, were the natural symptoms of such a belief.

[1] Price's tale of his witnessing in 1937 the materialisation of the nude figure of a little girl of six (who had died in 1921, according to his account) was published in his *Fifty Years of Psychical Research* in 1939, without a shred of corroborative evidence. The location of the house and the names of those present at the séance were all concealed. The affair was critically examined by Dingwall and myself in our *Four Modern Ghosts* (London, 1958) and Joad's letter to Price about it is quoted on p. 53 of that book with the permission of his executors. Mr Douglas Craggs, O.B.E. wrote to me on 16 April, 1952, 'You will remember my review of his book in which he described the Rosalie materialisation. This, in my view, was a complete invention and unworthy even of Price. When I sent him an advance copy of the review in which I criticised the Rosalie chapter he forbade me to publish it, and instead of the usual "Dear Douglas" he began his letter with "Dear Sir". I ignored his letter and the review duly appeared. About five months after the publication of the review he wrote to me in a very friendly strain saying he was sure that I was right and that he should never have put Rosalie into print.' Price evidently realised that even he had gone too far, and on p. 293 of *Search for Truth*, in the only paragraph in that book in which 'Rosalie' is mentioned, he said that he was not 'entirely satisfied' with the case, which he had published 'against my inclination'. It is instructive to compare these comments with the original account published only three years previously.

XIX

The Borley Medals

The Haunting of Borley Rectory. A Critical Survey of the Evidence (London, 1956), by Dr Dingwall, Mrs Goldney and myself, contained (pp. 61–4) a documented inquiry into the mystery of two medallions of French origin (one Roman Catholic), alleged by Price in his two books on Borley[1] to have been supernormally 'apported' into 'the most haunted house in England' one evening in 1929. The incident is of great interest, being apparently directly linked, according to Price, with the dramatic supposed historical background of the haunting of the Rectory by the spirit of a French Roman Catholic nun, 'Marie Lairre', whose alleged name and religion, her origin in Le Havre and brutal murder at Borley in 1667 were first revealed in planchette (automatic) writings in 1937. It was naturally argued by believers in the Borley 'phenomena' that since the first mention of a French Roman Catholic nun occurred in the planchette data in 1937, any hypothesis of trickery on Price's part in 1929 by the introduction of appropriate 'apports' to bolster up the story of 'Marie Lairre' is untenable on the face of it, since it would imply supernormal foreknowledge by him in 1929 of the coming events of 1937.

I was responsible for the investigation of the medallion affair over twenty years ago, and as I consider it to be one of the most striking and proven examples of Price's manipulation of evidence, I think that it should be included in the present work. The comment on the incident on pages 94–5 of *The Ghosts of Borley* by Paul Tabori and Peter Underwood, to which I shall refer, is in my opinion a fair example of the standard of scholarship of that book.

---

[1] *The Most Haunted House in England* (London, 1940), referred to in this chapter as *MHH*, and *The End of Borley Rectory* (London, 1946), referred to as *EBR*.

The first matter to be mentioned, I fancy, before the details of the affair of the medallions are considered, is that in Price's *Fifty Years of Psychical Research* (London, 1939) published ten years after the appearance of the alleged 'apports' at Borley, but one year before the publication of *MHH*, he wrote (p. 29), '*Apports.*—Objects brought abnormally into the séance room or elsewhere, from the French verb *apporter*, to bring, produce. Like "spirit" photographs, the evidence for apports is bad.' On page 201 of the same book Price added to this criticism, 'Very few serious investigators of to-day accept "apports".'[1]

Despite what he had written in *Fifty Years of Psychical Research*, a year later Price claimed that the medallions appeared super-normally in Borley Rectory on the night of 5 July, 1929, during the incumbency of the late Rev. and Mrs G. Eric Smith. Price was accompanied on this visit to the rectory by his secretary, Miss Lucy Kay at that time, and Lord Charles Hope.[2] Price wrote of the occasion (*MHH*, pp. 59–60):

One evening, a party of us was present when incessant bell-ringing occurred. This was accompanied by the usual *Poltergeist* manifestations consisting of the throwing of small pebbles, a shower of several keys (which appear to have been collected by the *Geist* and then projected into the hall); a small gilt medallion, such as are presented to Roman Catholic children on their Confirmation; and another medallion or badge, dated 'AN VIII' (*i.e.*, A.D. 1799) issued in Paris after the French Revolution. The origin of these medals is not known, and I will remark in passing that many of the phenomena at Borley are connected in some way with Roman Catholicism: the 'nun' and monks; the medallions; France; the 'messages' on the walls (of which I will speak later), and so on.

In *EBR* (p. 33) he wrote:

I visited the Rectory several times in 1929 and witnessed many phenomena under perfect conditions of control. In addition to the incessant paranormal bell-ringing, I saw showers of pebbles and keys coming from nowhere, and on one occasion a Roman Catholic

---

[1] These comments are not mentioned in *The Ghosts of Borley*, and *Fifty Years of Psychical Research* is not included in the index of that book.

[2] The name of Lord Charles Hope is not included in the index of either of Price's books on Borley.

medallion, and a badge struck during the French Revolution, came
tumbling down the stairs in a good light.[1]

Also in *EBR* (pp. 212–13) in Chapter XIII, 'Clues and
Indicators', Price wrote:

First of all, there is every indication that the nun was *French*. She
tells us she is French; that her name is 'Mary Lairre' (one Planchette
signature was *Marie* Lairre), a French name; and that she came
from Havre. It has been objected that she writes (Planchette)
'Havre' and not 'Le Havre'. But the definite article is frequently
omitted. As I write, I have a Continental time-table (1938–39)
before me, and in the index 'Havre' is printed *without* 'Le'.

Then we have the two French medallions that 'appeared' during
Mr. Smith's incumbency: a Roman Catholic pendant, as issued to
French children when they are confirmed. It was made in Paris,
but was found at Borley in 1929. With it came another medal,
dated 1799, issued in Paris during the French Revolution.

Price's determination to convince his readers of the connexion
between the French medallions of 1929 and the tragic story of
the French nun 'Marie Lairre', first revealed at a planchette
séance in 1937, is left in no doubt by these quotations. From
the point of view of the sceptic, the facts that Price was an
amateur conjurer and a collector of coins and medals remove
any doubt that it would have been perfectly practicable for
him to have produced the two French medals at Borley in 1929
by normal means. It was the chronological sequence of events
that raised such formidable objections to the hypothesis of
fraud. An investigation of other documents, however, both
published (but not in the two Borley books) and unpublished,
began to place a very different complexion on the matter. Every
single item of this new evidence (some from Price's own pen in
1929) showed that the first mention by Price of the two French
medallions was in *MHH* in 1940. The same documents demon-

---

[1] The late Mrs Mabel Smith, the wife of the Rector, was present during
all these striking 'phenomena' described by Price. During Price's lifetime,
a letter from Mrs Smith in regard to Borley Rectory was published in the
Church Times of 19 October, 1945, saying that she wished 'to state definitely
that neither my husband nor myself believed the house haunted by anything
else but rats and local superstition'.

strated, with equal precision, that it was a *single* quite different medallion, having no connexion whatever with France, that had 'appeared' at Borley on 5 July, 1929.

In the chapter 'Topography and Legends' in *The Haunting of Borley Rectory*, my co-authors and I wrote (p. 13):

There are two principal legends connected with Borley Rectory which play their part in the story of the alleged hauntings. The first of these was the one published, apparently for the first time, in the *Daily Mirror* and other papers in June, 1929, and was based on the assumption that the rectory was built on the site of a 13th-century monastery. This story was presumably current in the district for some time before its publication, and it has been suggested that it was established prior to the building of the rectory in 1863, and that the dining room fireplace with its monk's head effigies was installed by the Rev. Henry Bull to perpetuate a legend in which he may have believed. There are several variants of this first story, which we may loosely describe as the 'Monastery, Monk and Nun Legend', but in general terms the story is that some 700 years ago a monk from Borley Monastery eloped by coach with a novice from Bures Nunnery, some eight miles away. The legend says that the result of this ill-fated expedition was that the elopers were caught, the would-be bridegroom hanged or beheaded, and the novice bricked up alive in her own convent, which presumably accounts for the story of the phantom coach, the headless man, and the ghostly nun.[1]

The second and later legend, which Price ultimately adopted, arose in embryo from certain selected passages from planchette writings obtained by the Glanville family in October 1937, in which the late Sidney H. Glanville (who presented to me his unique *Locked Book* on Borley containing the séance transcripts) told me he had not the slightest belief. My co-authors and I wrote (p. 15):

The story in brief is that a young French Roman Catholic nun, Marie Lairre, was induced to leave her convent at Le Havre to

[1] Before the publication of *MHH* Price gave a lecture on Borley to the London Ghost Club, which included some of these details. Critical correspondence ensued in the columns of *The Times* on the mythical bricking up of live nuns, and on equally mythical pre-Reformation coaches in England.

become the wife of one of the Waldegraves of Borley, and was strangled by him in a building [an earlier rectory in this later legend] previously on the site of Borley Rectory on 17 May, 1667 and her body buried beneath the cellar floor. The suggestion was that the spirit of this unhappy young person was responsible *inter alia* for the rectory wall-writings, the loss of Mr. Shaw Jeffrey's French dictionary,[1] and the production of various 'apports', including two medals of somewhat suspicious provenance, an old coat, a piece of rotten wood, and a dead frog, in order to establish her identity and the whereabouts of her remains.

Price contributed an account of his adventures at Borley Rectory to the *Journal* of the American Society for Psychical Research in August, 1929, one month subsequent to the incident under scrutiny. It was his earliest story of the events of 5 July of that year. He described the rectory as being built 'on the vaults and cellars of a 13th century monastery. The ruins of a nunnery are close by'. There was not a word of truth in the story of the monastery, but Price still believed in it as late as 1936, when his *Confessions of a Ghost-Hunter* was published, containing a chapter, 'The Most Haunted House in England'. On page 26 he wrote, 'The house is not an old one, having been built about 1863. It was erected on the site of a twelfth-century monastery, the crypt of which is still preserved'. On 3 November, 1938, however, the late Sidney H. Glanville wrote to Price:

I have at last received a definite reply from the Secretary of the Essex Archaeological Society in which he says, 'There was certainly

---

[1] The late P. Shaw Jeffrey (1862–1952) wrote to Price in 1942 after reading *MHH* to say that when he was an undergraduate in 1885 he stayed at Borley Rectory with Harry Bull, and that among other experiences he lost a French/English dictionary. The wall-writings at Borley, associated by sceptics with Mrs Marianne Foyster, were in English. One of the principal believers in Borley, Dr W. J. Phythian-Adams, who contributed two chapters to *EBR* (and was described by Price on p. 13 of that book as a 'brilliant thinker'), wrote in an article 'Plague of Darkness' (*Church Quarterly Review*, January-March, 1946, p. 214), 'Am I seriously contending that a French girl (the "Nun") was haunting Borley all those years and that she collected words out of a dictionary in the 1880s for an appeal [the wall-writings] which had to wait another half-century? I am *contending* nothing. I simply ask whether any other explanation will fit the facts.'

no religious house at Borley; nor is there any record of a chapel or ecclesiastical building other than the church having existed there'. So there goes the monastery and nunnery legend. Unfortunate, but there it is.

Sidney Glanville might well have added with equal truth, 'There goes also the Monastery, Monk and Nun Legend'. In 1929, however, this story was the only one extant. Eight years were to elapse before Marie Lairre and her tragic history were to become available to Price. In his article on Borley in the *Journal* of the American S.P.R. in August, 1929, Price wrote:

We have experienced all the usual typical poltergeist manifestations such as the throwing of pebbles and other objects, and on the occasion of my last visit—I was then accompanied by Lord Charles Hope—we received a shower of ten keys which had been extracted from as many doors in various parts of the building. Amongst the keys was a brass Romish medallion, which the rector could not identify.

In this earliest account, written one month after the event, no other medallion was mentioned. The incidence of a *single* medallion, moreover, was confirmed in a puzzled letter from the Rector, the Rev. G. Eric Smith, to Lord Charles Hope dated 25 July, 1929:

Yes, the keys fitted the doors, but the upstairs lavatory key has never been found. Incidentally, the medallion that was hurled downstairs has never been seen before by anyone at the Rectory.

We learn more about the medallion from an unpublished contemporary account prepared by Lord Charles Hope from notes made on 6 July, 1929, five quarto pages in length, and headed, 'Visit to Borley Rectory, July 5th, 1929'. Lord Charles said that the visit was made with Price and Miss Lucy Kay, and that the house was occupied by the Rev. G. Eric Smith and his wife and one young resident maid, Mary, whose young man was allowed to visit her in the evenings. Lord Charles described the incident with which we are concerned on the second page of his account:

The next phenomenon was a crash in the hall. I was still near the bells [in the kitchen passage] but HP [Price], I think, had just gone from the back passage into the hall. The drawing room door opened and to my surprise the Smiths, followed by Mary and the boy, came out into the hall. On the floor near the drawing room door we found six or seven keys and a medallion with some Latin words on it and the head of a monk.

We recall that at the end of his account of the events of the night of 5 July, 1929, Lord Charles Hope wrote:

I should add that although I did not feel certain, I left Borley with the definite suspicion that Mr. Price might be responsible for some at least of the phenomena which had occurred while I was present.

This suspicion does not seem to have diminished with the passage of time, for we also remember that when in 1932 Price was about to give his lecture on Borley to which reference has already been made, Lord Charles wrote to him to say that he did not wish his name to be mentioned, accompanied by the proviso that if it was, Price was to say that Lord Charles had not been impressed by his experience at Borley, 'and thought the phenomena were produced by normal means'.

One thing was clear. The *single* medallion that Price, Lord Charles Hope and the Rev. G. E. Smith separately recorded shortly after 5 July, 1929 as having been thrown on to the floor of the hall at Borley Rectory on that night, did not fit the descriptions of either of the *two* medallions that Price described in some detail in the story in *MHH* eleven years later. The latter supported the 'Marie Lairre' story, which had been available for three years when *MHH* was written. The single medallion which actually appeared on 5 July, 1929, described by Lord Charles Hope as having 'some Latin words on it and the head of a monk', supported, it may be thought, the earlier 'Monastery, Monk and Nun' legend to which Price had tenaciously clung until it was demolished by Sidney Glanville's correspondence with the Essex Archaeological Society in 1938.

After Price's death a brass medallion was found in his collection. It is octagonal in shape, measuring 2 inches by $1\frac{1}{2}$ inches. The obverse shows a head and shoulders effigy of

St. Ignatius Loyola clad in the garb of a pilgrim and holding in his hand a book representing the rule of the Society of Jesus. The lettering on the obverse reads, 'S. Ignat. Lol. Soc. Jesu. P.' The reverse shows a representation of the Holy Trinity, with the single word 'Roma' underneath. It is believed to be a pilgrim's badge, in all probability struck in large numbers for one of the Holy Years, 1650, 1675 or 1700, to be sold or given to those visiting Rome for the Holy Year. It is, I am informed, neither valuable nor particularly rare. It is, quite clearly it may be thought, the single 'brass Romish medallion' described by Price in the *Journal* of the American Society for Psychical Research of August, 1929, as having appeared at Borley during the previous month.

The evidence of Lord Charles Hope apart, further positive identification of the St. Ignatius medallion with the events of the night of 5 July, 1929 came from Price's former secretary, Lucy Kay (by then Mrs Meeker) in two letters of 24 and 30 January, 1951 to Mrs C. C. Baines, a member of the S.P.R. who was interested in the historical aspects of Borley. Mrs Meeker wrote:

> It is the only medal or medallion I remember appearing in the early days, and quite undoubtedly this is the one that 'appeared' on the same night as the keys. I picked it up, said 'isn't that lovely' and, either that evening or a day or two later HP said I could have it . . . I am quite sure that only one medal turned up on the night of the keys, and I know that both HP and Lord Charles were there.

When, near the end of Price's life, Mrs Meeker heard that Price was writing a third book on Borley, she returned the St. Ignatius medal to him. Whether his former secretary's admirably clear memory of the events of the night of 5 July, 1929 and her production of the evidence pleased Price is a matter for conjecture.

In *The Haunting of Borley Rectory* we showed as Plate II[1] a photograph of the St. Ignatius medallion, in juxtaposition with photographs of the French Roman Catholic confirmation pendant and the French Revolution medallion or badge of 1799 that Price instead claimed had appeared at Borley when

---

[1] Reproduced in the present work as Plate 11.

he wrote *The Most Haunted House in England*. It bore no resemblance whatever to either. It is difficult to imagine a more complete example of decisive evidence of deliberate fraud, with an obvious and clear-cut motive.

We need waste little time, I fancy, on Tabori's account of the St. Ignatius medallion on page 266 of his biography of Price. We may presume that he found it among Price's collection of Borley material when he became literary executor. Something had to be written about it, and we can only conjecture that it was as a matter of convenience that Tabori decided to include it in his account of the clutter of miscellaneous objects found during the excavations at Borley in 1943. He described the brass St. Ignatius medal in this chosen context as being 'of poor quality gold'. Mrs Meeker's comment on this in her letter of 1951 was brief:

I notice the remark on p. 266 re the St. I. Brass being dug up. Silly man. I told him quite plainly that it was found with the keys in the early days.

In 1973, in *The Ghosts of Borley*, Tabori and Underwood repeated Price's story of the events of the night of 5 July, 1929, with the comment:

It has been suggested—though with little force of conviction—that Price lent some 'assistance' to the appearance of the objects, having picked the medals from his numismatic collection. His intention, the accusers said, was to bolster the legend of the Borley hauntings and the ghostly 'Nun'.

It is evident that we were not sufficiently lucid in our suggestion in regard to what we felt sure Price did, to be within the comprehension of Dr Tabori and Mr Underwood. The reader can decide for himself whether we ever believed that Price took the two French medals to Borley in 1929. We did not think it probable that they even entered his mind in connexion with Borley until 1937 or 1938 at the earliest, for reasons that are sufficiently obvious. The French medals were not introduced into the Borley legend by sleight of hand, but by a dishonest pen. Our critics do concede, however, that Price did rather oddly describe 'a brass Romish medallion' in the *Journal* of the

American S.P.R. The whole curious business, however, was in their view just an innocent muddle on Price's part. 'It is worth remembering,' it is stated on page 95 of *The Ghosts of Borley*, 'that Price was writing *The Most Haunted House in England* in difficult conditions after War had been declared and reference to his original papers was not easy.'

XX

The Story of a Library

The assembly of a large library containing a substantial number of rare and valuable items requires both money and leisure, and the late Harry Price enjoyed both these advantages as a result of his fortunate marriage to Constance Mary Knight in 1908. Nothing seems to have been publicly known of Price as a conjurer, a book-collector or a psychical researcher until 1920 when, twelve years after his marriage, he joined both the Magic Circle and the Society for Psychical Research at the age of nearly forty. By 1920, however, his interest had become centred on old conjuring books and by 1922 at latest, as we shall see, he had already assembled an important library of about 1500 items. Four articles by Price were published in *The Magazine of Magic* in 1920, with titles such as 'Some Magical Rarities, Ancient and Modern' and 'Mornings amongst the Cobwebs, or Hours in a Magical Library'. He contributed 'Five Hundred Years of Magic. A Wonderful Magical Scrap-book' to the same journal in February 1921, and his 'My Library' followed in *The Magic Wand* of October/November, 1923. These articles, and many others, all appeared in magazines read by professional and amateur conjurers. Price added to his status in this field of activity by joining the Magicians' Club and becoming its Hon. Librarian during this period.

The late Leo Rullman of New York, a bookseller specialising in rare works on magic, in the seventh of his monthly essays 'Books of Yesterday' in *The Sphinx* of June, 1928, described his visit during the previous month to Price's self-styled National Laboratory of Psychical Research, opened on 1 January, 1926, at 16 Queensberry Place in South Kensington. Rullman wrote:

On the top floor of the building, at the head of four flights of stairs, are located the laboratory, work-shop and library of Mr.

Price. However, it is with the latter only that we are concerned for the moment, the wonderful collection of magical and psychic literature that is at once the envy and the despair of every collector with similar interests. To those of my readers who may be interested in the scope of this collection, let me say at once that Mr. Price estimates 'the entire lot at more than 5,000 titles, which number necessarily contains a considerable number of works bordering on the occult. Personally, I counted some sixty-odd shelves of the sectional book-case type, all filled with books and pamphlets, which I understand to be only a part of the entire collection, many more volumes being in Mr. Price's home outside London.

Rullman went on to describe some of the principal treasures of the library, which included 'a practically perfect copy' of the first edition of Reginald Scot's *The discoverie of witchcraft* (London, 1584) 'beautifully bound in full crushed morocco gilt, with gilt edges'. Other items which attracted Rullman's especial attention were the second issue of Samuel Rid's *The art of jugling or legerdemaine* (London, 1614), 'bound in choicest polished tree calf, with armorial crest in gilt at front and rear',[1] together with the first edition of *Hocus pocus junior. The anatomie of legerdemain* (London, 1634)[2] and 'a long run of the so-called Hocus Pocus books written by or attributed to Henry Dean, from the first edition on down the line'.[3]

[1] *The art of jugling* was published in 1612, and was re-issued with a new title-page only in 1614. It was almost wholly copied from the chapter on conjuring in Scot, but without the illustrations. Price bought his copy at the Christie-Miller sale in 1925. At this auction specimens of both issues were offered. That of 1612, the Bindley-Heber copy (Lot 623) was bought by Dr Rosenbach for £45 and is now in the Henry Huntington Library. Lot 624, the Britwell Court copy of the 1614 issue, was bought by Price for £22 and is now in the University of London Library.

[2] *Hocus pocus junior*, once described by the late Leo Rullman as 'the hope and the despair of the seeker after rare magic books' (*Greater Magic*, Minneapolis, 1942, p. 928) was the first illustrated book wholly devoted to conjuring. Price bought his copy for £25 at the sale of the library of the Earl of Powis in 1923. The only four copies known of the first edition are now in London University Library, the Bodleian Library, Princeton University Library and the Henry Huntington Library.

[3] Rullman was not quite right about this, for Price never owned a first edition of Dean's *The whole art of legerdemain, or, hocus pocus in perfection* (London, 1722), of which the only three copies known to me are in the British Museum, Glasgow University Library and the Walter Hampton

In a later essay in the same series (the twentieth) Rullman returned to the subject of the 'Harry Price Library of Magical Literature', as its owner now called it, in *The Sphinx* of July, 1929. The collection had evidently grown appreciably during the thirteen months separating the two essays. Rullman said that the library now boasted 6,000 titles, and included 'books on spiritualism, psychology, clairvoyance, mediums, trances, thought transference, automatic writing, telekinesis, hauntings, 'spirit' paintings and crystal gazing, to name only a few'.

Rullman's second essay on the Price library had been inspired by the receipt of a copy of Price's first printed *Short-Title Catalogue* of the collection, which was Part II of Volume I of *Proceedings of the National Laboratory of Psychical Research*[1] (London, April, 1929). This list showed that in addition to the extremely rare and valuable books mentioned by Rullman in his first essay, Price owned many other very desirable conjuring items. One example was Philip Astley's *Natural magic: or, physical amusements revealed* (London, 1785), which Rullman had described in *The Sphinx* of February, 1928 as 'one of the rarest of the English-printed conjuring books', an opinion which I endorsed on pages 157–8 of my *Old Conjuring Books. A Bibliographical and Historical Study*. Price also possessed the second (1635) and third (1654) editions of John Bate's *The mysteries of nature and art*. The *Short-Title Catalogue* listed three different editions of *Breslaw's last legacy* published between 1792 and *c.* 1806 and, more importantly *The conjuror's magazine, or magical and physiognomical mirror* (2 vols., London, 1791–3), the first periodical to contain conjuring tricks. Price's copy boasted a complete set of the Lavater plates, a condition of perfection in which this item is extremely hard to find.

Price owned H. van Etten's *Mathematicall recreations* (London, 1653), the second English edition of one of the rarest and most desirable of early conjuring books,[2] together with the fourth

---

Memorial Library of the Players Club of New York. His earliest edition was the second (1727), as his printed catalogues show.

[1] Of which Price was the self-styled Honorary Director.

[2] It is unfortunate that Price erroneously dated it 1753 on both p. 175 of the *Short-Title Catalogue* and on p. 22 of his booklet *Exhibition of Rare Works from the Research Library* published in 1934.

French edition, published at Rouen in 1629. In addition to possessing one of the only four known copies of the first edition of *Hocus pocus junior* (London, 1634), Price also owned a fine copy of the fourth edition of 1654, and three German editions of the same extremely rare book. His shelves contained the first and second editions of Thomas Denton's *The conjurer unmasked*, 1785 and 1788,[1] and Thomas Hill's *Legerdemain: or, natural and artificial conclusions; and hocus pocus improved* (London, *c.* 1710), all of which are exceedingly difficult to find. Pinetti's *Physical amusements and diverting experiments* (London, 1784) is a rare book in either the English or French versions, and Price had both, together with the first edition of *Gale's cabinet of knowledge* (London, 1796). He owned the second edition (1653) of Sir Hugh Plat's *The jewel house of nature and art*, which is a prize in any book collection, and a fine copy of Porta's *Natural magick* (London, 1658). In addition to the *editio princeps* of Scot's *The discoverie of witchcraft*, Price possessed one of the two issues of the second edition published in 1651,[2] and the third, folio edition of 1665. He boasted an impressive run of John White's seventeenth century *A rich cabinet, with variety of inventions,* and examples of the early eighteenth-century adaptations of the same book entitled *Art's treasury of rarities and curious inventions* and *Hocus pocus, or, a rich cabinet of legerdemain curiosities.* An enviable item of similar size and period, and of exceptional rarity, in Price's catalogue is *Sports and pastimes: or, hocus pocus improved.* The library contained many examples of attractive early nineteenth century booklets with gaily imaginative hand-coloured frontispieces, and books published later in the same century which are rare because of their limited printings, such as *Second sight simplified* (London, 1883) and *Second sight for amateurs* (London, 1888), published respectively in 50 and 25 copies only.

By the end of the nineteen-twenties, however, the size and composition of the collection had changed, just as Price's writings about conjuring books had died away to give place to

---

[1] Price's false claim that his second edition was uniquely dated 1838, and the remarkable photographic evidence that apparently supported it, is discussed in my *Old Conjuring Books*, and in the present work (pp. 110–11).

[2] A third issue of the second edition was published in 1654.

the start of his immense output of books, and articles in psychic journals and newspapers, solely concerned with matters of occult interest. That Price's rare conjuring books, of which the foregoing paragraphs describe the most important, were ultimately greatly outnumbered by his assembly of occult works is demonstrated by his booklet, *Exhibition of Rare Works from the Research Library*, to which reference has already been made. This catalogue listed Price's selection in 1934 of the 500 most rare and valuable items in his collection, a sample which is sizeable enough to be significant. Nearly three-quarters of the entries related to books on spiritualism, psychical research and occultism in general. Many of these items were of considerable value and rarity, but they do not concern the collector of conjuring books. The reason for this imbalance (from my point of view) as I have already suggested, is that it was only in the early years of his collecting that Price's interest in the acquisition of old conjuring books was at its height. It is of interest in this connexion that Price displayed his qualification of Hon. Librarian of the Magicians' Club on the title-page of *Revelations of a Spirit Medium*. *Facsimile Edition with Notes, Bibliography, Glossary and Index*, published in 1922 and edited by Price and Dingwall. By 1930, when the second edition of this work on the tricks of fraudulent mediums was published, however, Price no longer used this distinction, and described himself instead on the title-page as the Founder and Honorary Director of the National Laboratory of Psychical Research.

When Price's collection was taken over by the University of London Library it was found to consist of less than 11,000 books, pamphlets and volumes of periodicals. Price's assertion on page 12 of his autobiography that his library contained 17,000 titles was superseded five years later in his last entry in *Who's Who* before his death in 1948, when the number had risen to 20,000 volumes. In the biography published in 1950, however, it was said that his library, which he had bequeathed to the University of London, consisted of 'some thirteen thousand volumes'. These later varying estimates are understandable for two reasons. First, Price was a vain and devious exhibitionist, to whom pointless and often reckless fabrication seems to have been habitual when writing on the subject of himself and his possessions. Only an exhibitionist, it may be thought, would boast of having amassed 20,000 press-cuttings about himself in 40 folio volumes.[1] Secondly, in both his printed catalogues Price failed to distinguish between books and newspaper and magazine cuttings, and the meagre information he furnished makes it impossible for the reader to separate the entries. When Dr Dingwall received a copy of Price's *Short-Title Catalogue* he wrote to its compiler on 1 June, 1929:

> Firstly, you will, I fear, cause untold annoyance by not telling the reader which are excerpts from periodical publications and which are not. For example, one never knows whether an entry is something one can consult outside the Laboratory or not. Moreover, it will set people hunting for items which they will never find in any trade catalogue, and which they can read in any library IF they know where to look. This is really infuriating.

As an example of Dingwall's point of criticism I may say that a rare and interesting history of conjuring entitled 'Mediums under other Names' was published on pages 130–7 of Part 36, April 1862 of the magazine *All the Year Round* edited by Charles Dickens. Price's entry for this anonymous essay on page 276 of his *Short-Title Catalogue* is simply:

Mediums under other Names. London, 1862.

This trick of listing a magazine article as if it is a book, of which there are hundreds of examples in Price's two catalogues, makes an entry, such as that quoted, totally valueless to the student, who will never find a book answering to the title and is not told where to locate the magazine article. Archdeacon Ellison's comment in the penultimate sentence of his chapter on Price's numismatic activities is very apt in this connexion. We recall that he observed that Price's concern in his writings seemed to be 'not so much the edification of his readers as the glorification of Harry Price'. In the present matter the 'glorification' was the claim in *Who's Who* that the library consisted of over 20,000 volumes when it was in fact not much more than half that size. It may be thought that my own comment on the

---

[1] *Search for Truth*, p. 54.

matter six years ago was restrained. On page 21 of *Old Conjuring Books* I wrote:

The late Harry Price published a catalogue and a supplementary list of his great library, the entries being without pagination, publishers or title-pages. Despite their frequent inaccuracies, and confusing lack of discrimination between conjuring books, occult works and newspaper and magazine cuttings, our knowledge of magic books would have been noticeably the poorer without these two publications, the pages of which were graced by reproductions of half-a-dozen title-pages of early conjuring items. However, they should, I think, be regarded as handbooks to the Harry Price Library of Magical Literature in the University of London, which makes available to the student an immense mass of raw material, rather than as reliable sources of bibliographical information in themselves.

I have tried to give some account of Price's library in reasonably small compass, so that with the background sketched in we may give our consideration to his claim in his auto-biography as to the reason for its assembly, and to its very interesting history from the early nineteen-twenties to Price's death in 1948. According to his own account, when he was twenty-one years old he had five ambitions in life, all of which he claimed were ultimately realised 'with no conscious effort or intention' on his part. He wrote:

(1) I wanted to be a writer and to write especially for the *Encyclopaedia Britannica*; (2) I wanted to appear in *Who's Who*; (3) I wanted to collect the largest magical library in existence; (4) I wanted to be offered a doctorate, *honoris causa*, of some uni-versity; (5) I wanted to possess a Rolls-Royce car.[1]

The eleventh chapter of Price's autobiography, which we recall was published in 1942, is entitled 'University of London and Psychical Research: The History of a Proposal', and in his opening sentence he wrote:

The chief reason why I founded the National Laboratory was to interest the universities in psychical research. Owing to the great

[1] *Search for Truth*, p. 54.

success that attended our work, I found this easy to accomplish—unofficially.[1]

In the same place Price claimed that he was determined upon 'turning psychical research into an *official* science',[2] and later in the same chapter related how in 1933 he offered as a gift to the University of London (a) his library (b) the equipment and furniture of his National Laboratory and (c) £500 per annum in perpetuity for research work, on condition that the University would establish a Department for the study of so-called psychical phenomena. He observed:

> The value of the proposed gift, including the laboratory equipment, library, etc., and the Endowment Fund necessary to produce an income of £500 per annum for research work, was about £30,000.[3]

From Price's point of view this would no doubt seem a generous offer, it may be thought, when we recall that when he died in 1948 his total estate, including the library, was proved at £17,618. Price's proposal was not accepted by the University, but the library did ultimately come to rest in the Senate House after a series of vicissitudes commencing in the nineteen-twenties, almost wholly omitted from Price's account.

In the early months of 1922 Price, who had been a member of the Society for Psychical Research for two years, was reported in the S.P.R. *Journal* of May, 1922 as having 'offered to place on permanent loan in the Society's Rooms his magnificent collection of books on magic and witchcraft. The offer was gratefully accepted by the Council, and so through his generosity Mr Price has given the officers of the Society the benefit of being able to consult what is generally considered to be the most complete library of magical literature in Great Britain, if

---

[1] *Search for Truth*, p. 97. [2] *Ibid.*, p. 98.

[3] *Search for Truth*, p. 98. On p. 93 of the same book Price said that the equipment and furniture of the National Laboratory were valued for insurance purposes at £3,000. It is quite clear, therefore, that in his estimation the book collection was by far the largest and most important physical property of the Laboratory. Its value was stated to be 'about £10,000' in 1936.

not in Europe'.[1] The article recording the acceptance of the collection on permanent loan was entitled 'Mr. Price's Library' and gave some account of the books,[2] which were to be catalogued, and either made generally available for reference by members or (in some cases) reserved for the use of the Officers of the Society.

Five years later a short note appeared in the S.P.R. *Journal* which said that during the re-organisation of the Library (which had been undertaken by Theodore Besterman) it had become clear 'that additional space was urgently needed for the Society's own books, and that it would therefore be impossible both to meet this demand and also to house in the Society's rooms the Library on Magic which Mr. Price some years ago kindly lent to the Society'. The Council was therefore 'reluctantly compelled' to request Price to remove his books from the Society's premises.[3] We recall in this connexion that Price's National Laboratory of Psychical Research was opened on 1 January, 1926, and that when Leo Rullman inspected the book collection in May, 1928 it was installed on the top floor of 16 Queensberry Place in South Kensington.

The London Spiritualist Alliance (which until 1884 had been known as the British National Association of Spiritualists)[4] owned its headquarters at 16 Queensberry Place, and Price's National Laboratory was the L.S.A.'s tenant on the fourth floor. In April, 1929, three years after the establishment of the National Laboratory of Psychical Research (founded, according to Price, in *Search for Truth*, 'to interest the universities in psychical research') he suggested an amalgamation of the National Laboratory with the L.S.A.[5] The spiritualists were

[1] *Journal*, S.P.R., May, 1922, p. 270.

[2] It was stated in the account that 'the books number about fifteen hundred items', and that 'the bulk of the volumes consist of works on magic in the sense of legerdemain'. This confirms, it may be thought, my remarks earlier in this essay in regard to the shift in Price's collecting interests after the early nineteen-twenties from conjuring to occultism.

[3] *Journal*, S.P.R., October, 1927, p. 114.

[4] It was in the rooms of the British National Association of Spiritualists that the Society for Psychical Research was founded in 1882.

[5] Tabori, *op.cit.*, p. 149. As I have shown that Tabori's reliability as a biographer is vulnerable to criticism, it should be pointed out that his account of the vicissitudes of the library consists almost wholly of quotations

not enthusiastic. Their answer, dated 26 April, 1929 and signed on behalf of the Council by the Secretary, Miss Mercy Phillimore, was that 'the success of both parties might be better assured if we continue as now, but with closer, friendly, unofficial co-operation as opportunity presents, rather than amalgamation'.

By June, 1929, Price was engaged in negotiations with the Institut Métapsychique of Paris,[1] offering to present his library, apparatus and furnishings to that organisation. Dr Charles Richet, the President, thanked Price for his 'generous offer', and suggested more detailed discussions between Price and the Director, Dr Eugene Osty. On 4 June, 1929, Price wrote to Osty, 'I am delighted to hear that your Council is agreeable to the principle of amalgamation, the suggested details of which we will have to discuss when next we meet'. Despite this favourable start, the negotiations broke down, and the library and equipment remained at 16 Queensberry Place.

In the early weeks of 1930, Price made a second approach to the London Spiritualist Alliance, and was again rebuffed.[2] Foolishly, perhaps, he made his next offer to another spiritualist body, the so-called British College of Psychic Science,[3] with

---

from Price's correspondence files at the University of London. Where his dates and details are less precise than one might wish, I have made the necessary corrections, and occasionally enlarged the quotations by reference to the original letters.

[1] The Institut Métapsychique was founded in 1918. It was the French equivalent of the Society for Psychical Research, with distinct leanings towards spiritualism. Its first Director, Dr Gustave Geley, was killed in an aeroplane accident on 15 July, 1924, a few days after his last séance with Franek Kluski of Warsaw, a materialising medium in whom Geley implicitly believed. Geley was a convinced spiritualist, believing in survival, reincarnation and communication with the dead. He was succeeded by Dr Eugene Osty.

[2] Tabori, *op.cit.*, p. 149. Tabori's date of 'in February' may just be possible, but the correspondence shows that Price was in negotiation with the British College of Psychic Science during the early weeks of that month.

[3] The British College of Psychic Science, which at the relevant time had its headquarters at 15 Queen's Gate, S.W.7., was founded in 1920 by Mr and Mrs Hewart McKenzie, who were ardent spiritualists. The College engaged mediums for the use of its members, and published a quarterly journal, *Psychic Science*.

whom he had been involved in disputes in the early nineteen-twenties, principally in connexion with William Hope, a carpenter in Crewe, who claimed psychic powers as a spirit photographer. Price caught Hope in fraud at the British College, and published the result in the S.P.R. *Journal* of May, 1922, and in booklet form.[1] The College, as might have been expected, turned the offer down. 'I cannot honestly say the idea has been received with enthusiasm', wrote the honorary Principal, Mrs McKenzie, to Price with restraint on 14 February, 1930.[2]

In March, 1930 (one month after the rebuff from the British College) Price tried for a third time to persuade the London Spiritualist Alliance to take over the library and equipment. The Council considered the offer for two months, but finally turned it down in a letter to Price dated 30 May, 1930, signed by Miss Mercy Phillimore, in which the terms of the Council's resolution were set out:

(1) To decline the offer made with this object by Mr. Harry Price.
(2) To enter into no further negotiations with regard to this offer.
(3) To instruct the Secretary to inform Mr. Harry Price of their decisions with an expression of their appreciation of his offer and of their regret at their inability to accept it.[3]

While the ultimately abortive negotiations with the London Spiritualist Alliance were going on, Price made a formal approach to the Rector of Göttingen University in May, 1930. His letter is quoted by his biographer:

[1] Harry Price, *Cold Light on Spiritualistic "Phenomena"* (London, 1922). It was Price's first published work in this field, and is now an exceedingly scarce pamphlet. On p. 6 he recorded that he 'ingratiated himself in every way' with William Hope and his companion Mrs Buxton, who were members of the Crewe Circle of spiritualists, telling them (oddly, we may think) that 'my people were natives of Shropshire'.

[2] Tabori, *op.cit.*, pp. 149–50.

[3] Tabori does not refer to this letter, and infers on p. 150 that the offer of March, 1930 was still under consideration several months later. He quotes Price as saying, 'I still want to help the L.S.A. in particular, and psychical research generally, and I repeat my original offer that I am willing to loan the Laboratory and its contents, the library, etc. for an indefinite period with the idea, if things go smoothly, of bequeathing the same to the London Spiritualist Alliance'.

In England the machinery of the universities is too slow and cumbersome for the Laboratory and library to be made suitable use of. My property would be wasted. I am, therefore, offering the entire equipment and library, value £10,000, to the Department of Psychology of Göttingen University subject to a few conditions— such as my access to it during my lifetime—which I shall be pleased to discuss with you in person, and would visit Göttingen specially for that purpose. I would pay all the expenses of removal. Why I have chosen Göttingen is because I consider it the most modern, scientific, elastic and progressive university on the continent of Europe. Also, the fact of it having been founded by George II of England likewise influenced me.

The university took almost four months to acknowledge this letter, and in the event nothing came of Price's offer.[1]

On 20 September, 1930 Price approached the London Spiritualist Alliance for the fourth time (not the third, as Tabori suggests) by writing to the Secretary, Miss Mercy Phillimore:

Unless someone takes over the Laboratory as a going concern, I shall be compelled to dismantle it at the end of the present year. My heart, which I badly strained two years ago, is not yet right and I feel I cannot devote the time and energy to the affairs of the Laboratory which I should like. When the idea of amalgamation was discussed some time ago a misunderstanding arose which made further negotiations impossible. But I am not now going into this matter: this letter is to offer the members of the L.S.A. the use of the Laboratory and its equipment etc., under the management of your Council, for an indefinite period.

In her reply of 26 September, Miss Phillimore wrote that the Council had considered the renewed offer, and had 'resolved that they are regrettably unable to collaborate with you'.

In October, 1930 Price made the same offer to the Society for Psychical Research (of which he was still a member) through the Hon. Secretary. His proposal was flatly turned down by the Council. On December 15, 1930, Price sent a circular letter to every S.P.R. member, which read in part:

I very much regret to inform you that I have failed in my

---

[1] Tabori, *op.cit.*, pp. 169–70.

endeavour to instil into the London Society for Psychical Research some new and active blood. I am confident that the acceptance of the free offer of my Laboratory, library and personal influence with mediums all over the world would have greatly benefited the Members of the S.P.R. and would have restored the usefulness of this Society—which for years has been living on its traditions. On personal grounds I was against the amalgamation, but a strong sense of duty prompted me to make the offer. I argued that as I had the only fully-equipped psychic laboratory in existence, and possessed the most valuable and complete research library in the world, it was my duty to offer it to British Psychical Research.[1]

At the end of this bitter communication, which appears to have been written to discredit the Council in the eyes of the members for rejecting the offer, Price added a threat that he might 'hand over my property to a foreign organisation'. The circular achieved no result.[2]

At the end of 1930 Price moved the National Laboratory from Queensberry Place, and rented a ground floor office at 13 Roland Gardens, South Kensington. I have already described how in 1933 he offered the University of London £500 per annum in perpetuity, the library and the equipment of the National Laboratory, if the University would form a Department of Psychical Research. His biographer said that 'Harry Price wanted nothing less than a Chair of Psychical Research'. Whether that be true or not, in his letter to Professor J. C. Flugel, the Secretary to the Board of Psychology, Price wrote:

I expect you know the broad idea of the scheme, which is to endow a 'department' which will examine the many facets of a subject which we are pleased to call 'psychic'. I suppose that the sum which I offer (£500 per annum in perpetuity) is not very large for the purpose, but it is a nucleus and undoubtedly more money would be forthcoming later. In addition, I have offered the University the entire Laboratory equipment, furniture, and library of about 11,000 volumes—a collection I commenced forming when I was eight years old.[3]

In February, 1934, Price's offer was declined by the University of London, as I have indicated earlier in this book.

---

[1] Tabori, *op.cit.*, pp. 151–2.   [2] *Ibid.*, p. 153.
[3] *Ibid.*, p. 154.

In his autobiography Price told the story of his negotiations with the University of Bonn, following the rejection of his offer by the University of London:

In April, 1936, Dr. Hans Bender, of the Psychologisches Institut, University of Bonn, called upon me in London, in order to see our Laboratory, etc. At that period more than two years had elapsed since Sir Edwin Deller informed me that the University of London found itself 'unable to accept' my offer and proposal to establish a Department of Psychical Research. During Dr. Bender's visit I related to him the history of my proposal, with its unsatisfactory sequel, and suggested to him that the authorities at Bonn might be interested in considering a similar offer by me, if it were made.[1]

Meanwhile, at the end of 1936, as Price's biographer tells us, 'the lease of the Roland Gardens premises was running out, and a new home had to be found for the Laboratory'. Tabori continued:

Harry Price decided to approach the University 'from a different angle' and suggested to Mr. Reginald A. Rye, Goldsmiths' Librarian of the University of London, that the University should house his library and make it available for students. Both the Senate and Court of the University voted unanimously in favour of accepting this offer and by the end of 1936 the library was transferred to the University.[2]

On page 159 of his biography of Price, Tabori referred to 'the Library and Records being transferred by gift to the University of London in November, 1936'. I found this difficult to credit, in the light of Price's negotiations with the University of Bonn, which continued in 1937, and I am much indebted to my friend Alan Wesencraft for placing the facts at my disposal.[3] On 11 November, 1936 the Library Committee considered a proposal by Price to 'place his Library on permanent loan in the University Library'. Of the conditions, the most interesting

---

[1] *Search for Truth*, p. 111.   [2] Tabori, *op.cit.*, p. 157.
[3] I remain astonished that Price recorded in his autobiography how in 1937 he discussed with the University of Bonn the transfer of his library and equipment to the Rhineland, when his property had already been accepted on permanent loan and insured by the University of London in 1936.

were that the collection was to be styled 'The Harry Price Library of Magical Literature' and so described on a plate to be placed 'in a conspicuous part of the room', that the collection was to be insured by the University at its full value (stated to be 'about £10,000') and that Price was to be allowed to nominate 'up to twenty-four friends who, with himself, shall have access to the Harry Price Library'.

The Committee recommended to the Senate that Price's offer be accepted on his conditions, 'and that the cordial thanks of the University be conveyed to him for his generous benefaction'. It was also recorded that in response to Price's request, the Librarian was authorised to remove the books and bookcases from Roland Gardens to temporary accommodation in the University building at South Kensington on a date before Christmas, 1936 agreeable to Price. The latter's difficulty over the housing of his collection at the end of his lease was solved.

According to Price's own account, at the end of February, 1937, one of Dr Bender's colleagues, Fräulein Dr J. Wichert, called upon him in London 'with the agreeable news that the German Government, after the fullest inquiry, had recognised psychics as an official science and had given permission for a Department of Psychical Research to be established at Bonn University'.[1] Dr Bender wrote to Price on 20 March, 1937, confirming what Dr Wichert had said:

The importance of your offer, and of the scientific principles involved in a decision, needed long deliberations. I am glad to repeat to you now what our collaborator has already been telling you in London: that the German Government and the University have decided to accept in principle your original offer. They authorise the establishment of a Department for Abnormal Psychology and Parapsychology (*Forschungsstelle für psychologische Grenzwissenschaften*) and think of special interest to this Department, besides the Research work, questions of social hygiene in occult matters. As acknowledgment of your possible gift, and considering the importance for public health, the German Government would confer upon you the *Rote-Kreuz*-Medaille I. Klasse (order of the Red Cross, 1st Class). This would not exclude the University's honouring you in some other way.[2]

---

[1] *Search for Truth*, p. 112.   [2] *Ibid.*, p. 113.

Price recorded in his autobiography that he visited Bonn in April, 1937 'as the guest of the German Reich and University in order to discuss with the officials there details of the proposed new Department'. During a motor tour of the neighbouring Rhineland (after a luncheon in his honour) he narrowly escaped encountering Hitler while tea was being taken at the Rhein-Hotel Dreesen at Bad Godesberg. Price remarked:

As for the University's 'honouring me in some other way', as suggested in Dr. Bender's letter, a doctorate, *honoris causa*, was mentioned, and I was to have been made an '*Akademischer Ehrenbürger der Universität Bonn*'—i.e. 'an academic honorary citizen' of Bonn University—an honour that has been bestowed only about ten times since the foundation of the University in 1818.[1]

Price said that he could make no final decision during his visit to Bonn because he was still waiting 'for London University to make a move in taking more than an academic interest in psychical research'.[2] His biographer observed:

How close England was to losing the great Harry Price Library, would be difficult to determine. The worsening international situation made him go slow, and in the end all these proposals were dropped.[3]

It is to be assumed that the negotiations with the University of Bonn were abandoned by October, 1938, for it was in that month, Mr Wesencraft tells me, that the library was moved from its temporary storage in South Kensington to the newly completed Senate House in Malet Street. It is of great interest that the University Library records show the precise composition of the collection. It consisted of 4,376 books, 5,343 pamphlets, 725 volumes of periodicals, 1,300 photographs, 741 negatives, 618 lantern slides and 140 framed pictures. It filled 87 packing-cases and was conveyed in 4 van-loads.

---

[1] *Search for Truth*, pp. 114–15. It is to be presumed that it was to this occasion that Price was referring in the passage on p. 54 of *Search for Truth*, already quoted, in which he said that an offer to him of an honorary doctorate had been made 'with no conscious effort or intention' on his part.

[2] *Ibid.*, p. 114.   [3] Tabori, *op.cit.*, p. 172.

The circumstances in which the Harry Price Library came to the University of London differed from most benefactions of this kind. Had the collection not previously been refused by the London Spiritualist Alliance (four times) the Institut Métapsychique, the British College of Psychic Science, the University of Göttingen and the Society for Psychical Research, it seems safe to say that it would not have been 'housed' by the University of London when Price's lease of Roland Gardens ran out. There is at least the probability that in the late nineteen-thirties the library might have been removed to Bonn, but for the worsening international situation of which Hitler's Nazi Germany was the storm centre. In the event, the books were left in the possession of the University of London throughout the war. The University scrupulously observed its side of the agreement, insuring the collection and arranging the dispersal of some of the more valuable books to safer locations during the bombing of London.

Price worked entirely from his home in Pulborough throughout the war and until his death in 1948. In his will he bequeathed his library to the University together with a variety of chattels, including the photographic and other equipment originally forming part of the National Laboratory of Psychical Research. The assembly of his book collection was, in my opinion, Price's most useful achievement during his life.

INDEX OF NAMES, PLACES &
PUBLICATIONS